The Jew: Assumptions o

Lily Markiewicz, from *Places to Remember II*, 1995. Black and white photograph on steel. Reproduced with kind permission of the artist.

The Jew: Assumptions of Identity

JULIET STEYN

CASSELL

London and New York

Cassell
Wellington House, 125 Strand, London, WC2R 0BB
370 Lexington Avenue, New York, NY 10017–6550

First published 1999

British Library Cataloguing-in-Publication Data
A catalogue record for this book is available from the British Library.

ISBN   0-304-70031-2 (hardback)
        0-304-70032-0 (paperback)

Library of Congress Cataloging-in-Publication Data
Steyn, Juliet.
        The Jew : assumptions of identity / Juliet Steyn.
            p.   cm.
        Includes bibliographical references and index.
        ISBN 0-304-70031-2. — ISBN 0-304-70032-0 (pbk.)
            1. Jews—Identity.   2. Jews—Great Britain—Public opinion.
        3. Public opinion—Great Britain.   I. Title.
        DS143.S76   1999
        305.892'4041—dc21   98-35840
                                                                             CIP

Typeset by Ben Cracknell Studios
Printed and bound in Great Britain by Biddles Ltd, Guildford and King's Lynn

Contents

Figures

Preface and acknowledgements

To be a Jew is to constitute a problem, for Others and hence for oneself.

Mary McCarthy[1]

Of all the criticism my work has provoked to date, the most painful is that which has sought to classify me as a Self-Hating Jew. This criticism is probably occasioned by the fact that I share nothing with those who would seek to essentialize the Jew, Jewish identity, Jewish experience, Jewish thought and Jewish history. I am not attempting to rescue the Jew from oblivion, to heroize or denigrate his position. I am trying to understand the category *Jew*[2] and 'real' Jews – as both subjects of and subject to institutions and discourses. Perhaps I am identifying with the 'aggressor' – anti-Semite, Jew or other – but I take this as the necessary and inevitable risk that is entailed in my attempt to grasp, to decipher and to describe the conflicting emotions which the idea of the *Jew* arouses.

The dilemma of the Jew in Modernity spins inexorably between two poles: identity and non-identity. The Diaspora has prompted and intensified the anxiety posed by this predicament. However, this is the modern condition, the condition of Modernity, and is shared by Jew and Gentile alike. Nevertheless, I do not mean to signify here that they are the 'same as'. Rather, I am concerned to inaugurate the possibility of thinking 'singularity' and 'particularity', but now to be understood as connoting *both* identity and transformation.

I have embarked upon this work in the spirit of Antonio Gramsci's demand:

The starting-point of critical elaboration is the consciousness of what one really is, and is *knowing thyself* as a product of the historical process to date, which has deposited in you as an infinity of traces, without leaving an inventory, therefore it is imperative at the outset to compile such an inventory.[3]

His use of the second person, 'thyself', is crucial here: it offers the prospect of critical reflection and distance. Gramsci's recognition also allows us to put in tension and doubt the assumed chasm between 'objectivity' and 'subjectivity' in historical analysis. My own work invades the 'space' that his thoughts about history permit and bring to light. Subjectivities are already invested in history. History is an interpretative practice and is connected to social practices. Conceived in this way, as a series of discursive texts, history can itself be subject to scrutiny which reveals its own assumptions and practices.

In *The Writing of History,* Michel de Certeau distinguishes between the idea of making history – that is to say, history as an act or a process – and the idea of history as a noun, notionally divorced from making or production. History can be understood as vacillating between two poles: the first of which refers to a practice (reality); the second, to a closed discourse which is the text itself. This text as a form of production, organizes and creates a mode of intelligibility. De Certeau also suggests that language 'not so much implicates the status of reality of which it speaks, as posits it as that which is other than itself'.[4] To describe the past historically does not mean to write it the 'way it was'. It means to grab a piece of the past, and separate it from the course of history and, as Walter Benjamin urges, 'to seize hold of a memory as it flashes up at a moment of danger'.[5]

My book proceeds through an examination of what I call episodes, including: a family photograph album; legislation on alien immigration in Britain; art exhibitions staged in London and New York; the Holocaust 'industry'; figures such as Mark Gertler, Clement Greenberg and R. B. Kitaj, each of whose work alerts us to the stakes of *Jewish* identity. Above all, I am concerned to dismantle old myths of identity. *The Jew: Assumptions of Identity* is inevitably caught in a paradox; in so far as it initiates a critique of identity and identity politics, it also demands and necessitates a working through, a repetition of, those problematics. So it is in danger of reiterating those very discourses it seeks to disrupt and disturb. Affirmations of sheer identity are put in question so as to offer ways in which identity and its corollary, non-identity, might be thought.

This book is the outcome of a prolonged project, which started as a doctoral thesis at the University of Kent at Canterbury. I am indebted to my then supervisor, David Reason, whose guidance through a labyrinth of critical theory was crucial to this work. Others whose participation was invaluable at that early stage in this protracted work include John Gange, John Hayes and Lewis Johnson. I thank Sue Andrew and Ursula Hedgley both for their practical help and, more important, for their encouragement. I wish also to thank Simon Moretti for his initial sketches for the book cover. I am particularly grateful to Janis Jeffries, Joan Key and Brian Sedgemore for their critical comments, support and advice. My debt to Christopher Kool-Want for his thorough reading and trenchant criticisms is inestimable. Above all, my thanks to Richard Appignanesi whose support has made me braver and whose imaginative ideas have informed this text and indeed often surpassed it.

Earlier drafts of parts of this study have appeared as: 'Painting another: other than painting', in Juliet Steyn (ed.), *Other Than Identity: The Subject, Politics and Art,* Manchester University Press, 1997; 'The subliminal Greenberg', in Alex Coles and Richard Bentley (eds), *de -, dis -, ex: Excavating Modernism*, Vol. 1, London: Backless Books, 1996; 'Charles Dickens' *Oliver Twist*: Fagin as a sign', in Linda Nochlin and Tamar Garb (eds), *The Jew in the Text*, Thames & Hudson, 1995; 'Inside-out: assumptions of English Modernism in the Whitechapel Art Gallery, London 1914', in Marcia Pointon (ed.), *Art Apart: Art Institutions and Ideology across England and North America*, Manchester University Press, 1994; 'The mythical edges of assimilation', *Mark Gertler: Paintings and Drawings,* Camden Arts Centre, London, 1992; 'Yids, mods and foreigners', *Third Text*, no. 15, Summer 1991; 'The complexities of assimilation in the exhibition *Jewish Art and Antiquities*, London 1906', *Oxford Art Journal*, Vol. 13, no. 2, 1990; 'The loneliness of the long distance rider', *Art Monthly*, February 1988.

Notes

1. Mary McCarthy, 'Hannah Arendt and politics', *50th Anniversary Partisan Review*, 1984, p. 733.
2. Throughout this text I use the typological convention that wherever Jew is italicized it refers to the regulating idea of Jew. Usually I write 'Jew' in the singular to connote something of the violence that can be associated with the histories of Jews and *Jews*. Similarly, the use of 'Other' signifies the regulating concept, while 'other' refers to 'real' others.
3. Antonio Gramsci, *Selections from the Prison Notebooks,* London: Lawrence & Wishart, 1971, p. 324.
4. Michel de Certeau, *The Writing of History,* trans. Tom Conley, Cambridge: Cambridge University Press, 1988, p. 21.
5. Walter Benjamin, 'Theses on the philosophy of history', in *Illuminations*, trans. Harry Zone, London: Fontana, 1973, p. 257.

*For my mother, Zena, and
in memory of my father, Bernard Steyn*

1

Introduction: the banal Jew

In this book, if I may coin a word, I *banalize* the Jew. However, my perception of the banal is at least twofold. It connotes writing about the Jew as seen in everyday life, the individual alone and together with others, the Jew at home, at work or in society. In this sense, the banal encourages us to remember what may seem trivial and mundane details: a family photograph album; the connotative power of the tie-pin worn by Raphael Shackman when photographed in London, in 1910; the evidence that the caretaker William Walker gave in 1902–3 to the Royal Commission on Alien Immigration; a painting by Solomon Hart of 1873. In the other sense that I give it, the banal signifies that which we have overlooked or taken for granted. Thought of in this way, it can provide us with a definition of ideology as that which we have forgotten: the ordinary or the familiar is naturalized, and paradoxically comes to stand for the norm which has hidden or repressed questions. The crux of the difference between these 'banals' lies in the vexed question of remembering and forgetting. The choice for Jews – as for non-Jews – is not a question of the past as given and therefore overlooked but rather what *kind* of past shall be had.

In *The Jew: Assumptions of Identity* I am concerned with those micro-stories that constitute the lives of people and their *selves*. I have chosen each chapter to animate the plight of my subjects who, I believe, were desperate to achieve citizenship, to belong, to accomplish an identity easily. I am writing about people who were struggling to achieve and to learn to use, as well as – in some instances – to challenge, institutions in their attempts to make 'home'. Without doubt, the Jewish question was a problem for enlightened Emancipation: the ability of some Jews to adapt to modern life, civil society and the burgeoning nation states was as threatening as the resistance of others to change and to assimilation.

Moreover, the banal in *The Jew: Assumptions of Identity* stands against those histories which set the Shoah as the founding moment of Jewish history and as the framing identity for the *Jew* in Modernity. Here we are faced with the most difficult example of the ways in which unpredictable historical events and historical processes can retrospectively get fatally trapped in interpretations of destiny. Writing about Jewish themes that occurred before the Shoah produces a very particular tension. It is tempting to read them as predictions: as if the Final Solution were an already accomplished fact. So, when we witness Theodore Herzl's dilemma in 1903 as he gave evidence to the Royal Commission on Alien Immigration, we may be tempted to agree with him that the foundation of a state of Israel was the only way to protect the Jews. However, it is important not to interpret the past through what we now know was to be the future. At the same time, histories of Jews in Modernity cannot minimize the plight of those people and their direct or indirect experiences of pogroms and the Shoah. In human society there will always be conflict, but it is the links between ideology, Jewish identity and the conditions in which 'ordinary' hostility turns into murder which are at stake here.

The fabric of Jewish identity has been interwoven with the complex formations of anti-semitism. Emmanuel Levinas reminds us that the symbolism attached to *Jew* is linked to primary psychic and social processes and is outside the grip of biological essentialism. His thought points us to that recurring question: why are the Jews hated so much? Levinas describes anti-semitism as

> a repugnance felt for the unknown within the psyche of the other, for the mystery of its interiority or, beyond any agglomeration within an ensemble or any organization within an organism, a repugnance felt for the pure proximity of the other man, for sociality itself.[1]

Levinas is firmly bringing the problem of anti-semitism into the realm of ethics and is steering us towards the equally chimerical and complex world of the Other which highlights the proximity of the image of the other to the self.

In psychoanalytic terms the Other is conceived as an entity made and accomplished in the disavowed elements of self. The psychic mechanisms that are at stake here are 'identification' and 'projection'. Identification arises out of the twin processes of desire and denial. An ambivalent structure of relationship, it is conceived as a process which describes our capacity to empathize with others, to attribute to others aspects of our own experience. It also refers to a defence mechanism that in its pathological sense is active in the forms of persecution interpreted by Melanie Klein as characteristic of racism and sexism.

Projection is a form of protection, a defence that entails the expulsion of the subject's disowned aggression in order to distance it from the self. According to Klein's description, projection refers to the earliest actions of the ego in which the self and the surrounding world are recreated to minimize the fear and distress which endanger itself or the loved others. These fantasies are projected out of the self so as to escape from them. Aspects of the self which are disowned and repudiated may be attributed to the concept of 'not-self'.[2] The Other, in this case, is a narcissistic projection of self which is experienced as belonging to someone or something else in the outside world. The Other comes to function as the 'bad' object, at once dismissed, but nightmarishly capable of reappearing. Jews have serviced this role. The *Jew* is invested with unconscious desire.

Despite the difficulties of Jacques Lacan's terminology, he has contributed greatly to our understanding of the Other by a suggestion that man's desire is the desire of the other:

> What he desires presents itself to him as what he does not want . . . he transfers the permanence of his desire to an ego that is nevertheless intermittent, and inversely protects himself from his desire by attributing to it these very intermittences.[3]

My work looks at these intermittences.

Structures of social conflict are described by the philosophers Theodor Adorno and Max Horkheimer, in their polemical but still seminal book, *Dialectic of Enlightenment*, written in 1944. This work intertwines two major strands of modernist thought: Marxism and psychoanalysis. From psychoanalytic theory, they borrow Freud's notion of 'projection' and the distinction he makes between those forms of identification which enrich our lives and their opposite: those in which we over-identify and lose our ability to distinguish between the self and other, the inner and outer world. They argue that the life of reason takes place as 'controlled projection' which they distinguish from 'false projection'. The latter

> confuses the inner world and outer world and defines the most intimate experiences as hostile. Impulses which the subject will not admit as his own, even though they are most assuredly so, are attributed to the object – the prospective victim. The actual paranoiac has no choice but to obey the laws of his sickness.[4]

When a subject is not able to return to the object he loses his ability to differentiate and reflect. False projection, or paranoia, is that which in ourselves we refuse to recognize.

Marxism brings a socio-political dimension to Adorno's and Horkheimer's theory of the human psyche. They quote Karl Marx's association of the Jew with finance and his identification of the Jew with capitalism, but they point out:[5]

> The Jews remained objects, at the mercy of others, even when they insisted on their rights. Commerce was not their vocation but their fate. The Jews constituted the trauma of the knights of commerce who had to pretend to be creative, while the claptrap of anti-semitism announced a fact for which they secretly despised themselves. Their anti-semitism is self-hatred, the bad conscience of the parasites.[6]

Through their analysis of production and consumption, the 'body' of capitalism is revealed as a confidence trick, a rip-off. Adorno and Horkheimer claim that 'the people "know" this: And so the people shout: stop thief – but point at the Jews.'[7] Yet despite this knowledge – the fact that the thief is already known to be capitalism – the finger of blame is pointed at the Jews.

Anti-semitism reveals the extent of the limits of radical liberalism which was heralded by the Enlightenment. Whilst people desire justice and equal rights for all, they also hate the idea that others might be getting away with something they do not deserve. Vicious feelings are projected onto those others who are pushed away, outside or into the margins. The Other is made up of those who are precisely disallowed. However, the other has already heard the call to come inside, to become alike, to identify, and risks rejection and condemnation for attempting to do so. Those on the inside wish to control the outside and thereby to neutralize the power the Other is imagined to possess. By keeping him outside, the fantasy of control and power is preserved. The liberal state was constituted by this double-bind, which for the Jews at least was a promise and a curse. Emancipation, with its corollary assimilation, depends upon exclusions which produce the need for scapegoats, enemies and victims. Anti-semitism in its specific modern form reveals the dark side of the Enlightenment project and, as Adorno and Horkheimer argue, is a social disease. Envy is its neurotic condition: the physical extermination of the Jews its outcome, if not its inevitable consequence.

Enlightenment was in part a fantasy and spoke in barbed tongues. Reason is both the instrument by which humankind has freed itself from nature and superstition and also the very means by which Europe subjected others to domination. Above all, Adorno and Horkheimer insist, the rational spawns the irrational. Moreover, the reason of rationalism requires social categories – such as the Jew, the alien, the criminal, the insane, the scapegoat or the Other – against which to define itself. They show how it was that *Jew* became a category ripe for exploitation: how it was that, for some, the Jew was installed as the archetypal capitalist – as he who produces nothing and consumes everything. Economic injustice was attributed to the Jew, who was cast as rapacious as capitalism itself. Yet again, for others, he was the Bolshevik menace that destabilizes the state.

To begin to understand Jewish history through interpreting the ways in which – in the subjective worlds of Jews and non-Jews – anti-semitism has become the principle which has shaped Jewish history and the Jews' representations of themselves could, I think, offer alternatives to the ideology of the victim so dominant in representations of the Jew. The image of the Jew as victim of history provokes distrust or, worse still, is itself used as an incitement to violence. We should also be aware that it is through the very *assumptions* of Jewish identity that past memories are often evoked to legitimate and explain today's defensive nationalism so vividly enacted in Israel by both Israelis and Palestinians, by fundamentalists of either side. These need taking apart lest the Jew remain forever a victim and fail to come to terms with the consequences of power. The particular problem here for the Jews, as the author Ilan Halevi maintains, is that by making anti-semitism the sole evil principle, Jews are forever innocent, not only of responsibility for their own sufferings but also for what in other places and other times, they may make others suffer.[8] These are, I know, unbearable thoughts for some. Nevertheless, they are the ones that give my project – to dismantle old myths and themes of Jewish identity – its urgency. The writer of Jewish history, Yosef Hayim Yerushalmi, warns us,

> Myth and memory condition action. There are myths that are life-affirming and deserve to be interpreted for our age. There are some that lead astray and must be redefined. Others are dangerous and must be exposed.[9]

My intention is neither to deny nor to elevate the history of the Jew in Modernity: rather, as I have already mentioned, it is to banalize it, to prise it open, expose and explore the ever-changing, yet historically grounded definitions of the Jew and identity. It is to redescribe *Jewish* identity, in its 'singularity' as both repetitious and subject to change and transformation. So I ask in *The Jew: Assumptions of Identity*, and the questions come out thick and fast: where and when – in what contexts – are *Jewish identities* discussed and invented? In what and whose terms? I also consider the values attached to the differences constructed between *Jew* and *Other* in the hegemonic culture and its discourses. Therefore, my interest is also to identify and to understand the practices of institutions and discourses that both mediate and use *Jew* as a category.

An examination of these mediations is to remark on the political, the state and civil society. The constitution of European nation states have shaped and have been shaped by notions of *identity*. In the nineteenth century the nation state achieved pre-eminence as a form because it seemed at the time to offer relative political stability, social coherence, economic viability, the propensity for expansion, colonial or otherwise, and above all the ability to defend itself from outside. The formation of the modern state is interconnected with the structures of political and social groups and classes, and its relationships with other states. The union of peoples around the concept 'nation' was to preoccupy the newly formed states. The incorporation and consolidation of colonies and the integration of immigrants were crucial issues.

A major question for nineteenth-century liberalism, where my story begins, is 'who' has the right to belong? At the turn of the twentieth century in Britain this issue was clearly marked, and made vivid for us in the evidence presented to the Royal Commission on Alien Immigration (1902–3) which led to the Bill of 1905 that was to restrict alien immigration.

Later in this century Hitler, in his theory of *Lebensraum*, adapted previous notions of the nation state to encompass the idea of a superior people. German supremacy was based to a large part on ideas about 'race'. The alleged need for economic and social expansion was to be obtained by annexing other states at the same time as 'purifying' the population of the fatherland. Thus expansion could be justified on the grounds of purity. Accordingly, it could be argued European civilization would thereby be enhanced. When this theory was put into practice it was, as we know, disastrous for Jews, Communists, homosexuals and gypsies as the impure Others. Nationalism has created, indeed continues to create, appalling suffering in its name.

At the centre of the identity of the modern state lies its claim to represent and be accountable to its citizens. However, the modern state is not monolithic or homogeneous but consists of an array of small entities which form, shape and govern individual lives through those public institutions and private ventures which constitute civil society. I use the term *institution* sometimes in a narrow sense to denote that which is established or constituted in society, a *body* with a programme of public responsibility, for example, the Jews' Free School in London. On other occasions, I use institution to denote a governing ideology and a corporate project which works to legitimate, let us say in the case of the art world, particular forms of art. So, for example, I use the Whitechapel Art Gallery in London to describe how a particular institution legitimates certain ideas about *Jewish* and modern art, creates notional identities for those who view it, and promotes particular ideas of the *Jew* (for Jews and others) which are compatible with Englishness.

The philosopher Louis Althusser has argued that we are first united by institutions which he describes as the 'myths' and 'themes' that govern us without our consent.[10] In short, he provides us with a definition of ideology, again as that which we have forgotten or repressed, in other words the banal. His understanding of institution brings us close to the notion of discourse which has been given special meaning in the work of Michel Foucault, one of whose quests has been to discover the buried, yet present, positive unconscious of knowledge. Foucault is particularly concerned with knowledge as a socially instituted set of discourses.[11] Discourse is not just a text, but is a practice which operates on a number of levels and describes a domain of language use, a system of representation. Historical discourses make social identity explicit. It is the intervention of institutions and discourses which legitimate and frame identity. Hence discourse can be understood as an historical, social and institutional structure of categories and beliefs. *Jewish identity* is made, undone and made again: it does not exist in an essential sense. It has been constituted, however, in a number of discourses – in legislation, social policy, literary and visual culture, art theory and art exhibitions. It is these discourses which underpin the themes offered in this book.

I shall proceed with an examination of the art exhibition *Jewish Experience in Twentieth-century Art* and witness the making of certain Jewish identities in two major institutional settings. The show was first staged at the Jewish Museum, New York, in 1976, by Avram Kampf and then again in 1990, at the Barbican Arts Centre, London, with Kampf as guest curator. Although the London show changed many of the particular works, it maintained the approach of the original show, which Kampf claimed 'had been vindicated by a widespread rejection of formalism in favour of a search for roots and identity'.[12] Thereby both exhibitions elaborated a revision, or even a repudiation, of received modernist art history and historiography so as 'to shed light on the submerged context which thus far has been largely ignored by contemporary art historians and critics'. The key to understanding the exhibition was the Jewish origin, background, concerns and motifs of each artist. Included among the 360 works on show were works by David Bomberg, Jacques Lipchitz, Amedeo Modigliani, Lilian Lijn and Joseph Herman, as well as Marc Chagall and R. B. Kitaj (as the subtitle of the second version made plain). Kampf attempted to establish and thematize a social matrix in which all the artists worked, and out of which they emerged, into a version of art history through which he could speak of the 'essential' truths of European culture and the *Jewish* experience.

Jewish experience was identified with persecution, survival, migration, adaptation, the formation of Israel, the encounter with the biblical landscape and the rebirth of an ancient language. These experiences were thematized in the organization of the exhibition and the catalogue as: 'The Quest for a Jewish Style'; the 'Encounter with the West'; 'Paris'; 'the Holocaust'; the 'Evocation of the Religious Tradition'; and finally, 'Reaching for the Absolute'. The sequence of the works mapped out a route which led inevitably to the Promised Land and described how lives were reassembled after the Shoah. The force of the narrative worked to create Israel as the predestined outcome of the catastrophe and as a haven of liberty. It charted a succession of historical moments in terms of a projected revelation of meaning as a continuum. The texts of the exhibition presented a version of history in which Zionism was 'the centre, the Alpha and the Omega, the base and the end'.[13] In its effects, the show presented a political view of Jewish history shaped by the present exigencies of Zionism. This version of history provides the moral foundation for the Return selectively screened to present the idea of one nation.

The story told is the story of Ashkenazi Jews (as if they themselves possess a unitary history) and it passes over in silence the history of, for example, Sephardi Jews. Indeed, at an earlier time, David Ben-Gurion when faced with the task of building one nation in Israel is reported as saying, 'The culture of Morocco I would not like to have here.'[14] Assimilation of a European model of both culture and the nation state was vigorously enforced to create 'unity'. The battle over history and identity played out during this century is left unmentioned. The concept named as identity is neither as self-evident nor as transparent as Kampf presumes. It is not an already accomplished fact. Indeed as Robert Paine argues, there continues in Israel 'competition over tradition and because of the near impossibility of rebecoming, this identity is still in the toils of labour.'[15]

The exhibition in its effects perpetuates the assumption that whatever art is made by Jews, over and above the diverse contexts in which it is made and mediated, shares an unequivocal Jewish essence and identity. The story Kampf tells is a miraculous conflation of continents and moments of twentieth-century geography and history. A common language, religious tradition and family life, according to Kampf, hold the Jews together and these factors provide him with the basis for interpreting and creating the category *Jewish* art and artists.

To name a *Jewish* art, or an artist as *Jewish,* is to seek the basis for defining or classifying that which inevitably works to differentiate them from the 'norm'. I do not subscribe to those discourses which allege that there is a well-defined essence of the Jew, or indeed that there is an essential *Jewishness*. Nor do I agree with those who seem to know exactly whether some phenomenon or another is *Jewish* or not. I follow here Ilan Halevi, who points to a paradox:

At the very point when Jewish society was breaking up as an autonomous social system, disintegrating into a host of special social situations, the idea spread among Europeans, as among the Jews of Europe, of a single question: a question which always went back in the last analysis, to the idea that each had Judaism in general.[16]

Likewise in the *Jewish Experience* exhibition the Jew is already confirmed in an identity, recognized, characterized and thereby potentially 'known'. The search for roots is disingenuous, and overshadows the particular which is subsumed by the general.

The names of the artists 'Chagall and Kitaj' are used by Kampf as paradigmatic individuals who pre-figure a type. They represent models of Jewish identity already formed and realized. The type provides the myth with its own truth. It allows the dream that between the poles signalled by the names, Chagall and Kitaj the whole of *Jewish identity* can be embodied and possessed. Chagall comes to represent assimilation, primitivism, modernism, Russia, Europe, and Jewish essentialism. Kitaj, in contrast, is seen as representing separatism, urban sophistication, modernism, America, Europe, and again Jewish essentialism. In Kampf's argument the 'who', Chagall–Kitaj, comes before the subject. *Jew* is assumed to be already there, ceaselessly *a priori*. The subject is identical with identity. Chagall–Kitaj–Jew becomes the sign through which the works are read. However, they are not reducible to one set of meanings or identity: subjects are not identical with themselves.

Chagall's art is a product of deep ruptures: between East and West; Jewish and Christian; identity and non-identity. It is not reducible to the timeless (universal), nor to the essential (the seamless issue from his Jewish soul), nor to folk art (primitive), nor to a Parisian avant-garde (modernism). It is marked by an unceasing negotiation with identity. Although Kitaj's art enters history at a different moment and seems to test the limits of the assimilationists' dreams, it likewise bristles with the tension between *Jewish* identity and non-identity, and is correspondingly not essentially bounded (Figure 1). However, for Kampf, strong moral commitment marks it out as *Jewish,* a trait he believes Kitaj shares with other Jewish artists, especially those of the New York School.[17] Kampf describes the familiar tropes of *Jewish* identity: Jews have a propensity for moral and ethical values; a tendency towards abstraction and they are angst-ridden.

Many of the faces which have come to represent *Jewish* identity are reproduced and reiterated in the exhibition. On one level these were bound to fluctuate, since contingency is the only certain ground. Yet, on another level, the exhibition confirms existing post-Emancipation images – the uprooted, angst-ridden, perpetually threatened intellectual.

Figure 1.   R. B. Kitaj, *Germania (The Tunnel)*, 1985, oil on canvas,
183.2 × 214 cm, Marlborough Gallery, London. By kind
permission of the artist.

Dissimulation and assimilation are the critical axes around which the
notions of *Jewish* art and artist interminably spin.

The historical experience of the Jews is generalized: constant
repetition is the refrain whose effects give the theme, *Jewish art*, the
authority of 'tradition'. In his *Theses on the Philosophy of History*,
Walter Benjamin charges us to wrest tradition away from conformism
that will overcome it. He warns, 'the danger affects both the content
of the tradition and its receivers'. Endless repetition may give the
appearance of 'tradition', but it is not identical with it. As long as the
logic of identity remains, we can only ever move endlessly from the
Same (the already assigned) to the Other, inevitably and always under
the authority of the Same and of the foregrounding of the problematic

of identity. Thus we shall remain blind to that 'flash of danger' to which Walter Benjamin alerts us.[18]

The ideological demands for *Jewish identity* to be understood and categorized (coming from both Jews and non-Jews) were and continue to be great. The quintessential catalogue or inventory is the museum: the double-edged sword of banality. Jewish museums devoted to history and the politics of identity are proliferating, for example, in London (the Museum of Jewish Life); in Frankfurt (a museum of Jewish history); in Mechelen, Belgium (dedicated to remembering the deportation and extermination of Belgium Jews, which also includes Jewish resistance movements); and in Gerona, Catalonia (established with financial support from America and Israel). Whilst clearly on many levels these enterprises can be affirmed, nonetheless, I am increasingly wary of the notion of *identity* as a way of remembering and designating a people and ourselves which in itself inclines towards fixing 'them' and 'us' in a wretched space which marks identity. We 'belong' in a much more doubtful place, traceable 'somewhere' between identity and non-identity. There is also a danger that an over-determined preoccupation with identity, exemplified in museums such as the United States Holocaust Museum, which opened in Washington, DC, in 1993, can lead to the loss of distinction between 'idea' and 'act', between 'individual agency' and 'society', between the 'real' world and 'representation'.

This tendency is vividly evidenced in the display of the Holocaust Museum in Washington. It provides its spectators with what has been described by Richard Appignanesi as 'a Disneyland hypperreal tour of the past' and more 'a "theme park" stroll through genocide'.[19] Here, so-called hidden histories are reified and the drive to the cultural politics of identity leads to the glorification and seductions of sheer affirmation: the error of forgetting is superseded by that of spectacle, and memory is banalized. Moreover, as Jenny Bourne in 'Homelands of the mind' argues, 'Identity politics is all the rage. Exploitation is out (it is extrinsically determinist). Oppression is in (it is intrinsically personal). What is to be done has been replaced by who am I. Political culture has ceded to cultural politics.'[20] Hence, it can be argued that the difficult political problems of freedom and equality are avoided. Through this move, the further erosion of political will can be legitimated.

Jews, of course, live in the world at large. So it is impossible to understand Jewish history outside that context – just as it is impossible to understand the world without the Jews. Consequently, this book is both about *and* not about Jews. Jacques Derrida says we are all *Jews*, insofar as people in the contemporary world are nomads and displaced. I myself am interested in identifying *Jewish* dimensions which will expand our understandings of Modernity, in order to disrupt modernism's unifying effects in which Emancipation strove to assimilate *difference* to *identity*. Moreover, I also wish to challenge post-modernism's wholesale critique of this. Affirmations of differ-ence – in the name of pluralism – also produce limitations and dangers. The fixed opposition between *identity* and *difference* hides the degree to which they are interdependent concepts. The link which is established between them is hierarchical, with the former term ascend-ant and the latter subordinate, and hence inferior. The principal term, *identity*, relies upon the subsidiary term, *difference*, for meaning. Noting such binary oppositions makes us aware of the ways in which meanings are *made* to work.

The right to *difference* inevitably affirms the sequence: difference = equality = subordination. *Difference* is achieved through differen-tiation and is always constituted on the basis of exclusions. Inequalities are perpetuated because the institutions of power and the power of institutions reside within particular spheres of interest. Those who digress from or fall outside those spheres are marginalized. My study is sensitive to the claims of *difference* but not merely as a substitute for *identity*. Ideas about difference must move beyond the configuration, difference = identity, to a reaffirmation: to a 'yes / yes', which cannot rely upon a simple affirmation. A single 'yes' can only exist in opposition to 'no', in which the opposition between affirmation and negation is played out. The resolution of what I now see as the plight marked by the names *identity* and *difference* does not come from negating or justifying either term as it is normatively construed.

The notion of a single unitary subject understood as identical with itself has been the cornerstone of the modern Western philosophical tradition. Self-identity is a problem for both philosophy and philosophy's definition of itself. Identity here becomes a question for ontology.[21] However, if the 'essential' self is put in abeyance, another possibility of thinking the self becomes possible. It is in the sense of the emergence of self-as-continuous-becoming that traditional concepts of the self can be displaced and the 'singular' can be announced. I present identity as akin to culture which allows identity, but is not a guarantor of the subject. Hence, I argue that subjects are not identical with their assumed *identity*: they are not the same unto themselves. The questions that advance the chapters in this book entail questioning the very assumptions of identity and point to ways in which either *identity* or *difference* can be displaced and reconfigured by something which is neither one nor the other.

This book is a patchwork of little narratives, in and through which the grand narratives of modernism are brought into doubt. Episodic in form, it deals with the subject in representation, the politicization of social anti-semitism, the complexities and limits of the project of assimilation, the making of a putative normative culture and the processes of alienization. It traces and charts the Jews' and others' thoughts and preoccupations in racial, cultural, social and political fields. It shows that as a category, the *Jew* is both ripe for exploitation and essential for the creation of boundaries, national and other. It presents the Jew both as other and same simultaneously. It suggests that through an examination of these notions we can witness the limits of liberal democracy.

The Jew: Assumptions of Identity, the title of this book, acknowledges the assumptions, at the same time as dismembering the old myths of identity. It calls on us to go beyond the provocations of *identity*. It asks us to rethink identity as something made, as a process, as something that can never be complete, that is always becoming and contingent. It tells us that we should be concerned about the boundary between *Jew* as a regulating concept and real Jew and argues that the untroubled identification of *Jew* with Jew reiterates what Theodor Adorno has characterized as 'identity thinking', that is to say, an identity is presumed to be shared by subject and object.[22] The logic that governs this supposition is that the particular is subsumed under the general concept, just as the individual is subsumed under the plan. Once we affirm the diverse nature of the notion identity, then we can reappraise the ways in which we think about the self.

Above all, what may be important about the episodes recounted here is precisely that they allow us to glimpse other possibilities of thinking about the subject and identity, and to shed some light on the limits to and the processes of Jewish Emancipation, questions of assimilation and integration, and the dialectic of identity and difference. To dismantle the subject and identity may encourage the possibility of other configurations of thought to emerge. Thinking through *Jewish* identity as 'singular', as repetition and as transformation may allow us to move from that anguished state which marks *identity* and embrace the universal, which is after all just heterogeneous singularity. Thus the specific may be reconfigured. I do this in the hope that the project of enlightened democracy may yet be rekindled or begin anew.

Inventory

I recognised no Jew I knew. Shylock was revengeful and, against all humanity and reason, had insisted on his pound of flesh. Something was wrong. There came a moment when Portia announced that Shylock couldn't have his pound of flesh because it would involve spilling blood which was not called for in the contract, and I was struck with what I felt to be an insight. The real Shylock would not have torn his hair out and raged for being denied his gruesome prize but would have said,

'Thank God!' Thank God to have been relieved of the burden of taking life.[23]

Arnold Wesker

To follow Gramsci, let us attempt to make an inventory, and fabricate an ideological coral reef out of images of the *Jew*. Subjects are made in part through cultural inscriptions and historical representations. What is at stake in this inventory is not 'reality' as such, but representation, and the ideological implications of these perceptions. The chosen items are crude and familiar. Indeed they have been selected for those very reasons. In one sense they are arbitrary, in another they are representative. Indeed, many of these images will be encountered again and again. Moreover, as the inventory shows, the formation of *Jewish* identity involves an ensemble of dispersed desires and conjectural positions. It is, as I indicate in the various episodes in this book, overdetermined and saturated with meaning. It is both fascinating and appalling to see how *Jewish* identities have been and continue to be created and accomplished. Above all, the inventory is poignant: we know what happens when the Jew has been catalogued.

Item 1: *the killers of Christ*

At what cost to themselves has been the Jews' denial of Christ?[24]

Item 2: *ugly and smelly*

Is a picture of them required? Always sweating from running about selling in public squares and taverns; almost all hunch-backed, such dirty red or black beards, livid complexions, gaps in their teeth, long, crooked noses, fearful, uncertain expressions, trembling heads, appalling frizzy hair; knees bare and pocked with red; long, pigeon-toed feet, hollow eyes, pointed chins . . .

Prince de Ligne[25]

Item 3: *uncivilized and wicked*

In *The Merchant of Venice*, William Shakespeare figures the Jew, Shylock, as vengeful and against all humanity and reason. Arnold Wesker discovered that Venetian law demanded that no citizen could have dealings with a Jew unless a contract existed. Gentlemen's agreements were unacceptable. Thus it appears that the Jew was no gentleman.[26]

In the nineteenth century, Charles Dickens invented the irredeemable villain as the *Jew*, Fagin. In the mid-twentieth century, David Lean's film of *Oliver Twist* recreated Fagin as a sinister yet lovable rogue but nonetheless a Jew. Between these two poles the mythology persists that the Jew is evil by nature, which, again in the nineteenth century, the image of Jack the Ripper confirmed.

In the public eye, validated by circumstantial evidence, the Ripper was an East European Jew. Scrawled on a wall close to a blood-covered apron associated with one of his horrific murders was the message, 'The Juwes are The men That Will not be Blamed for nothing'. A high proportion of the 130 men interviewed in the Ripper case were Jews. Sander Gilman explains that a powerful connection existed between the proletariat, anarchists and Jews which combined to create the image of Jack the Ripper as a Jewish worker, 'marked by his stigmata of degeneration as a killer of prostitutes'. Gilman goes on to suggest that the chain of accumulated associations, Jew = lepers = prostitutes = blacks, presented the ultimate rationale for the Jewish Ripper.[27]

Item 4: *degenerate*

The nineteenth-century criminologist Cesare Lombroso, following the received opinions of his day, claimed that Jews evidenced a 'curious' superabundance of 'lunatics', 'four or even six times . . . as [many as] the rest of the population'.[28]

Item 5: *feminine, hysterical and mad*

George Eliot created the equivocal, feminized hero, Daniel Deronda. The 'feminine' is the ubiquitous other of modernity so we find in this figure a double other. Deronda himself 'could not escape (who can?) knowing ugly stories of Jewish characteristics and occupations'.[29]

By the end of the nineteenth century, it was commonly accepted that Jews were more prone to hysteria than other 'races'. Jews, like women, are rendered as hysterical. Jean-Martin Charcot concluded his Tuesday lecture of the 23 October 1888 with the remark:

> I already mentioned that this twenty-one-year-old patient is a Jewess. I will use this occasion to stress that nervous illnesses of all types are innumerably more frequent among Jews than among other groups.[30]

Charcot argued that this tendency was because of a 'weakening' to the 'nervous system' due, he thought, to endogamous marriages. Lombroso accepted the general thesis that the Jews were particularly prone to mental illness. He, however, differed from Charcot in his interpretation of the causes. He advanced the theory that they were due to the 'residual effects of persecution', which in his view constituted Jewish identity.[31] In other words, Jewish identity in the nineteenth century became a psychological quality.

Item 6: *witty*[32]

L. M. Büschenthal wrote what was, according to Sander Gilman, probably the first collection of Jewish jokes, *Collection of Comic Thoughts about Jews, as a Contribution to the Characteristics of the Jewish Nation*, in 1812. The introduction to the collection maintained:

> Necessity and weakness – this the female sex teaches us – give rise to deception, and deception is the mother of humour. Therefore one finds this much more frequently among persecuted and poor rural Jews than among rich ones.

Jews when persecuted can only assault verbally. They are like women, whose lack of power is counteracted by their humour.

Otto Weininger defined the source of all humour 'as the ability to transcend the empirical world'. He argued that Jews are unable to possess true wit. Accordingly, 'Jews and women are devoid of humour but addicted to mockery'. As Gilman goes on to suggest for Weininger, 'Jewish discourse and feminine discourse merge and overlap in the world of satire, for true humour is possessed only by men'.

In a letter to Wilheim Fliess (1897) Freud reported that he had compiled 'a collection of profound Jewish stories', which were to form the basis for his book, *Jokes and Their Relations to the Unconscious* (1905). His study of *Jewish* jokes, of humour and its relation with the unconscious, was a source for his study of the nature of psychopathology. Laughter was for Freud 'the means of expiating Jewish self-hatred'.

Item 7: *emotional*

For the art critic John Berger, writing in the 1950s, it is the suffering of the Jews which give them their identity. *Jewish* art is for Berger 'the result of acute suffering and intense yearnings'. The Jewish artist becomes identified with or perhaps even the prototype of the angst-ridden genius. Berger's response to the 1953 exhibition *Russian Emigré Artists in Paris*, which included works by Chagall, Soutine, Zadkine, Mané, Katz and Chapiro, was to identify emotion, sensuality and nostalgia as the unifying connections between Jewish artists and their art. Accordingly, these artists become 'almost hysterically intoxicated and hopelessly impetuous'.[33] These characteristics, he maintained, arose as a direct consequence of their Jewish history of persecution, along with 'pride with which they have withstood persecution'.

Edward Carter, in the preface to Helen Rosenau's *A Short History of Jewish Art*,[34] repeats the theme of emotion as a way of identifying Jewish art: 'an interesting feature of Jewish art is the capacity of so many Jewish artists to inject dynamically powerful charges of emotion into abstract or near-abstract forms.'[35]

Item 8: *clever and modern*

The image of the modern *Jew* is often represented as bookish, intellectual, secular if not atheist, with a tradition of abstract thought, assimilated, cosmopolitan, with leftish or anarchist political tendencies. However, according to Helen Rosenau, the importance of the 'book' in Jewish tradition has resulted in the 'one-sided development of the intellectual against the aesthetic sensibilities'.[36]

Discussing the New York School, second generation, Leo Steinberg has argued that a common ground existed between Jewish life and modern art. He considered them both to be 'masters of renunciation', having given up 'all the props on which existence as nation or art seemed to depend'. Jewish religious ritual and abstract art are for Steinberg 'free of representational comment', self-fulfilling and established, as he put it, by 'uncompromising exclusiveness'. Jewishness is synonymous or coterminous with the modern.[37]

Item 9: *alienated*

In *Jewish Artists in the East End*, a film which focuses on David Bomberg, Mark Gertler and Alfred Wollmark, Richard Cork argues that a common identity existed between them as Jews: alienation is the condition they share.[38]

Item 10: *capitalist*

Karl Marx identified the Jew with capitalism. According to Marx, the god of the Jews had become secularized and the god of the world. Exchange or money had become this god. He described 'haggling' as the language of the Jew and the Talmud as the language of capitalism. Accordingly, for Marx the imaginary nationality of the Jew is mercantile.[39]

Item 11: *socialists and revolutionaries*

A popular ditty, recorded by the anarchist Rudolf Rocker, who was spreading his political message in French country villages in 1893, went:

> Those who would all things destroy
> Into the Jewish trap must fall.
> Yes! Even the Socialist dreamers
> Are led by a Marx and Lassalle.[40]

Item 12: *Jewish inventory*

If we proceeded with this would we inevitably arrive at the all-too-familiar catalogue that passes from the ideological to the museological – the detritus of the death camps?

What is dangerous about such an inventory is the taxonomy and the presumptions concerning classification. However, such an inventory is not just a question of labelling, rather it marks a concern with the ideological implications associated with the image of the Jew. As Sander Gilman suggests, what is at stake is how 'difference' is understood and how that understanding is integrated into the self-perception of Jews.[41] The question remains whether Jewish subjects can be spoken and interpellated, however precariously, without falling into the traps of identity which itself may have been marked by anti-Semitic rhetoric.

Jews are a group without a single foundation, a heterogeneous linking of the non-identical. *Jewish* identity, like all identity, is repetitious yet subject to negotiation, resistance and change. *The Jew: Assumptions of Identity*, while showing that identity is formed and validated in representation is concerned, nevertheless, to indicate that anything identified as *identity* is already in a position of acknowledging the possibility that it is other than its representation. Let us now proceed to consider a specific representation: a photograph, at once banal and enigmatic.

Notes

1. Emmanuel Levinas, 'Zionisms', *The Levinas Reader,* ed. Sean Hand, Oxford: Basil Blackwell, 1989, p. 279.
2. For a further discussion of this concept in the context of cultural theory, see Claire Pajaczkowska, 'The ecstatic solace of culture; self, not-self and other: a psycho-analytic view', in Juliet Steyn (ed.), *Other Than Identity: The Subject, Politics and Art*, Manchester: Manchester University Press, 1997, pp. 101–13.
3. Jacques Lacan, *Ecrits*, London: Tavistock, 1977, p. 312.
4. Theodor Adorno and Max Horkheimer, *Dialectic of Enlightenment,* trans. John Cumming, London: Verso, 1989, p. 187.
5. Karl Marx, 'On the Jewish question', in *Early Texts*, ed. David McLellan, Oxford: Basil Blackwell, 1972, *passim.*
6. Adorno and Horkheimer, *op. cit.*, p. 175.
7. *Ibid.*, p. 174.
8. Ilan Halevi, *A History of the Jews,* trans. A. M. Barrett, London: Zed Books, 1987, p. 158.
9. Yosef Hayim Yerushalmi, *Zahor: Jewish History and Jewish Memory,* New York, Schocken Books, 1989, pp. 99–100.

10. Louis Althusser, 'The Piccolo Teatro: Bertolazzi and Brecht', *For Marx*, trans. Ben Brewster, Harmondsworth: Penguin, 1969, p. 150.

11. Michel Foucault, *The Order of Things*, London: Tavistock, 1970, *passim*.

12. Avram Kampf, *Chagall to Kitaj: Jewish Experience in 20th Century Art*, London: Lund-Humphries/Barbican Art Gallery, 1990, p. 5.

13. Halevi, *op. cit.*, p. 158.

14. Cited in Robert Paine, 'Israel: Jewish identity and the competition over tradition', in E. Tonkin, M. McDonald and M. Chapman (eds), *History and Ethnicity*, London: Routledge, 1989, p. 132.

15. *Ibid.*, p. 121.

16. Halevi, *op. cit.*, pp. 129–30.

17. Kampf, *op. cit.*, p. 106.

18. Walter Benjamin, *Illuminations*, trans. Harry Zohn, London: Fontana, 1973, p. 257.

19. Richard Appignanesi, *Postmodernism for Beginners*, Cambridge: Icon Books, 1995, p. 122.

20. Jenny Bourne, 'Homelands of the mind', *Race and Class*, Vol. 29, Summer 1987, p. 22.

21. See Andrew Benjamin, 'Figuring self-identity: Blanchot's Bataille', in Juliet Steyn, *Other Than Identity*, pp. 9–32, for an elaborate exegetical study of this issue.

22. Theodor Adorno, *Negative Dialectics*, trans. E. Ashton, London: Routledge & Kegan Paul, 1973.

23. Arnold Wesker, *The Birth of Shylock and the Death of Zero Mostel*, London: Quartet Books, 1997, p. xvi.

24. Pointed out by Andrew Benjamin, 'A place of refuge', *Times Literary Supplement*, 10 October 1997, p. 31, in a critical appreciation of George Steiner's autobiography, *Errata: An Examined Life*, London: Weidenfeld & Nicolson, 1997.

25. Quoted in Leon Poliakov, *The History of Anti-Semitism*, trans. M. Kochan, Vol. 3, London: Routledge & Kegan Paul, 1975, p. 48.

26. Wesker, *op. cit.*, p. xvii.

27. Sander L. Gilman, *The Jew's Body*, London: Routledge, pp. 113, 127.

28. *Ibid.*, p. 131.

29. George Eliot, *Daniel Deronda*, London: Panther Books, 1970, p. 196.

30. Quoted in Sander L. Gilman, *Difference and Pathology: Stereotypes of Sexuality, Race and Madness*, Ithaca, NY: Cornell University Press, 1985, pp. 154–5.

31. Sander L. Gilman, *Jewish Self-Hatred: Anti-Semitism and the Hidden Language of the Jews*, Baltimore: Johns Hopkins University Press, 1990, p. 290.

32. All examples in this item come from *ibid.*, pp. 257, 267, 262, 265.

33. John Berger, 'Jewish and other painters', *New Statesman and Nation*, 12 December 1953, p. 53.

34. Helen Rosenau, *A Short History of Jewish Art,* London: James Clarke, 1948.
35. *Ibid.,* p. 12.
36. *Ibid.,* p. 71.
37. Leo Steinberg, *The New York School: Second Generation,* New York: Jewish Museum, 1957, cited in Kampf, *op. cit.,* p. 163.
38. Richard Cork, *Jewish Artists in the East End,* video, London: Whitechapel Art Gallery, 1985.
39. Marx, *op. cit.,* p. 112.
40. Quoted by William Fishman, *East End Jewish Radicals 1875–1914,* London: Duckworth, 1975, p. 231.
41. Gilman, *The Jew's Body,* p. 2.

2

Neither/nor:
the Shackmans portrayed

A photograph's *punctum* is that accident which pricks me (but also bruises me, is poignant to me).

Roland Barthes[1]

Upon his arrival from the Ukraine in 1870, Isaac Perkoff opened the St Petersberg Studio on the Commercial Road, London.[2] He had learnt his trade from his father, Michael, in Kiev. Isaac and his studio assistants photographed members of his own family in a variety of situations – from formal studio ones, such as that of Isaac himself with his wife, Anuta, and their son Ben (taken by Rube Mason) (Figure 2) to informal pictures, like those showing Anuta with her eight children (Alec, Victor, Michael, David, Ben, Bella, Rebecca and Rachel) throwing snowballs in the garden of their home in Lea Bridge Road, Clapton (Figure 3). Photographs and snapshots, it seems, were part of their everyday life, and their album of photographs was one of the seemingly natural attributes of their family life.[3] In this chapter I consider what kind of *Jewish* subjects were in the process of being made in London, in the eye of the camera, in the latter part of the nineteenth and early twentieth century.

These fragile images respond eagerly to my caption 'London Jews circa 1900'. I am wary of the violent effects of such a name: it is already too restrictive, too loaded and secure. Titled thus, these photographs can be read too easily as documents. How can these people be identified as 'Jews'? What or who do Jews look like? Of course there have been those like Francis Galton, who developed a system of classification to identify the Jewish type, who have claimed to know (Figure 4). The categorization of people into racial groups was a quintessential nineteenth-century project, a technology of power and a disciplinary

Figure 2.   Rube Mason, *Isaac, Anuta and Ben Perkoff*, Perkoff family
archive. With kind permission of The Jewish Museum,
London.

technique. *Jew* as a category has been accessible and ripe for abuse and
'real' Jews as a consequence have been persecuted and even annihilated.
Jew is an overdetermined sign which is saturated with meanings.
Reading the photographs as representations of Jews is to walk on
quicksand and risks reiterating already existing assumptions of identity.

A photograph is an emanation of a past reality which offers itself
today, now, as evidence. Photographs insist upon their status as
recorders of events, as providers of proof. Absorbed in and by history,

Figure 3.   Isaac Perkoff, *The Perkoff Family*, Perkoff family archive.
With kind permission of The Jewish Museum, London.

yet curiously estranged from it and uprooted, they cry out for location
and historical specificity from which meanings may be induced and
derived. The aura of a photograph comes from its power to co-opt the
truth of a moment: yet we know everything in the image has been
composed. A photograph is a trace without facts while at the same time
it elicits them. However, the photographs could be understood also as
'recollections forward':

> Repetition and recollection are the same movement only in opposite
> directions; for what is recollected has been, is repeated backwards,
> whereas repetition properly called is recollected forward.[4]

Through Kierkegaard's formulation we can begin to see that the
images are neither simply representations and repetitions nor solely
fixed and frozen repositories of memories, recollections. As neither
one nor the other, their singularity can be discerned. Hence the photographs can be considered as a way of disturbing the assumed boundary
between *Jew* as a category and that other equally anxious classification,

Figure 4. Francis Galton, *Composite Portraits of the Jewish Type*, 1885, University College, London. With kind permission University College, London.

'real' Jew. My interpretation of photographs from the Perkoff family album relies on both the troubling acknowledgement of *Jewish* identity and a refusal of it. Uncovering a Jewish story which may be said to be both veiled and discernible in the photographs is not to say that such a history and identity is 'essential', rather, it is to enable a going-beyond (insofar as going-beyond necessitates a working-through, a repetition).

If, as Roland Barthes suggests, there are four possible repertoires for imaging a person – 'the one I think I am, the one I want others to think I am, the one that the photographer thinks I am and the one he makes use of to exhibit his art[5] – then who did Tsippa and Minnie (nieces of Isaac) think they were (Figure 5)? What did they want others to think? Whom did Isaac Perkoff make use of for his artistry?

Tsippa and Minnie were not expecting to be photographed when this picture was taken, sometime in 1895, the year the family moved into the house on Lea Bridge Road.[6] They had been scrubbing the kitchen floor and were interrupted to have their photograph taken. Tsippa's blouse is untucked and Minnie still wears an apron. They face the camera smiling and appear at ease. This was twenty-five years after the family's arrival from Kiev.

Isaac's business must have been successful enough for the family to move out of the *Jewish* East End to Clapton, although by then it had changed from a genteel middle-class suburb into a district occupied by 'respectable' working-class people. Lea Bridge Road, judging from the census returns of 1891, was a street almost exclusively occupied by working- or lower-middle-class English people. The census recorded a number of labourers, clerks, milliners, shopkeepers and washer-women as living there.[7] However, the family name appears neither in the census return nor in the *Kelly's Directory* for that decade, suggesting that the family were not owner-occupiers but tenants, possibly precariously positioned in the quest for upward class mobility.[8]

The girls pose as if bound together, holding a book, its pages opened half-way. The image suggests that books were a 'natural' part of their family culture. Associations with housework, the low, are disturbed and displaced. Here dirt has evaporated in the move from 'work' to 'leisure', which again confuses the assumptions we may have about class. The book is a complex signifier which may allow us to read it as an image of aspiration. It would seem thus to affirm the value of reading for young working-class women as something which is easy and relaxed – an entertainment. The public and social expectations established through the categories of *working* and *leisured* classes are unsettled. From their facial expressions it appears that we witness an ordinary event: neither Tsippa nor Minnie has dressed for the occasion. On that day, momentarily, they have been interrupted from their book to face the camera. The photograph marks a moment in which to

Figure 5.   Isaac Perkoff, *Tsippa and Minnie Perkoff*, 1895, Perkoff
family archive. With kind permission of The Jewish
Museum, London.

commemorate them. It commits their image to memory. And it also
seems to stage a question – what will these young women-of-the-book
become? The photograph resonates with the possibility of becoming
and may be seen to mark a Utopian moment which resists the memorial
(or even death) through a sense of the future which is always, already
inscribed within it. The question nevertheless remains: who are they?

The photograph itself cannot answer that question. But suppose for a moment that there was a caption which read, 'Idle moment in an East End brothel'?

Referring to portrait photography in the nineteenth century, John Tagg has argued that a portrait is 'a sign whose purpose is both the description of an individual and the inscription of social identity.'[9] In his argument the photograph is a tool in the project of bourgeois social regulation. Power, for Tagg – as indeed for Foucault before him,[10] is described as diffused and differentiated. It is maintained and mediated through particular forms, procedures and technologies. Individuals are subject to the regulative powers of the state and its various institutional forms, which include photography. The photograph, in Tagg's argument, is a powerful site for the making of 'docile' subjects. Indeed it may be so: but not simply thus. Tsippa and Minnie are not just subject to but are subjects of the photograph which slips and slides around the categories established by Tagg, precisely refusing a simple codification. The photograph poses itself and is posed in ways which both accept and deny such a totalizing manoeuvre. The image constitutes the object which is also its subject. Accordingly, there is always the possibility of a reversal of the power of the gaze.

Photographs may ape social conventions but may also transgress them. This is a 'private' photograph and may escape the confines of the formal public gaze. Private life is precisely a zone, as Barthes suggests, where an image may escape the limits of conventional codes.[11] In excess of these, a supplementary narrative bursts forth. The connotative power of the image lies in its precarious relationship with the boundaries provided by rigid systems of classification. The photograph has been composed and presented as if its future was to be a public document (which it has now become). But this too is an uneasy reading: its public outcome could not have been known. The split between the public and the private is disrupted by the girls who seem to mimic posing itself. The photograph of Tsippa and Minnie is transgressive: it clarifies the ruling conventions at the very moment that it posits a space for new ones.

Tsippa and Minnie may well have attended the Jews' Free School which, like all schools, played an exemplary role as transmitter of the values – in this particular case of Anglo-Jewry. Assimilated Anglo-Jewry comprised an élite group which tended to prosper in banking, investment and business. Its 'members' created the institutional infrastructure of Jewish life. These private individuals assembled into public bodies which transmitted the needs of English and bourgeois society to those of the state. Through these processes political exigencies were transformed into a social 'order' which appeared as the norm.

The activities of the Jews' Free School were entirely consistent with English secondary school education of the time. The curriculum aimed to produce people with 'sound bodies' and 'agile minds'. Healthy bodies were perceived as a contribution to the well-being of the nation and a sign of patriotism. The school also provided religious classes, whose main purpose was provide moral and social guidance. However, there were many parents who were critical of what they perceived as the inadequacies of the religious instruction offered there.[12] Indeed 70 per cent of the pupils also went to a Talmud Torah or Chedar after school. The Chief Rabbi, Adler, was contemptuous of this. He argued that the education given in these classes had not changed for two hundred years. His concern was with the rapid modernization of Jewish immigrants, their adaptation and assimilation to an English and preferably middle-class form of life. Nevertheless, he reluctantly supported their continuing existence, insofar as he could see that the religious classes, however outmoded, would provide yet another opportunity to instil the appropriate standards of morality in the pupils. A speech of 1902 clearly spells out his fears:

> Every Jewish scamp, every Jewish money-lender, every Jewish cheat, does more harm to Judaism than a Christian scamp, a Christian money-lender, a Christian cheat does harm to Christianity. Contrariwise every Jewish hero does us more good. This is the necessary condition of minorities. So you may recognize and understand your importance and your responsibilities.[13]

He stresses communal responsibilities, accepts and reinforces the opposition between Christian and Jew, and perhaps displays embarrassment. After all, it appears that no amount of education would have been enough to free the Jewish élite from the stigma attached to the newer Jewish immigrants, miscreant or other. Inevitably, Jewry was itself split into a myriad of parts: it was divided by class interests, by differences in religious interpretation, by attitudes towards Jewish nationalism, by earlier constellations of history which depended upon the settlers' country of origin and, of course, by attitudes towards England and assimilation itself. As Halevi has noted, in the space of two generations the status and place of European Jews had undergone changes on an unparalleled scale: from the *shtetl* to modern citizenship. However, he also reminds us that there were those who had not been given any opportunity to assimilate. The Jews of the Pale in the Russian Empire tended to favour Jewish nationalism whether secular or religious. They considered Western Jews to be traitors to the essential cause of Jewish identity in their desire to integrate.[14] This was a view shared by the novelist, Israel Zangwell, for whom acceptance into English society could only be at a cost:

Judea prostrated itself before the Dragon of its hereditary foe, the Philistine, and respectability crept on to freeze the blood of the orient with its frigid finger, and to blur the vivid tints of the East into the uniform grey of English middle-class life.[15]

Language was seen as the key to successful assimilation. In the Jews' Free School, children were forbidden to speak any language but English. An article in the *Daily Graphic*, in 1895, praised the school for its achievements:

It is essentially a foreign school and the immense majority of the children on entering the school cannot speak a single word of English. When they leave, after passing the successive standards, they all speak English with a regard for grammar and a purity of accent far above the average of the neighbourhood.[16]

The success of the school was thus measured in terms of the language accomplishments of its pupils, and it was emphasized that the pupils did not just speak English but a particular kind of English: one which was pure, devoid of nuance or local accent. The article continued with a case history, providing the evidence of the efficacy of the education provided:

As another instance of the completeness of the English education given in this school, I may mention the case of a gentleman to whom I was introduced as the manager of another Jewish institution. After a few minutes 'conversation' I could not help asking him how it happened that he, an obvious John Bull, came to be connected with the Jews. He explained that his parents were Polish Jews, that he came to London with them at the age of four, and that he had received the whole of his education in the Jewish Free School. That is typical of the work the school does. This school, supported by Jewish subscriptions and Jewish endowments, is in effect a huge factory for the production of English citizens from foreign material.[17]

Schools are the intermediary space between home, the private sphere and the public domain. Assimilation was their main goal and social engineering their practice. So the idea of a school as a 'factory' was indeed an apt metaphor. The headteacher, Louis B. Abrahams, in his speech to parents at the annual prize giving in 1905, emphasized parental responsibility in the successful adaptation of their children to English values:

Strengthen the effort of the teachers to wipe away all evidences of foreign birth and foreign proclivities, so that [your] children shall be identified with everything that is English in thought and deed, that no shadow of anti-Semitism might exist, that [your] boys and girls may

grow up devoted to the flag which they are learning within these walls
to love and honour, that they may take a worthy part in the growth of
this great Empire, whose shelter and protection [I hope] will never be
denied them.[18]

He claims that foreignness is the key problem and anti-semitism is
the inevitable consequence of not assimilating. Abraham's message,
then, was become alike, become English and anti-semitism will
disappear. Assimilation, it seems, was managed and consented to, in
part at least, on the basis of fear. Jews should be eternally grateful to
be offered a place in British society. If Abrahams was right, it follows
that any signs of refusing to assimilate would themselves create anti-
semitism: it would be the Jews' own fault, something they brought
upon themselves. This is not a simple choice, but a repetition of the
question 'who' to become in the 'host' society. A certain image was
needed to give back to the host both what it is and is not.

The Perkoff family chose the route of assimilation. Yet to assimilate
may perforce be to imitate, which is itself ambivalent. In the case of
the portrait of Raphael and Anne Shackman (née Perkoff), a marmoreal
effect is created and as a consequence the figures resemble statues
(Figure 6). This fixing creates stasis, which is also the promise (or
deception) of representation itself. It is very different in its effects from
the photograph of Tsippa and Minnie in which, if you have accepted
my interpretation, the girls pose at posing. The Shackmans by contrast
are akin to monuments. Their very presence relies on the prospect of
a stable identity.

The picture of the Shackmans disturbs ruling photographic
conventions but in a different way and with a different effect from that
of Tsippa and Minnie. It was taken at the St Petersberg Studio in 1910.
They were married in 1907. At first glance it looks like a conventional
bourgeois betrothal portrait, conforming more or less exactly to Tagg's
notion of the portrait photograph as 'description' and 'inscription', in
other words as inescapably an image of social regulation.[19] But again,
with reference to Barthes, who did the photographer think the
Shackmans were? What did he himself use to show his art?

The accoutrements of the St Petersberg Studio pictured in the
Shackman photograph include a French-style eighteenth-century chair
and table. From the 1840s in England this style had been revived.
Ferdinard de Rothschild described it as

> not classical, it is not heroic, but does it not combine as no previous
> art did, artistic quality with practical usefulness? . . . French eighteenth-
> century art became popular and sought for, because of that adaptability
> which more ancient art lacks . . .[20]

Figure 6.   Isaac Perkoff, *Raphael and Anne Shackman*, 1910, Perkoff
family archive. With kind permission of The Jewish
Museum, London.

The Rothschilds' London home and Halton House in Buckingham
were decorated in this way and his defence of what was, after all, the
style of his own homes rests primarily upon the improbable grounds of
utility. Both houses were condemned by such establishment figures as

Lady Frances Balfour and Mary Gladstone as 'vulgar'.[21] Such critical derision may itself have prompted Rothschild's extravagant affirmation of his good own taste. The choice of furnishings for the St Petersberg Studio may well be understood as connoting high achievement exemplified by the Rothschild family, but it may also have conveyed tasteless or indeed 'vulgar' extravagance to the English ruling class.

The Shackmans themselves pose, and are posed, in accordance with the conventions of bourgeois portrait photography. They face us, who now witness them. Pierre Bourdieu has suggested that this is the pose which gives the subjects a sense of self-respect: 'striking a pose means respecting oneself and demanding respect.'[22] The Shackmans have dressed up for the occasion in what may well have been their wedding garb. She wears a blouse trimmed with lace inserts and ribbons; the sleeves are long, full and ruched, the collar is high, the skirt long, with a few inches touching the ground. Her hair is swept up into a chignon. Around her neck is a velvet ribbon with a small heart hanging from it. In all, her costume was à la mode in 1906, but already dated by the time the photograph was taken. Certainly by 1910 fashion for women had changed to narrower, more tailored costumes with shorter skirts which touched the instep. The 'ideal' contour of women, perceived hitherto as 'mature', was being remoulded to a more svelte form.[23]

For men, by 1907 single-button fastening was common. Raphael Shackman's suit was in the mainstream of male dress, which was less subject to change than that of women. However, subtle shifts to it were occurring. In 1900 separate collars of starched white linen up to about three inches (7.5 cm) in height were the accepted mode, but gradually the height declined to about one inch (2.5 cm) and unstarched collars became acceptable.[24] Here a high starched collar is worn. His sleeves and trousers are a touch too long and Raphael also breaks one of the cardinal rules of contemporary dress – his tie-pin attracts too much attention and thus would have been perceived as vulgar by those concerned with creating and upholding strict standards established by codes of dress.[25]

The *punctum*, to borrow Barthes' term, or the jolt effect – that which focuses the entire photograph – is, for me, Raphael's hand, which grips the arm of the chair as if he is holding on to life itself.[26] Raphael and Anne's posture is rigid because they are burdened by appearances. They face the camera and thereby, according to Bourdieu, demand respect. But the promise of a demand is deceptive: it has already been circumvented. Anne rests upon Raphael, who is himself supported by the chair. The cleft between those who demand respect and those who can command it is unbreachable. Between a demand and a command lie different orders which themselves imply hierarchical relationships. What is caught in the photograph is an imitation.

Figure 7.   Isaac Perkoff, *Picnic in the Forest*, 1889, Perkoff family
archive. With kind permission of The Jewish Museum,
London.

The picnic in the forest at Chigwell, dated 19 May 1889, provides
another contrast (Figure 7). This photograph parodies, acts out self-
consciously, the pomposity of the bourgeois group portrait. Wit and irony
are figured particularly in the poses of the men, who seem to ask: who
do you think we are? Here, to mime is a vivacious and pugnacious act
and comes close to Homi K. Bhabha's description of mimicry as dis-
rupting authority and estranging the normality of dominant discourse.[27]
Mimicry is not just imitation but works as a metaphor for 'excess'. It is
the fugitive and ephemeral interval between image and identification.
The photograph is caught at the moment of deviant defiance. Its subjects
are indeed subject to but are they subjected by its gaze?

The photograph as a public statement, paid for and taken in a studio,
conferred status upon the sitters. John Tagg has argued that having
their portrait taken was an act through which the subjects could make
their social mobility visible both to themselves and to others.[28] Thereby
people could see themselves classed among those who possessed and

enjoyed social status. From the Shackmans' portrait can we infer that they want to be accepted, assimilated, to 'make it' as something which may transcend Jewry, as something else, as something which is negotiable?

Writing nearly thirty years later in 'The work of art in the age of mechanical reproduction', Walter Benjamin, having seen sweeping changes to the reproduction and dissemination of images, identified a possible repercussion of the reproducible image as the democratization of forms of representation. [29] He affirmed the loss of what he called the 'aura' of art (uniqueness, authority, authenticity and distance) insofar as he considered that technological reproduction released art from its parasitical dependency on ritual to bring it closer to the masses. Thus, in this logic, it could be argued that people were armed with the weaponry of self-representation. The allure of the photograph for Benjamin lay in its liberatory prospect, in the possibility that it was a site of resisting and resistant subjectivities. However, Benjamin's essay is more equivocal than I have been suggesting: it has contradictory impulses and connotations. For not only did he welcome the loss of aura but he also lamented it. He could see its inherent danger, insofar as this very 'loss' allows politics to become more spectacular and thrilling. Spectacle subsumes critical distance: socialist or fascist? asks Benjamin in a dramatic turn which brings his essay to a close.

Moreover, people represent themselves in languages and through conventions which they themselves have not necessarily established, in which they are both subjects of and subject to pre-established codes and conventions. The Shackmans are photographed within and seemingly desirous of the conventions of high art: the studio setting is the art world in which the photographer himself creates his own art. The Shackman portrait uses the conventions of painting but a stable and secure message could not be communicated through its signs. If the photograph was potentially an agent of democracy then it becomes clear, in the Shackman portrait, that the gap between the world of the bourgeoisie and of democracy was unbreachable. In such an abyss the camera, the image, cannot tolerate the strain. In the gaze of the camera, the Shackmans are ill at ease in the conventions. Furthermore if, as Bourdieu suggests, the sense of frontality displays the 'need for reciprocal deference' then such reciprocity is lacking.[30]

Roland Barthes has argued that photographic connotation, like every well-structured signification, is an institutional activity in relation to society overall. Its function is to integrate man, to reassure him.[31] Still, it does not follow that there is always a simple, direct or immediate identification with those values or institutions which will permit or produce a 'reassuring' image. The photograph of the Shackmans shows the limits of strict codes and conventions. The motivation to assimilate, conform, seek reassurance and identity may have been there for the Shackmans themselves and the photographer Isaac Perkoff, yet the image once again escapes the limitations of its frame. It may itself cite the 'universal', insofar as that condition permits the very possibility of *meaning*, but it is also a condition of its very universality that it allows us to witness the breaking of the codes and expose fake unities. The universal, after all, is only heterogeneous singularity.

Thus we are able to glimpse the Shackmans in their singularity and the limiting and limited possibilities of representation, identification and even assimilation itself. To destabilize conventions means to confront the social and symbolic order which is itself based on the supposed identity of subject and concept. The Shackmans are not identical with *English* or *English Jews*, assimilated or otherwise: their bearing marks an unnameable body.

Acceptance of the Jews in Britain meant their successful assimilation. This was the main line of defence in the evidence given to the Royal Commission on Alien Immigration.[32] The Commission was established in 1902 as a response to the MP, Major William Evans Gordon's Parliamentary Amendment: 'To represent the urgent necessity of introducing legislation to restrict the immigration of destitute aliens in London and the cities of the United Kingdom.'[33] As the proceedings of the Commission show, 'destitute aliens' equalled Jews. Several headteachers from the East End of London were called as witnesses. They all accepted and reinforced the view that assimilation was the key to solve the problems perceived to have been posed by immigrants. They set out to prove that the second-generation children were indeed striving with success to become Anglicized. J. M. P. Rawden of Deal Street Board School, which had on its roll 335 Jewish boys out of a total of 340 pupils, confirmed that in his school:

> Practically the whole of these children are of foreign parentage. Not withstanding the fact, the lads have become thoroughly English. They take a keen and intelligent interest in all that concerns the welfare of our country. They are proud to be English boys.[34]

Again it is the successful mastery of the English language that is affirmed as the way to become assimilated. But patriotism is also a principle at stake here. These themes were also taken up in Lord Rothschild's questions to Sir Samuel Montague, who, on the basis of a visit to the Jews' Free School, was able to offer reassurances to the Commissioners:

> I went with a Polish doctor to the Jews Free school which is the largest school, and has the most foreign children, and had the greatest difficulty in finding one child (although they held up their hands that they were

the children of foreign parents) who knew the Polish or Yiddish language . . . They had become so thoroughly English from the tuition of the free schools that they had lost all their foreign characteristics, except, probably in their own homes, where they would be teaching their parents English.[35]

The children of the immigrants proved their Englishness through their identification with the language. But if 'home' was still a problem, it was one which the future would overcome. Yiddish was the mark of Otherness, so, Louis Abrahams in his prize-giving speech mentioned earlier urged his audience to give up Yiddish, 'that miserable jargon which is not a language at all'. In his view it created the dividing line between the English and the Jews. He told them to throw off their 'foreign habits' and 'foreign prejudices and become English – truly English'. For Abrahams and indeed others, Yiddish was the ultimate sign of Otherness and something for which they showed nothing other than fear, expressed as disavowal and contempt. Yiddish was the pre-eminent declaration of Jewish identity and was as such either decried or celebrated.

The status and significance of Yiddish was paradigmatic of the struggle over Jewish identity. For some it represented the ghetto – it was the very language which kept the Jews apart – for others it was the language of 'the people' and carried with it socialist connotations. For others again, as we have seen, it was 'jargon', an impure language and a source of shame. Language contributed to the perception of the Jew as *essentially* different. A Yiddish-speaking Eastern-European Jew, or a Jew speaking English with the traces of a foreign tongue, was the sign of a despised incomplete symbiosis with the 'host' nation. Visibility was also a question of sounding different. Hence speaking Yiddish, it was believed, impeded the way to full unconditional citizenship. Assimilation seeks to consume everything that is unlike, to remake it in its own image. As a process, it relies on the assumptions of a given identity.

So when Raphael and Anne Shackman posed for their portrait it may have been a sign of their desire to assimilate, but the image was also a sign of the limits of that very project. It may point to a rift in bourgeois notions of assimilation and identity. However, to make claims such as these is also to ignore the heterogeneity of the photograph's address and to assume that the meaning of photographic representation is hegemonic. The photograph presents merely the possibility of meaning and, as Allan Sekula has suggested, it is 'polysemic' in character.[36] So to and for themselves as assimilating Jews, the image could have been seen as a mark of their social achievement, while for a Rothschild, perhaps, it could have elicited the satisfaction of self-emulation. Or, for others again, perhaps a religious Jew, it could have been understood as a sacrilegious act. Or again, perhaps for an anti-alien campaigner such as Arnold White, the photograph might have constituted a threat: an image of another who has slipped into the same and who, by becoming alike, presents a menace. Or yet again, perhaps for a Lady Balfour or a Mary Gladstone, it may have been yet more evidence to confirm the idea of the Jew as vulgar.

The vulgar Jew has been described by Hannah Arendt as the *parvenu*, which she defines against the *pariah*.[37] The pariah (embodied for her in the figures of Heinrich Heine, Franz Kafka, Sholom Aleichem and Charlie Chaplin) self-consciously brings Jewish existence into the unsympathetic world of the non-Jew (the world in which he must live), but he neither denies nor idealizes his Jewish heritage. The parvenu does *either*: he is the opportunist in excess. To which typology do the Shackmans belong? To both and to none: to neither/nor. Is this a tragic condition? Neither pariahs nor parvenus, they resist classification, thereby refusing total incorporation by or in the gaze.

The processes of assimilation were not monolithic. There were spaces in which resistance to its assumed totalizing power were also a possibility. For both Zangwell and Dr Theodore Herzl, Jewish nationalism was the only possible form of resistance to assimilation, which they understood as bringing an end to the Jew. On Monday, 7 June 1902, Herzl was called to give evidence to the Royal Commission on Alien Immigration. He was asked to define assimilation: 'By assimilation I understand verbally what the word implies – to become assimilar – that you are no more distinguishable. That is assimilation.'[38] Herzl did, however, support the view – and here he comes close to Abrahams – that in the present circumstances Jews 'should accept English hospitality gratefully', implying both subservience to the 'host' and a transitional stage. As long as Britain was seen and indeed represented itself as the 'host', the rights of the Jews, he argued, could never be guaranteed. Hence Herzl maintained that the Jews should set up their own homeland in Palestine, a place where they could achieve autonomy and civil rights. The 'rights' granted in Britain were, he thought, inevitably precarious as long as the Jews were perceived as aliens and they saw themselves as and were seen as 'guests'.

A month before, in his diary (9 June, London), Herzl voiced some of the problems facing the Commission, some of which he feared would cause him difficulties in replying to their questions. He felt he was walking a tightrope:

> My testimony before the Royal Commission, which will throw into relief the horns of a dilemma that now perplex them; either to break with the glorious tradition of free asylum, or leave the working class defenceless.[39]

Beforehand Herzl had met privately with Rothschild, who alerted him to the reasons he had been called as a witness. He warned Herzl that his reputation as an expert on the Jewish question would be used and exploited. Indeed, as the following extract in a letter from Max Nordau (27 June 1899) to Alfred Austin in London shows, Herzl had already acquired an awesome reputation:

> You will see in him one of the most remarkable men of our time, less so as yet by actual achievement than by grandeur of purpose. His mental qualities are those of a poet and a statesman welded into one. His character is of almost Anglo-Saxon staunchness and of puritan severity. He is an idealist in conceptions, a realist in execution – withal a born leader.[40]

Herzl's authoritative position and in particular his well-known view that 'a Jew can never become an Englishman' made him especially useful to the anti-alienists' campaign. Rothschild also warned him not to mention the plight of the Jews in Romania where Jews must, in Herzl's own words, 'either die or get out'.[41] On the basis of this view, Rothschild was anxious that it would be assumed that thousands more Jews would arrive in Britain and this fear alone would inevitably lead to restrictive legislation. Herzl, however, refused to heed Rothschild's advice and reported in his diary:

> I would be a wicked person, if I confined myself to saying things that would lead to a restriction of immigration. But I would incidentally be one of those wicked persons to whom English Jewry might well create a monument because I saved them from an influx of Eastern European Jews, and also perhaps from Anti-Semitism.[42]

The 'expert' witness set out his reasons for Jewish nationalism before the Commissioners in the following terms:

> I myself was an assimilated Jew and I speak from experience. I think the Jews have rather a tendency to assimilate, they have a natural tendency to assimilate; but there comes the moment when they are in a very good way on the road to assimilation, and then at that moment comes Anti-Semitism. The whole history has taught us that never have Jews been in a happier condition than when they were in Spain before the events which led up to the Inquisition and the Expulsion in the fifteenth century; they were to Spain all they could be, and they had all they could have.[43]

Herzl expresses a choice or a no-choice situation – whether or not to assimilate, or to belong to a 'historic nation'. For him it was a choice to be made by each individual Jew. A nation in Herzl's terms was 'a historical group of men of a recognizable cohesion, held together by a common enemy'. The common enemy for the Jews was anti-semitism. Herzl created the architecture which combined Jewish nationalism with the modern state. According to Herzl, anti-semitism produced Zionism. His Zionist vision is a response both to the limits which he saw as endemic to the project of assimilation and liberal democracy and the pogroms. Jewish nationalism was established on the basis of European nationalism and replicated its logic with all the contradictions. Paradoxically, it was the very identity of liberal democracy which both promised and betrayed the commitment to equal rights. Herzl's thinking repeats the misconceptions of identity as either/or. He is trapped in the logic of identity and difference.

Modernization and assimilation were negotiable at least for some. Assimilation could not be a hegemonic project even though it set out to be so. It constituted a radical and liberating strategy for those who took the opportunity to reshape and create new forms of life. It enabled them to leave the ghetto and participate in the public life of the nation. For them, including perhaps the Shackmans, it must have felt as if their unending demand for a home was granted. They may have been able to balance the losses with the rewards that assimilation proffered. For some it may also have been subordinating: assimilation was, after all, a middle-class project. Assimilation could be productive of its own forms of violence from inside Jewry itself: those Jews who consented to its discipline in some instances betrayed those Jews who were unwilling or unable to enter that class. So there were inbuilt and powerful restrictions which inevitably set limits.

The photographs from the Shackman family album were taken during a period of intense anti-alien agitation in Britain culminating in laws to restrict immigration which entered the statute books in 1906. During the years 1902–3 the Royal Commission gathered evidence to support its claims that unfettered immigration was dangerous and evil and that Jews were a threat to *Englishness*. The *Jew* was by this process subjected to the alienizing gaze of both Jews and others, including police, clergy, schoolteachers, doctors, shopkeepers and various professionals, who were living with sets of assumptions which claimed to know and to identify the most intimate traits, habits and customs of all Jews. Through this discourse the *Jew* (and to a certain extent other foreigners) was named: rendered as fixed, as knowable and indeed as representable.

I myself have named the series of photographs discussed here 'London Jews circa 1900', which has itself yet again repeated the possibilities of representation. Using that very label has made my fictions possible: indeed, not to have named might have been not to have written. But the name itself is featureless. Yet it has been that very name which has distinguished those people, their *otherness*, their

Jewishness. In order to have made apparent the limits of naming, the name itself has had to be named as impossible. Jew is not simply a representation: there are real Jews that are *real* by virtue of their singularity made manifest through the name which is itself not representable yet always represented.

Notes

1. Roland Barthes, *Camera Lucida*, trans. Richard Howard, London: Fontana, 1984, p. 27.
2. This information came from the depositor of the photographs and was conveyed in a letter to me from Colin Dilkes of the London Museum of Jewish Life (17 August 1988). I am extremely grateful to him for his help.
3. Archive, the London Museum of Jewish Life.
4. Søren Kierkegaard, *Repetition: An Essay in Experimental Psychology,* New York: Harper & Row, 1964, p. 33.
5. Barthes, *op. cit.*, p. 13.
6. Letter, Colin Dilkes.
7. Census returns, 1891, Rose Lipman Library, London Borough of Hackney.
8. *Kelly's Directory* was published annually. I searched through those dating from 1890 to 1905.
9. John Tagg, *The Burden of Representation*, London: Macmillan, 1988, p. 37.
10. See especially the Michel Foucault of *Discipline and Punish.*
11. Barthes, *op. cit.*, p. 15.
12. Eugene Black, *The Social Politics of Anglo-Jewry, 1880–1920*, Oxford: Basil Blackwell, 1988, p. 127.
13. *Ibid.*, p. 129.
14. Ilan Halevi, *A History of the Jews,* trans. A. M. Barrett, London: Zed Books, 1987, p. 134.
15. Israel Zangwell, *Children of the Ghetto,* London, 1892, p. 2.
16. *Daily Graphic,* London, 1895, in the Archive, Stepney Green Library, Tower Hamlets, London [no page].
17. *Ibid.*
18. *Jewish Chronicle,* July, 1905, cited in E. C. Black, *The Social Politics of Anglo-Jewry 1880–1920*, Oxford, Basil Blackwell, 1998, pp. 110–11.
19. Tagg, *op. cit.*, p. 37.
20. Ferdinard de Rothschild, cited in Joanna Banham, Sally Macdonald and Julia Poster, *Victorian Design*, New York: Crescent Books, 1991, p. 204.
21. *Ibid.*
22. Pierre Bourdieu, *Photography: A Middle Brow Art,* Cambridge: Polity Press, 1991, p. 80.

23. Joan Nunn, *Fashion in Costume, 1200–1980*, London: Herbert Press, 1984, p. 175.
24. *Ibid.*, p. 402.
25. *Ibid.*
26. Barthes, *op. cit.*, p. 47.
27. Homi K. Bhabha, *The Location of Culture*, London: Routledge, 1994, p. 86.
28. Tagg, *op. cit.*, p. 37.
29. Walter Benjamin, 'The work of art in the age of mechanical reproduction', in *Illuminations*, trans. Harry Zohn, London: Fontana, 1973, p. 226.
30. Bourdieu, *op. cit.*, p. 80.
31. Roland Barthes, 'The photographic message', in *Barthes: Selected Writings*, introduced by Susan Sontag, London: Fontana/Collins, 1983, p. 210.
32. The findings of the Royal Commission on Alien Immigration (hereafter RC) are published in four volumes: i: *Report*, cd. 1742 (1903); ii: *Minutes of Evidence*, cd. 1742 (1903); iii: *Appendix*, cd. 1741 (1903); iv: *Index and Analysis to Minutes of Evidence*, cd. 1743 (1904). Source: House of Commons Library. I am extremely grateful to Brian Sedgemore, MP, for arranging permission for me to use this library.
33. RC, i, p. 5.
34. RC, ii, Rawden, 18866. (All references forthwith are given with the number referring to the first line of evidence.)
35. RC, ii, Montague, 16766.
36. Allan Sekula, 'On the invention of photographic meaning', in Victor Burgin (ed.), *Thinking Photography*, London: Macmillan, 1982, p. 91.
37. Hannah Arendt, *The Origins of Totalitarianism*, London: George Allen & Unwin, 1958, p. 56.
38. RC, ii, Herzl, 6244.
39. Martin Lowenthal, *The Diaries of Theodore Herzl*, New York: Dial Press, 1956, p. 391.
40. Letter, Max Nordau to Alfred Austin, in Cecil Roth (ed.), *Anglo-Jewish Letters*, London: Soncino Press, 1938, p. 321.
41. Lowenthal, *op. cit.*, p. 365.
42. *Ibid.*, p. 366.
43. RC, ii, Herzl, 6244.

3

The figuration of a Jewish type:
Fagin as a sign[1]

In short, the wily old Jew had the boy in his toils. Having prepared his mind, by solitude and gloom, to prefer any society to the companionship of his own sad thoughts in such a dreary place, he was now slowly instilling into his soul the poison which he hoped would blacken it, and change its hue for ever.

Charles Dickens[2]

What fantasies will the *Jew* have aroused to become in Charles Dickens's *Oliver Twist* such an examplar of hatred, of desire and of fear? What is made to seem repellently alien in the figure of the villainous Fagin is in fact all too familiar: Fagin is a reiteration of the medieval image of the Jew as demonic (with red hair, a large nose and a toasting-fork), of the Jew as child murderer (seeking rich offal), of the Jew as 'avaricious', harking back to Shylock (pp. 52, 115, 76).

The story of Oliver Twist is one of salvation. It describes the rite of passage of the young boy, Oliver, whose life journey takes him from the deprivations of an orphanage, to the lure of criminality, to the discovery of love and family and the virtues of bourgeois life. Belief in justice underpins this moral tale but this can only be achieved through the ultimate sacrifice, the annihilation of evil in the figure of the Jew, Fagin.

The image of the Jew-as-evil possesses a prolific history in popular and literary imagination and was available for Dickens and George Cruikshank, who illustrated *Oliver Twist*, to plunder. Myths about the Jews were powerful enough to be a substitute for reality or indeed to have become reality. Both Dickens and Cruikshank were able to call upon a rich repertoire of signs, attributes and references through which to identify Fagin and represent and typify the *Jew*. Physiognomy and other external signs such as clothes, language, and social and hygienic codes, especially odour, were used to mean Jew. The subject, Fagin, is presented as identical with all Jews.

Fagin stands for all Jewish people, past, present and future. The figuration of a Jewish type is a model both of and for identity – an identity formed and realized. Dickens assembles the idea of the Jew through an elaborate synthesis of imagery from the past, made credible in the present and viable for the future, through his application of social and racial theories.

In the nineteenth century the identity of the Jew was determined by race: '[Fagin] is called "The Jew", not because of his religion, but because of his race.'[3] So wrote Charles Dickens to Eliza Davies. His comment was a response to Eliza Davies's admonishment for encouraging in *Oliver Twist*, as she put it,[4] 'a vile prejudice against the despised Hebrew'.[5] Dickens's reply was to justify himself in the following terms:

> If I were to write a story in which I pursued a Frenchman or a Spaniard as the 'Roman Catholic', I should do a very indecent and unjustifiable thing; but I make mention of Fagin as the Jew because he is one of the Jewish people and because it conveys that kind of idea to him, which I should give my readers of a Chinaman by calling him Chinese.[6]

By 1863, when Eliza Davies presented her challenge to Dickens, Social Darwinism was providing him with the evidence that each and every Jew could be classified and understood according to the exigencies of the science of race. Indeed, *Oliver Twist* was written at a moment when scientific investigations were introducing the processes of elaborating empirical and descriptive evidence to define differences between races that were considered 'essential', that is to say differences of nature or kind. Human nature, behaviour and language, it was argued, sprang directly from biology. Biology, intelligence and physical attributes were made central to definitions of racial identity and supported the idea of racial hierarchies.

Discourses of race had seized the imagination of the European mind and sensibility. So much so, as Edward Said points out, that people as 'unlike each other as Matthew Arnold, Oscar Wilde, James Frazer, and Marcel Proust' not only agreed with racial categories but actively fabricated and used them,[7] as did the enlightened, radical writer, Dickens.

Eliza Davies criticized his attitude to the Jews, by contrasting it with his well-known position of championing the causes of the oppressed. The anger and anxiety she shows in her letter reveals that she considered the Jews in Britain to be generally despised and subjugated and as such, indeed, more than worthy of Dickens's usual philanthropic stance: 'Fagin, I fear admits of one interpretation; but [while] Charles

Dickens lives the author can justify himself or atone for a great wrong on a whole though *scattered nation*.'[8] As a way of marking his atonement, Eliza Davies suggested to Dickens that he gave his support to a Convalescent Home for the Jewish Poor which was to be a named memorial to Lady Montefiore, wife of the financier Sir Moses.[9] Dickens's reply was to offer a nominal sum of money to the charity.[10] However, he made it plain in no uncertain terms that his donation was not to be understood as an admission of the validity of her complaint. Rather than 'atone' for his depiction of the Jew, instead Dickens chose to 'justify' himself: 'Fagin in Oliver Twist is a Jew, because it unfortunately was true of the time in which the story refers, that that class of criminal almost invariably was a Jew.'[11] Dickens confidently represents Fagin, not only as a Jew but as a criminal. He had further elaborated his reasons for doing so in the Preface to *Oliver Twist*:

> It appeared to me that to draw a knot of such associates in crime as really did exist; to paint them in all their deformity, in all their wretchedness, in all the squalid misery of their lives; to show them as they really were, for ever skulking uneasily through the dirtiest paths of life, with the great black ghastly gallows closing up their prospect, turn them where they might; it appeared to me that to do this, would be to attempt a something which was needed, and which would be a service to society. And I did it as I best could.[12]

We can understand 'best' in this context as the accurate and true depiction of characters. These in themselves were to be understood as reflections of what actually existed, that is to say, for Dickens, reflections of reality itself. Evil is here rendered specific, as anti-social and criminal behaviour – as a sociological fact – with all the conviction that Enlightenment science could muster.

Dickens defended his fiction on the grounds of realism. For many mid-nineteenth-century writers and artists, realism was connected, through a sequence of complicities and associations, to scientific materialism, which had itself come to be understood as constituting the truth. Realism promised enlightened understanding and the possibilities of social reform. From this point of view, *Oliver Twist* is concerned with the 'realities' posed by the particular time and space of Victorian London and can be read thus as a critical and moral comment on the harsh and inhumane Poor Laws and their debasing effects on people when treated solely as 'bodies'. Here Dickens the social reformer speaks: the novel was itself a social commentary and moral didacticism was for him a social duty. The realistic portrayal of the criminal Fagin, the *Jew*, was a way of articulating a threat to social reform.

However, Dickens's view of the *Jew* was not the only one possible in Victorian England. In *Daniel Deronda,* George Eliot sketches

Deronda's own ideas about Jews and introduces us to a range of *Jewish* types which the novel will later unmask:

> Spite of his strong tendency to side with objects of prejudice, and in general with those who got the worst of it, his interest had never been practically drawn toward existing Jews, and the facts he knew about them, whether they walked conspicuously in fine apparel or lurked-by in streets, were chiefly of a sort most repugnant to him. Of learned and accomplished Jews he took for granted that they had dropped their religion and wished to be merged in the people of their native lands . . . Deronda could not escape (who can?) knowing ugly stories of Jewish characteristics and occupations.[13]

Here we are introduced to three types of *Jew*: the ostentatious *Jew*, the parvenu, the one who is always visible and in excess; then the slimy *Jew*, the one who lurks in the side streets (and harks back to Fagin), who is there but not quite there; finally, the educated *Jew* who can, through his intelligence, choose to assimilate, become alike and disappear. Their representations may appear fixed from reading the passage quoted above, but through Deronda's meeting with Mirah Eliot creates a crisis in those very categories.

Mirah herself conforms to none of those identities. Neither, of course, does Deronda, but it is only as the plot unfurls that Deronda's Jewish origins become known. Perhaps Mirah comes closest to Hannah Arendt's typology. As a 'pariah' she accepts her inheritance with equanimity and grace. Mirah, the 'good' *Jew*, is fabricated through identification with her mother. Her own father is rejected as uncouth and vulgar. Eliot constitutes the 'good' *Jew* as 'feminine', a characteristic which is also striking in her presentation of Deronda himself. The gendering of *Jew* as female renders Deronda at once more and less threatening. He becomes an equivocal figure, both sensual and powerless, and is an object both of desire and disavowal. Eliot's philosemitism may be subject to the same or similar tropes as Dickens's more manifest anti-semitism and point to the limits of a discourse restrained by the régime of identity and difference.

In 1829, just a few months before Dickens himself started to work as a reporter in the House of Commons, the Liberal Member of Parliament Macaulay (later the famous historian Lord Macaulay) had argued, when advocating Jewish rights, that being Jewish was like being born with 'red hair' and was, as such, an unimportant accident of birth:

> If all red-haired people in Europe had, for centuries, been outraged and oppressed, banished from this place, imprisoned in that, deprived of their money, deprived of their teeth, convicted of the most improbable crimes on the feeblest of evidence, dragged at horses' tails,

hanged, tortured, burned alive . . . what would be the patriotism of gentlemen with red hair? [14]

The point of politics, Macaulay goes on to argue, was to make all people – irrespective of their specific histories – into patriotic citizens. In a speech in the House of Commons in 1830 he claimed that the history of England is 'made up of wrongs suffered and injuries endured by them'.[15] Explicit in his thinking was the notion that people are moulded socially and can thereby be changed.

Against such liberal voices, Dickens in *Oliver Twist* changes the significance of the red hair to reiterate its traditional demonic connotations. Indeed, Fagin's red hair becomes one of the determining signs of Fagin's physical and racial identity. Fagin was born demonic. In the novel, Sikes declares that being with Fagin reminds him

> of being nabbed by the devil . . . There never was another man with such a face as yours, unless it was your father, and I suppose *he* is singeing his grizzled red beard by this time, unless you came straight from the old 'un without any father at all betwixt you: which I shouldn't wonder at a bit. (p. 276)

It would seem, then, that the Jew was condemned by birthright: he was born evil and hence could not be changed. Throughout the narrative, Dickens refers to Fagin as the 'Jew'. It is only in direct speech that he is given his proper name. If ever he is called 'Jew' to his face it is only in a derisory manner. Again and again, *Jew* is remarked upon in a language of scorn and loathing. When, for instance, a young Jew appears in the novel, he is already figured by and in the image of Fagin and is described as 'nearly as vile and repulsive in appearance' as Fagin himself (p. 91). With age, because of his biological inheritance he would necessarily achieve the vileness of his mentor. If the young Jew replicates Fagin, then it is already determined that Jews are heinous: this is their Jewish inheritance, their biological destiny. So it is again that Dickens promotes the idea of the *Jew* as defined and determined by the already existing characteristics of a race.

Not only is the Jew condemned by birthright, he is a stranger to civility. Fagin in an exchange with Nancy says, 'We must have civil words.' Nancy replies, 'Civil words, you villain'(p. 100). He is beyond the pale of civilized life. The *Jew* is a threat to order and Fagin is a throwback to an earlier, 'primitive', pre-enlightened form of life.

The philologist Ernest Renan described the Semite as 'primitive' and deficient, thus subordinating him to the Indo-European race. It is through the category Semite that *Jew* becomes classified as a race. Moreover, what the Semitic Jew is seen to lack is precisely what defines the Indo-European as superior:

In all things the Semitic race . . . appears an incomplete race by virtue of its simplicity. The race – if I dare use the analogy – is to the Indo-European Family what a pencil sketch is to a painting; it lacks that variety, that amplitude, that abundance of life which is the condition of perfectibility. Like those individuals who possess so little fecundity that, after a gracious childhood they attain only the most mediocre virility, the Semitic nations . . . have never been able to achieve true maturity.[16]

In this account the male Semite is the child of humankind, ineffectual and weak. The Semite is incomplete: he is intellectually and sexually immature. Benjamin Disraeli transmutes the negative image of the primitive into a positive image of the *Jew*, in which the 'primitive' connotes wisdom and civilization. Again using theories of race, he promoted the Semites to the rank of the 'aristocracy of nature', and he claimed such luminaries of European culture as Kant, Mozart and Napoleon as belonging to the *Jewish* race. His thinking marks a defensive attempt to represent the Jews, not just as 'better' than others, but as the 'best'. In a speech he delivered to the House of Commons (1847), he demanded the admission of the Jews not on the basis of the liberal principles of tolerance or equality but as a privilege due to the 'People of God':

On every sacred day you read to the people the exploits of Jewish heroes, the proofs of Jewish devotion, the brilliant annals of past Jewish magnificence. The Christian Church has covered every kingdom with sacred buildings, and over every altar . . . we find the tables of Jewish law. Every Sunday – every Lord's day – if you wish to express feelings of praise and thanksgiving to the most High, or if you wish to find expression of solace in grief, you find both in the words of the Jewish poets. All the early Christian were Jews. The Christian religion was first preached by men who had been Jews until they were converted; every man in the early ages of the Church by whose power or zeal, or genius, the Christian faith was propagated was a Jew.[17]

Born of Judaism, Christianity is steeped in it. The Father gave to his progeny not only spiritual guidance, but the Law from which morality and ethics are derived.

Jews are supposed to be ancient and wise, primitive and stupid. Fagin too is an embodiment of the 'primitive'. Dickens's description of him is complex and contradictory. He is drawn as ossified, and shrewd and cunning. Such accounts of the 'primitive', marked by longing and denial, are a register of the mixed feelings and fears that the *Jew* aroused. *Jew* marks the point where social insecurity and instability assume a vibrant form.

Oliver Twist has twenty-four illustrations which all closely relate to the written text. A particular verbal and visual conjunction is set up in which the relationship between words and pictures is symbiotic, and as our gaze strays between the words and the pictures, the one informs the other. When *Oliver Twist* was serialized in *Bentley's Miscellany* it was broken into twenty sections for popular reading, which imposed upon its author the need for recognizable threads, compact narrative episodes, and the interplay of powerful textural as well as textual references. Dickens gave Cruikshank precise instructions for the overall orchestration of the texts. Writing to Cruikshank about *Mr. Bumble and Mrs. Corney taking tea,* he explained: 'I have described a small kettle for one on the fire – a small black teapot on the table with a little tray and so forth – and a two-ounce tea canister. Also a shawl hanging up – and the cat and kittens before the fire.'[18] Indeed, the picture includes all those items which are described, in similar detail, in the narrative on the facing page. However, the interplay across the two sites (words and pictures) is contiguous, not homogeneous. Although Dickens tries to defend his text against ambiguity in his pursuit of the real, there can be no guarantees for the 'correct' reading. Meanings are adduced, 'reality' demonstrated and authenticated, moral truths imparted and learnt in that uncertain space between words and pictures (traversing both). Paradoxically, the rich and vivid interplay of verbal and visual imagery works to conflate realism with myths, the myths about and fears of the Jews.

Ambivalence is inscribed in the very structure of the novel in which two orders, the real and the fantastic, are connoted. Fantasy is played out in Fagin's psychic and physical domain, a nightmarish, supernatural place. When the supernatural is brought into the fiction it could perhaps indicate, as indeed it has been argued, that Dickens's own concerns were moving away from realism.[19] Nevertheless, I think this argument is to miss the point. It was, for Dickens, imperative that the danger of the Jews was perceived as actual. Furthermore, it is only through the representation of the extremes, fantasy and reality, that Dickens can present one as that which is not the other. And that which is not the dangerous stinking world of the Jew is also the real – with all the moral tones that realism carried. Crucially, however, these worlds cannot be kept apart: they permeate each other. As in the process of osmosis, each destabilizes the identity of the other, causing dangerous reverberations.

Fagin's power is described as pervasive. He is 'in-sati-able'(p. 76): his desires are invented as unquenchable. One way in which this is achieved is through the descriptions of Fagin's nose. Physiognomy is used as a key to understanding Fagin's character. A large nose is itself a 'representation of the hidden sign of sexual difference'.[20] Big nose,

Figure 8.   George Cruikshank, *The Jew and Morris Bolter begin to understand each other*, first published in *Bentley's Miscellany*, 1837–9.

with its phallic connotations, has come to denote *Jew*. Cruikshank, in *The Jew and Morris Bolter begin to understand each other* (Figure 8), highlights Fagin's nose: it is the only illuminated part of his body. And Fagin's nose is not any old large nose. The way in which it is drawn conforms exactly to Eden Warwick's contemporary description of the Jewish nose, which is always 'very convex, and preserves its convexity like a bow, throughout the whole length from eyes to the tip. It is thin and sharp.' Sharpness, as Gilman reminds us, connotes shrewdness.[21] Indeed, Fagin himself is described as 'sharp' by Noah (Morris Bolter), who applauds him for recognizing that he and his wife are from the country (p. 263). Fagin is described as striking the side of his nose with his right forefinger. This knowing gesture is frequently invoked by Dickens to signal *Jew*. Noah, wanting to be seen to be as astute as Fagin, tries to mimic his gesture but fails: his own nose, we are told, 'not being large enough for the purpose' (p. 263). Fagin's nose is pointed to and pointed out again and again in pictures and obliquely referred to in the narrative by contrasting its size with that of other noses. The illustrations work to substantiate the written text, which illuminates the picture in a never-ending cycle. The Jewish nose, produced as the ultimate visual sign of difference, is a threat, a lethal concoction of intelligence and potency. It is an ambivalent and menacing image reminiscent of a primal sexuality that is simultaneously loathed and envied.

Dangerous sexuality is signalled in our first introduction to Fagin. The scene is dirty:

> In a frying pan, which was on the fire, and which was secured to the mantelshelf by a string, some sausages were cooking; and standing over them, with a toasting-fork in his hand, was a very old shrivelled Jew, whose villainous-looking and repulsive face was obscured by a quantity of matted red hair. He was dressed in a greasy flannel gown with his throat bare; and seemed to be dividing his attention between the frying pan and the clothes-horse, over which a great number of silk handkerchiefs were hanging. (p. 52)

The squalor and the smell of the setting described by Dickens evoke impurity. The urge to cleanliness, according to Freud, originates in the compulsion to get rid of excreta, which is associated with a shameless, abandoned, animal sexuality. Fagin is dressed in a 'greasy flannel gown'. Freud points out that a person who is unclean (who does not hide his or her excreta) offends other people by showing them no concern. Fagin's dirtiness, his bad smell, is both a reminder of the primitive sexuality associated with the *Jew* and a threat to sociality or, to follow Freud, to civilization itself.[22]

There is a long history connecting the Jew with a particular smell – the *foetor Judaicus*. For medieval anti-Jewish rhetoric, the smell of the Jews was their special distinguishing feature. It was also associated with the sexualized image of the goat: Jews, like the devil, are horned. They share other similarities – a tail and a beard. Bad smells were also linked to the plague, which Jews were blamed for spreading. By the eighteenth century, Jewish smell had been disconnected from the supernatural but became instead an issue of uncleanness. By the nineteenth century the racialized science of biology labelled the *foetor Judaicus* as one of the natural, inherent signs of Jewish difference.[23]

Figure 9. George Cruikshank, *Oliver introduced to the respectable old gentleman*, first published in *Bentley's Miscellany*, 1837–9.

Throughout *Oliver Twist* bad smells are metonymically evoked. Not only are the subjects that Dickens catalogues redolent of odour but Cruikshank's illustrations to the text, time and time again, make great play with smoke and other visible vapours. *Oliver introduced to the respectable old gentleman* (Figure 9) depicts a smoke-filled room. Fumes are emitted from the pipes smoked by the lads, the candle which burns on the table, the sausages being fried in a pan on an open fire, which also smokes. In sum, the Jew's room is shown to be rank, and the walls and ceiling are described, in both images and words, as 'black with age and dirt' (p. 52).

Dickens makes use of the sign 'bad smell' in his representation of the Jew, whose relationship with the world is connoted primarily through smell. Not only is his abode filthy but the very air of Fagin's neighbourhood is 'impregnated with filthy odours' (p. 51). Fagin is contagious: bad smells emanate from him. Smell is pervasive and escapes rational control. Through smells individuals merge, boundaries dissolve: the self permeates and is permeated by the Other. Bad smells denote the material nature of existence. 'Uncivilized' and rotten, they are devices of differentiation and exclusion. The 'low' and the 'dirty' are at the outer limits of civilized life. Dickens was writing at the moment of modernizing the city, where separating the 'healthy' from the 'contaminated' – 'good' from 'bad' odours – was a social and medical concern. Through bad smells, Fagin is identified with nature rather than culture. Paradoxically, however, Fagin is situated against nature by being in the city, again confusing the boundaries between nature and culture.

The city, the site of modernity, of progress, and of what was perceived as the unassimilable masses, was in *Oliver Twist* both exciting and dreadful: it was a decaying, degenerate and devouring place. The city is alive, uncontrollable, debasing and tainting to its inhabitants. Desire for order and intelligibility are, in the novel, projected onto the country. The text contrasts people who live in the city with country-dwellers. People who can see 'sky, and hill and plain, and glistening water' are bound, Dickens suggests, 'to feel uplifted' and experience 'a foretaste of heaven' and 'memories . . . not of this world'. In the town beauty is defiled and people become 'pain-worn dwellers in close and noisy places' (p. 195). The country is understood as a haven, a lost paradise, and the city an unyielding hell. The inhabitants of each are determined by the other. These extremes are important: but each seeps into the other, disturbing boundaries yet again. Country people, like the Boulters, are corrupted by the city through their encounter with the smelly Fagin – a noxious composite of nature and culture. Fagin is the one who creates havoc and confusion.

Fagin's city is a slimy underworld where 'the mud lay thick upon the stones and a black mist hung over the streets; the rain fell sluggishly down, and everything felt wild and clammy to the touch' (p. 115). Clamminess is an in-between state. Lacking stability and yet not flowing, it clings, it is an 'aberrant fluid or melting solid'. As such, it is judged as a base form of existence that falls outside the basic categories: it is anomalous, hence impure.[24] Impurity is that which departs from the symbolic order. Through identifying Fagin with the filthy city, yet another boundary is drawn – that of the other side. The opposition between order and disorder defines the limits to and boundaries of each as a category of the other. Anything which falls outside order, into that abyss of disorder and uncertainty, is reviled and becomes an object of revulsion.

There, on the other side, the repulsive Jew lurks and creeps about. Fagin only comes alive when others are asleep:

It was nearly two hours before daybreak; that time which, in the autumn of the year, may be truly called the dead of the night; when the streets are silent and deserted; when even sound appears to slumber, and profligacy and riot have staggered home to dream; it was at this still and silent hour. (p. 289)

Figure 10. George Cruikshank, *Fagin in the condemned cell*, first published in *Bentley's Miscellany*, 1837–9.

Fagin is chronicled as an alien estranged from the habits and values of contemporary life. His strangeness, his out-of-placeness, is illustrated for us in *Oliver introduced to the respectable old gentleman*, where he is drawn wearing a loose garment reminiscent of a kaftan, which was a relic of medieval middle-class costume: the present is shown literally as clothed in the past. Enlightenment, which realism desired so fervently, had to bury the reminders of the past before it could accomplish its dreams. In the picture of Fagin in prison, *Fagin in the condemned cell* (Figure 10), the night before he is to be hanged, his head is covered with a piece of knotted fabric resembling a kefia. The kaftan and the kefia, both with Semitic connotations, give substance to, and again provide the material evidence for, Fagin the Jew as being out of place in the modern civilized world; as a symbol of the repulsive underbelly of urban experience, he is a ghost which needs to be exorcised.

Thus, as would befit a ghost, it is in the cover of darkness that the Jew skulks

> stealthily along, creeping beneath the shelter of the walls and doorways, the hideous old man seemed like some loathsome reptile, engendered in the slime and darkness through which he moved: crawling forth, by night, in search of some rich offal for a meal. (p. 115)

Popular imagination associated Jews as a whole with participation in magic and bloody rituals, and from this point of view the rich offal touches on the idea of *Jew* as child-murderer.[25] Here Fagin is described as a pre-historic animal, a primitive creature; as such he is an object of loathing who defies or disobeys the rules of classification. In that hinterland between reality and prehistory, this not-quite-human, the unclassifiable lurks. Throughout the text Fagin is described variously as 'villainous-looking and repulsive', 'wily' with a 'hideous grin', as a body which displays 'earnest cunning' and is 'infernal' (pp. 52, 115, 54, 123, 75). He is 'lynx-eyed' or has a 'hawk's eye' and an 'evil leer' (pp. 243, 263, 77). His hand is a 'withered old claw' (p. 275). He is a 'blackhearted wolf' (p. 277). More, when Fagin 'bit his long black nails, he disclosed among his toothless gums a few such fangs as should have been a dog's or rat's' (p. 290). And again, 'the Jew sat watching in his old lair, with face so distorted and pale, and eyes so red and bloodshot, that he looked less like a man, than like some hideous phantom, moist from the grave, and worried by an evil spirit' (p. 289). This detailed cataloguing of Fagin's attributes is so excessive that it borders on the hysterical. The Jew is a hallucination. Fagin speaks with 'abject humility' (p. 76). He simultaneously 'beseeches and pulverizes'.[26] He is a figuration of disgust felt for the unknown within the psyche of the Other, a repugnance felt for the Other that is also the self. Fagin presents a desperate image: he is close but cannot be assimilated. The symbolism attached to the *Jew* is sinister, dark, dangerous and strange. A stranger who is a vision of disorder. Anything which falls outside the modern order into the abyss of disorder and uncertainty is reviled. It is noncontiguous and disturbs identity. That which does not respect order and system is ambiguous, a composite. This is Fagin.

Fagin is feared and he is fascinating. Through Fagin, Dickens presents a vision of power which does not arouse respect but lets loose various excitements. Fagin is as seductive as he is vile. Both Sikes and Nancy cannot stand the Jew, yet they are seduced by him. Bewitched, they give themselves over to imitate him. Had they not become entangled with him, they could have been saved. Imitation and the impossibility of identification lie at the heart of *Jew* loathing. Fagin is able to manipulate others to do his dirty deeds. He leads Nancy 'step by step, deeper down into the abyss of crime' (p. 304). Although they are themselves depraved, it is Fagin who must bear the responsibility for their sin. Nonetheless, Fagin also inspires loyalty. At first Nancy refuses to betray him, crying out as one who is enthralled, 'Devil that he is, and worse than devil as he has been to me, I will never do that' (p. 286). Fagin can also be very funny. The games he plays at first charm Oliver and provoke him to 'laugh till the tears ran down his face' (p. 57). He seems able to enter the child's world as an immature (primitive) creature might. He is witty and horrifying, desirable and despicable, crafty and intelligent. Fagin summons and repels and is himself hypnotic. Tempting the youth, Oliver, he says, ' "Delighted to see you looking so well, my dear" . . . bowing with mock humility' (p. 97).

Cruikshank's illustration, *Oliver's reception by Fagin and the boys*, cunningly reiterates the humble mien described in the narrative, but here what might have been seen as benign turns sinister under a large dark shadow that dwarfs the image of Fagin. He is the hatred that smiles. Dickens does not merely represent Fagin but projects him. Dickens's desire is disguised as repugnance: desire turns aside and becomes rejection. Fagin is funny and shrewd and repugnant – in summary, he is charismatic. His evil is set against equally stylized depictions of other characters, and all characterizations in *Oliver Twist* can be seen against this calibration. However, Sikes and Nancy, although wicked, are redeemable, since their crimes are represented as a consequence of social injustice. Fagin, by contrast, is doomed by virtue of his birthright.

The fusion of evil and criminality specifically identified with the Jews was itself symptomatic of the fears inspired by the perceived threat of uncontrollable, unassimilable, seething masses then gathering in metropolitan centres. The evils attributed to the Jews were prompted by the reorganization of urban life in the nineteenth century. The Jew was seen as the quintessential city dweller and became a body onto which those fears could be projected. Fagin, however, was not simply a criminal but one who preyed on innocent children. His deviancy was an attack on the future as much as it was an anti-social crime of the present. The *Jew* encapsulated fears which themselves anticipated and projected the impossibility of future progress. Fagin filled out and occupied that symbolically important place as Other. Although the category marked by the Other was ambivalent, there was no escape from it. The presence of the *Jew* gave sense to the Other.

The Jewish question was part of the general question of social reform and control yet differentiated from it. Nineteenth-century radical liberalism needed exclusions in order to support its very workings. *Jew* was installed as a distinctive category in which differences were used to define and maintain social order.

Oliver Twist reveals deep clefts in Enlightenment thought between progress and regress, the rational and the irrational. The Enlightenment was in part at least a dream and spoke in forked tongues. It is there, in that very place, lying somewhere between fantasy and reality – a murderous conjunction – that the dialectical tensions of the Enlightenment are re-enacted and then resolved through a synthesis in which evil, the criminal, the *Jew* is annihilated.

Fagin, the terrified and terrifying nomad, must be exterminated. Even on his last night alive, perhaps parodying Christ in the garden of Gethsemane, Fagin continues to inspire fear and hatred.[27] He

> started up, every minute, and with gasping mouth and burning skin, hurried to and fro, in such paroxysm of fear and wrath that even they – used to such sights – recoiled from him with horror. He grew so terrible, at last, in all the tortures of his evil conscience, that one man could not bear to sit there, eyeing him alone; and so the two kept watch together. (p. 330)

Fagin does not repent but curses about his condition. He does not, cannot, atone for his sins. The drawing of *Fagin in the condemned cell* shows a Bible resting unopened upon a shelf in a dark corner of the cell. There is no view through the barred window. A shaft of light illuminates the bench upon which Fagin sits, highlighting the very part unoccupied by him. Untouched by light, he bites his nails, his knees knock together, his eyes bulge white with terror. The *Jew* is irredeemable. In the *Merchant of Venice*, in the figuration of Jessica, Shylock's daughter, Shakespeare indicates that Jews are doomed by blood but can at least be saved by Christianity.[28] Dickens's Enlightenment fable does not, cannot countenance this prospect. In Hannah Arendt's sharp words, 'Jews had been able to escape from Judaism into conversion; from Jewishness there was no escape.'[29] Liberalism was put into jeopardy by the very existence and form of life of the Jews, since they threw into question (and doubt) the very generality by which liberalism was itself constituted. It was predicated upon the idea of reform or its possibilities, yet Fagin was not reformable. That was his role.

The Jew stood out as the disturbing feature in the projected harmony of the evolving nation. The liberal project offered, as an image of itself, the idea of the unity of man. While it promised radicalism and was predicated upon notions of freedom and equality – seeming to say that all people were welcome to share power – this could only happen if everybody abided by the same rules, which were marked out by the privileged group which itself constructed its Others. Jews heard enlightenment call, inviting them inside (to become alike) and some may have accepted the invitation but were condemned or rejected for doing so. Those desirous of maintaining or asserting control needed to restrain the 'outside' and thereby counteract the force the Others were imagined to possess. Thereby the fantasy of political power and ascendancy was maintained and preserved. The racialized sciences perfected the logic of exclusion.

Oliver Twist – a serialized story read by the man travelling daily from the suburbs into the city on the omnibus – played a part in rendering fantasies about the *Jew* familiar and further inscribing in the popular imagination the myth of Jew-as-evil. Of course, that which can be represented is also that which is assumed to be known: as soon as the *Jew* is represented there is always the possibility that the fears he has aroused may be contained. But are they? Slavoj Zizek argues: 'An ideology really succeeds when even the facts which at first sight contradict it start to function as arguments in its favour.'[30] Accordingly, ideology can work if it is not felt in conflict with reality, that is when it determines the very mode of our everyday experience of reality itself, another instance of banality as forgetting.

Notes

1. I am indebted to Tamar Garb, who, as co-editor of *The Jew in the Text: Modernity and the Construction of Identity,* London: Thames and Hudson, 1995, gave me invaluable advice for an earlier version of this text.
2. Charles Dickens, *Oliver Twist,* London: Chapman & Hall, n.d. [1842?], p. 124. Subsequent quotations in this text are from this edition with page numbers in parentheses.
3. Letter, Charles Dickens to Eliza Davies, in Cecil Roth (ed.), *Anglo-Jewish Letters,* London: Soncino Press, 1938, p. 91.
4. *Oliver Twist* was published in twenty parts in *Bentley's Miscellany,* 1837–9. It was the first novel to appear under Charles Dickens's proper name. Edgar Johnson, *Charles Dickens: His Tragedy and Triumph,* Toronto: Little, Brown & Co., Vol. 1, 1952, p. 223.

 5. *Ibid.*, p. 305.
 6. *Ibid.*, p. 306.
 7. Edward Said, *Orientalism,* Harmondsworth: Penguin, 1985, p. 145.
 8. Roth, *op. cit.,* p. 305.
 9. *Ibid.*, p. 304.
10. *Ibid.*, p. 306.
11. *Ibid.*
12. Charles Dickens, 'Preface', *Oliver Twist.*
13. George Eliot, *Daniel Deronda*, London: Panther Books, 1970, p. 196.
14. 'Statement of the civil disabilities and privations affecting Jews in England', London, 1829, reported in the *Edinburgh Review*, January 1831, p. 369.
15. T. B. Macaulay, 'The Jews', *Hansard,* House of Commons, 5 April 1830, p. 1309.
16. Ernest Renan, cited in Said, *op. cit.,* p. 149.
17. Cited in Leon Poliakov, *The History of Anti-Semitism,* Vol. 3, London: Routledge & Kegan Paul, 1975, p. 329.
18. Dickens, *Letter 1, 152* [1838] to Cruikshank, cited in Johnson, *op. cit.,* p. 216.
19. Michael Hollington, 'Dickens and Cruikshank as physiognomers in *Oliver Twist*', *Dickens Quarterly*, 7 (2), 1990, p. 216.
20. Sander L. Gilman, *The Jew's Body,* London: Routledge, 1991, p. 179.
21. Eden Warwick (George Jabet), *Notes on Noses*, 1848, in Gilman, *op. cit.*, p. 179.
22. Sigmund Freud, *Civilization and Its Discontents,* Harmondsworth: Penguin, 1987, p. 289.
23. Sander L. Gilman, *Jewish Self-Hatred: Anti-Semitism and the Hidden Language of the Jews*, Baltimore: Johns Hopkins University Press, 1990, pp. 174–5, 300.
24. See Mary Douglas, *Purity and Danger: An Analysis of the Concepts of Pollution and Taboo,* London: Ark Paperbacks, 1989, p. 38.
25. Gilman, *Jewish Self-Hatred*, p. 77.
26. Julia Kristeva, *Powers of Horror: An Essay on Abjection*, New York: Columbia University Press, 1982, p. 5.
27. Matthew 16 (King James Bible).
28. Jessica says: 'Alack what heinous sin is it in me/To be asham'd to be my father's child!/But though I am a daughter to his blood,/I am not to his manners . . ./I shall end this strife/Become a Christian . . . ', William Shakespeare, *The Merchant of Venice*, Act 2, Scene 3.
29. Hannah Arendt, *The Origins of Totalitarianism*, London: George Allen & Unwin, 1958, p. 87.
30. Slavoj Zizek, *The Sublime Object of Ideology*, London: Verso, 1989, p. 49.

4

Fried fish and matzo meal: representations of the Jew in the evidence presented to the Royal Commission on Alien Immigration, 1902–3

Southwark holds its time, with the City, with Whitechapel, with Clerkenwell, holds the memory of what it was: it is possible to walk back into the previous, as an event, still true to this moment. The Marshalsea trace, the narrative mazetrap that Dickens set, takes over, the figures of fiction outliving the ghostly impluses that started them. The past is a fiction that absorbs us. It needs no passport, turn the corner and it is with you.

Iain Sinclair[1]

By witnessing the witnesses who were summoned to give evidence to the Royal Commission on Alien Immigration, during the years 1902–3, we walk that tightrope and bear witness to a name, by naming what is after all unrepresentable, yet always represented. What we witness in the evidence is a discourse which works as ideology and is thus already assuming Jewish identity. Moreover, this also gives us the chance of testing the assumed distinction between explanation and witness. The evidence supplied by questioners and witnesses alike offers not so much 'truth' about the world but a construction and a projection of it. We find ourselves again somewhere in a confused world, in the hinterland between 'fiction' and 'reality'.

Dickens's *Jew* was born in the world of fiction. However 'real' this fiction was meant to be, *Oliver Twist* could work only because it is a gripping story which displays the ingenuity and consummate skills of the storyteller. It straddled fantasy and reality to create a dangerous concoction which bore witness to the *Jew*. We can situate the evidence presented to the Royal Commissioners at the opposite point in the same vein as *Oliver Twist*. It is likewise a fantasy-construction which supports 'reality'. Accordingly, the evidence is neither 'reality' nor 'fantasy'; it is a text that imitates, creates, recreates and replicates – in an almost endless cycle – the category *Jew*. It offers ideological evidence as given social reality, which in itself masks its nightmarish fears. This inquiry into the alien problem culminated in legislation to restrict what was perceived by many as the unfettered immigration of Jews from Eastern Europe. Through its practices and procedures, the Jew as alien-other was normalized in political and legal discourses.

Many historians have celebrated Jewish integration into British society, a society which has been seen as more tolerant than other European states. Recently Todd Endelman has claimed: 'Jewish integration into the mainstream of society proceeded more smoothly, with less resistance on the part of the majority, than in other European states.'[2] However, David Cesarani has identified and criticized Jewish historical research that has adopted what he calls an 'apologetic stance'.[3] This, he argues, has taken two very particular forms that are in themselves the outcomes of, and shaped by, Anglo-Jewry's particular route to modernity. The first devotes itself to showing that Jews in Britain had both earned and deserve full equality; the second has been fashioned to support, as he puts it, the 'Zionist revolution', and to show that the 'lessons' of history 'proved the inevitability of assimilation, enervation or annihilation'.[4]

As for anti-semitism, again there are conflicting readings of its significance, meaning, intensity and indeed presence in Britain. Leon Poliakov suggests in his classic three-volume study, *The History of Anti-Semitism*, that in the second half of the nineteenth century it was at a 'low ebb'.[5] If Eliza Davies is to be believed and Dickens's Fagin should be understood as a projection, then we have 'evidence' for the Jews being perceived as a real threat. Cesarani, in my view rightly, argues: 'The issues of anti-semitism in British society and related questions of culture were overshadowed by continental models and subtly marginalized, if not entirely dismissed.' Endelman, however, follows the pattern identified by Cesarani when he claims: 'Anti-semitism, while not uncommon in many social settings and in popular consciousness, remained largely outside the political arena.'[6] Against Endelman, I maintain that on the political point, as evidenced in the Royal Commission on Alien Immigration, anti-semitism was a significant issue. Enshrined within the weft and the weave of the evidence – its very texturing – was anti-semitism if we take it to be an ideology, involving negative views of the Jews (they are evil, smelly, uncivilized and so on), hostile attitudes towards them (they should be excluded, kept outside, or in their place and so on) and moral attitudes which pervade opinions and justify attitudes.

Whilst it is true that no systematic pogroms occurred in Britain, nonetheless anti-semitic discourses existed and were to a large extent officially legitimized by and in the evidence to the Royal Commission. The attitudes to Jewish integration, as exemplified by Endelman above, leave aside many questions and sidestep many of the problems. It figures as both a symptom and a product of social anti-semitism, which could have easily, as Hannah Arendt has argued in the context of Germany, 'paved the way for Jew-hating as a political weapon'.[7] John Garrard suggests that the crucial question is not whether the anti-aliens legislation was anti-semitic in intent, but that people thought it might be.[8]

According to the census returns used by the Royal Commission, there was an increase of 151,285 'aliens' between the years 1881 and 1900.[9] Not all of these people were Jews but their concentration in East London, in the two square miles from the City to Mile End Road, from Bethnal Green to Cable Street, made them especially visible in the metropolis and created the impression that the alien issue was both a Jewish problem and a question for the Jews. On the basis of this geographical microcosm, macro-political solutions were provided by legislation to restrict immigration. The Aliens Bill was passed in 1905.

The evidence presented to the Royal Commission called upon a variety of witnesses, Jews and non-Jews, who again and again produced images of Jews so as to contain the Other that is strange and to counter the fear which itself constituted the *alien*. The figure of the 'stranger' is hazy, endlessly shifting and unstable. He is, as Zygmunt Bauman suggests, 'neither friend nor enemy', yet indeed he may be both.[10] Because he is 'neither'/'nor', neither one nor the other, he threatens the social order, and life itself. The title cover of *The Illustrated London News* for 22 August 1903, 'The Alien Invasion and the British Exodus: Immigrants' (Figure 11), shows poorly clad foreigners with their meagre possessions, disembarking from a boat. This furtive image conjures up the instability which makes the stranger dangerous. Time and again the evidence presented to the Royal Commission invoked the figure of the strange-alien, signalling a less tolerant and more anxious society than the one represented by Poliakof and Endelman above. Indeed, Britain may well not have been a culture immune to anti-semitism in all its guises, rather more one that could be available for its expression.

Through the Aliens Bill, fear of the strange-alien was politicized. Late in the nineteenth century the anti-aliens movement crystallized what must have been a general sense of insecurity on the social and cultural domain by placing the immigration issue firmly within the political realm. The *Jewish Chronicle*, the official newspaper of Anglo-Jewry, carefully followed and reported the developments of the 'movement'. Ever-sensitive, forever anticipating criticism, on 18 September 1888, it warned:

Figure 11.   Max Cowper, *The Alien Invasion and the British Exodus: Immigrants*, from *The Illustrated London News*, 22 August 1903. With kind permission of the Illustrated London News Picture Library.

If poor Jews will persist in appropriating whole streets to themselves in the same district, if they will conscientiously persevere in the seemingly harmless practice of congregating in a body at prominent points in a great public thoroughfare like the Whitechapel or Commercial Road, drawing to their peculiarities of dress, of language and of manner, the attention which they might otherwise escape, can there be any wonder that the vulgar prejudices of which they are the objects should be kept alive and strengthened. What can the untutored, unthinking denizen of the East End believe in the face of such facts but that the Jew is an alien in every sense of the word – alien in ideas, in sympathy, and in interests from the rest of the population, utterly indifferent to whom he may injure so long as he benefits himself, an Ismael whose hand is against everyone, and against whom the hand of everyone may rightly be.[11]

The immigrants were condemned from inside the Jewish community – as well as from outside – for their visibility, for their differences, for just being there. Moreover, Jewry was split amongst itself. Anglo-Jewry was seeing and representing itself through the optic of middle-class England. Indeed, as Halevi has argued, 'Emancipation inaugurated the era when the Jew looked at himself in the eye of Western Christians and integrated the vision of the other into his own representations of himself.'[12] But Jewry could neither achieve nor accomplish the perfect match. Liberal democracies were not prepared to acknowledge what were, after all, explicit tensions in 'universalism' and the particular needs of socially differentiated societies and cultures. The desire for universal emancipation subordinated the concerns of the 'particular' to the totalizing dreams of the nation state.

The *Jewish Chronicle* in 1889 provided a description of one of the leading anti-alienists, Arnold White. He was, 'at once, apologist and accuser, a strange mixture of frowns and smiles, a veritable Janus at the Gates of Jewry . . . Mr. White seems to love and to hate us in a breath, to at once kiss us and scratch us with proverbial feminine inconsistency.'[13] The article – troublingly echoing anti-semitic characterizations of the Jew – announces powerful fears. Love and hate are dramatically opposed and made all the more dangerous by the feminization of these emotions. This is a discourse in which the feminine is produced as the uncontrollable, irrational and unpredictable element of human nature. White's attitude to the Jews are represented as precarious. As a figure of desire and denial, guilt is projected onto White, who takes on the role of scapegoat.

Representing the interests of established Anglo-Jewry, the *Jewish Chronicle* had a message for all Jews – assimilate. In editorials and news coverage it articulated concerns which must have contributed to arousing the anxieties of its readership. It must also have strengthened the divide between Anglo-Jewry and 'greeners' (new arrivals in Britain). The concerns voiced by the paper had some sort of foundation insofar as the anti-alien movement was gaining momentum. But, as we have seen, the twisted turns given by projection inaugurate disavowal and lead to sacrifice, in this case by the Jews themselves.

In May 1901 the British Brothers League was established by Major William Evans Gordon and Murray Guthrie, MP for Bow, as a response to complaints that the King's Speech omitted an Aliens Bill. In August of that year the 'Parliamentary Alien Immigration Committee' was set up and fifty-two MPs signed a letter to Lord Salisbury demanding legislation. A year later, in January 1902, Evans Gordon moved the Amendment to the Address and demanded legislation to restrict immigration.[14] Behind the demand that the Jew should be classified as alien from there on lay dubious nostrums from economic theory, particularly as regards theories of unemployment which blamed the Jew for creating social problems. The amendment, reflecting the urgency it presumed, was swiftly followed by the appointment of a Royal Commission which commenced sitting on 24 April 1902. The Commission was chaired by the Right Honourable The Lord James of Hereford. Its members were the Right Honourable The Lord Rothschild; the Honourable Alfred E. Lyttelton, KC, MP; Sir Kenelm E. Digby, KCB; Major W. E. Evans Gordon, MP; Mr Henry Norman, MP; and Mr William Vallance.[15] They sat for thirteen months. Their recommendations were not unanimous – Rothschild and Digby presented a minority report in which they argued that the restrictive measures proposed were inoperable and, in Rothschild's words, 'even if they are directly aimed at so-called "undesirables" they would certainly affect deserving and hard-working men'.[16] Nevertheless, in 1905 a Bill to restrict alien immigration was passed.

First, the case for restriction was presented to the Commissioners. It was organized by Evans Gordon. By and large the witnesses were in some way associated with East London. A variety of people – shop-keepers, doctors, charity workers, dockers, sanitary inspectors, costers, policemen, boot-makers and teachers – were called. In class terms, they were representative of a broad sector of the population. However, the number of women called was negligible. The Jews themselves were represented by Anglo-Jewry, that is to say, often by men from the second or third generations. The 'alien' Jew was not called to represent himself. Witnesses were described as 'qualified' or as 'experts'. Eye-witness anecdotes were presented as facts with universal implications. Looking does not take place in a neutral domain. What the Commissioners saw was already 'known' and re-presented for them by the questions which the witnesses were expected through their answers to confirm.

In considering the deliberations and Report of the Royal Commission it is important to remember that such Commissions had at that time enormous status and power in the British system of government. The Commission, advised by civil servants, could call upon experts in the relevant fields of inquiry. Yet in this case it can be argued that from the outset the Commission created the conditions as if aliens were on trial, rendering them guilty from the beginning. The fact that Anglo-Jewry was defensive, almost disassociating itself from the greeners, again suggests strongly that Britain was hardly free of prejudices.

The Commission framed its questions to the 175 witnesses called so that they could explore: 'The character and extent of the evils which are attributed to the unrestricted immigration of Aliens, especially in the Metropolis.'[17] Inscribed within the language itself was the inevitability of its own conclusions. The key word here is 'evil'. It seems that the amendment was based on the certain assumption that immigrants bode ill, cause trouble and are *a priori* bad. It was alleged that on arrival in Britain they were impoverished, unclean, insanitary in their habits and likely to be carriers of infectious diseases. It was argued too that they were liable, in higher proportions than the native population, to be criminals, anarchists and prostitutes. According to the mass of evidence presented, the immigrant Jews were destitute, criminal, fraudulent and evil and contaminated the population. Inscribed in the very structure of the questions set by the Commission was an outcome bound to lead to such characterizations. The witnesses were subject to, and indeed some of them subjects of, anti-semitic discourse at its crudest. Loaded heavily with assumptions about the *Jew,* the Commission seemed set on the course of not only replicating and reinforcing such identities but also re-inventing and creating new representations of the Jew.

The Commissioners were pledged to investigate 'destitute' immigration in general but in fact they focused on Jewish immigration. Their inquiry into 'destitutes' led them to distinguish between 'good' (the respectable) and 'bad' (the residuum–poor) and by extension 'good' and 'bad' Jews. The division of the social into good and bad maps out the divisions between civilized and uncivilized. These social categories were legitimized in, and rarely challenged by, the evidence presented to the Commissioners. People were to be granted the right to enter Britain and become a citizen in relation to what was perceived as their potential to become good citizens. This process entailed evaluating the kinds of people who were suitable and could be allowed to belong. Moral judgements were the means through which those decisions could be made.

Arnold White, who as we have seen was one of the major protagonists in the fight against the aliens, described the 'lowest type' of immigrants as persons who:

> have no regard to any provision for sanitation and scanty regard for
> cleanliness and for whom the conditions of life are very low; those who
> are comparatively indifferent to anything outside the mere sensual

indulgence of eating, drinking and sleeping, and those who have no hope or ideal in life, no pleasure in the past and amusements, and who really approach the condition of animal life.[18]

White is not just describing the immigrants but is projecting his own sexual desires and fears. By externalizing these, by ascribing them to others, they can then be counter-attacked. White displays the attributes of a noxious combination of lucidity and fear or fear made lucid. Seeing had whetted the gaze of this resolute Jew-watcher. In the world of 'false projection' as described by Adorno and Horkheimer, the 'ego sinks into the meaningless abyss of itself', and others become allegories of destruction.[19] The bourgeois subject continuously defined and re-defined itself through excluding what it assigned to the 'low'. Low is dirty, repulsive, noisy, polluting. It was, however, that very exclusion which was constitutive of its own identity. Again and again the Royal Commission's questions produced representations of the aliens as 'low', as people of bad character, in whom and through whom the English and other bourgeoisie could differentiate itself and produce itself as 'good'.

The image of the Jew as evil-stranger was reinforced with the allegation that the Jews did not intermarry with the 'native race' and so would remain a 'solid and distinctive colony'.[20] The immigrants were accused of congregating in large masses in certain districts, especially in the East End of London, particularly the Borough of Stepney. It was argued that here they had become a compact, non-assimilating community, and that the immigrants dealt exclusively in trade with their own 'race' and religion so that the native tradespeople would lose out.

But, somewhat contradictorily, at the same time it was feared that the population would be 'mongrelized' and become a hybrid and hence impure. The Earl of Dudley gave voice to this anxiety: 'They come to intermarry and this means necessarily a lowering of the whole moral and social standard of the population and those districts in which they settle.'[21] The law of natural selection, proposed and legitimated by the science of Social Darwinism had, it was thought, begun the processes of weeding out the 'strong' from the 'weak', the 'poor' from the 'degenerate'. But the influx of immigrants, it was claimed, disturbed and disrupted this process.

From the mass of evidence, I have selected three 'typical' witnesses whose testimonies sum up the main trends of thinking and indeed reiterate the fundamental themes. The first, George Brown, was a photographer's assistant (he may even have come across the St Petersberg Studio).[22] Brown described what he saw as the great changes which had taken place in East London since the arrival of the immigrants. He claimed that the English had been driven away and were consequently suffering great hardships. The Englishness of England was being undermined by the destruction of the English Sunday, which had caused 'pandemonium' in the district. The neighbourhood had become what he termed a 'foreign colony'. The traders dealt only with their own kinspeople.

My second witness was a house and insurance agent in Stepney, George Augustus Dix.[23] He spoke of the deterioration of the district, overcrowding and the displacement of shopkeepers. Ill feeling, he said, had arisen because of rent rises, immorality, coarse habits, socialistic principles and hostility to the country. The Reverend Ernest Courteney Carter, vicar of St Jude's, Whitechapel, produced a further inventory of complaints.[24] He alleged that feelings against the aliens were very strong due to the displacement of the indigenous people, to the aggressive conduct of the Jews, to their language, their attitude to the Christian religion and to their behaviour on Sundays. He conceded that dealings with the 'better class' of Jews were on a more friendly basis. His chief complaint, which he claimed to share with others, was the Sunday grievance.

A distinction within the working class between the 'respectable' and the 'rough' was in the process of being installed. Harold Perkins has noted that there was:

> A diagonal frontier running right through the working class from top to bottom but taking in more at the top and progressively fewer towards the bottom. To some extent it coincided with the divisions between the chapel- and church-going (chapel for the urban working classes was usually superior to church, which was for the more abject, dependent poor, and the Catholic Irish were automatically classed as rough).[25]

The Jews, clearly neither chapel- nor church-goers, and foreign moreover, could only be placed within this schema alongside the 'rough'. (Members of the Anglo-Jewry were anomalies within this framework, and tended to be judged as citizens, considered as 'rough' or 'respectable' depending on class and circumstance.) Jews wrecked the English Sunday and were thereby seen to threaten the social order. Through this chain of associations they were categorized as the residuum.

Yet another contradiction was to condemn them for being hardworking as well as lazy. Their willingness to work long hours for low pay, it was claimed, depressed the wage level and caused unemployment among the 'native' workers. The immigrants were blamed also for the levy of key money and for high rents, leading to overcrowding and the displacement of the local population. The evidence of R. Leavis Thomas provides a summary of such fears: 'At first aliens are far below the native people in habits and standard of life. They improve rapidly, but as others are pouring in there is always a permanent sub-stratum of people living under horrible conditions.'[26] Gareth Stedman Jones argues that the geographical separation between rich and poor was becoming ever more complex. Indeed, as he puts it, 'the poor themselves were becoming more closely crammed together regardless of status or character.'[27] Israel Zangwill put a possibly 'Jewish' view in his novel, *Children of the Ghetto*, where he wrote, 'England was well named, for to the Jew it was really ENGE-land, which in German signifies the country without elbow room.'[28] If the etymology is spurious, nonetheless the point is well made. The overcrowding of the poor was attributed less and less to economic exigency, even though during the years 1880–1914, according to Harold Perkins, inequality in Britain was at its height.[29] The distribution of income was more skewed and the economic distance between the classes was greater than ever before. He characterizes the cumulative effect as an overwhelming 'fear of the poor' which was managed by the state through forms of legislation designed precisely to contain and control that fear.[30]

Fear of social unrest was exacerbated by a language which dramatized the extent of immigration by calling it an 'invasion'. Poverty was attributed more and more to criminal fecklessness. Overcrowding, in this discourse, was not bad luck or an effect of social policy but a crime; and the people subjected to it were criminalized. It was argued that London was becoming a school of crime for the aliens. It was claimed that many of the immigrants who arrived there had not hitherto been 'believed to be criminals' but that in London they were educated in criminal practices.[31] On 24 July 1902 John Mulvavy, Chief Inspector of H Division for six and a half years, was called before the Commission.[32] H division, the so-called Jewish East End, extended from the City boundary, through Norton Folgate, to High Street Shoreditch, Warner Place in Hackney, to Squirries Street and White Street, across Bethnal Green Road, the Whitechapel and Mile End Roads to the Regents Canal and to the Thames. It included the whole of Stepney except a bit of Limehouse. Mulvavy described the changes he had seen in this district. In particular he noted an increase in the number of foreigners and what he described as the displacement of the native population. He claimed 'in certain parts, streets are wholly colonized now, if I may use the word, by foreigners'. The accusation that the Jews or foreigners 'colonized' a neighbourhood was a common theme: 'There is no end to them in Whitechapel and Mile End. It is Jerusalem,' said William Walker, a caretaker.[33] But at the same time it was feared that if indeed they assimilated they would become indistinct and concealed, and would insert themselves into the indigenous culture and state. The fear of territorial boundaries as indeterminate and unstable is again voiced here, and, as we have seen before, this same objection to separateness was usually accompanied by an equally strong objection to social mixing or to 'mongrelization'.

According to Mulvavy, of the 101 streets he claimed were 'colonized', 84 were occupied by persons of good character and 17 of those he designated as 'bad'.[34] He defined 'bad' as those people who ran 'disorderly' houses. Mulvavy did argue against the questioner who was pushing him to say that civil unrest would occur as a direct consequence of the foreigners. He would not commit himself to agreeing that they were inherently bad or worse than their English counterparts.

A development of the complaint against the assimilated or 'concealed' Jew was that if his 'true' identity was concealed then the true nature of his crime could never be known. It was also suggested that foreigners who did not speak English could more easily evade the police: 'It follows from that, does it not, that the foreign criminal has a certain advantage over the English-speaking criminal in this district, because it is more difficult for you and your officers, on your own statement, to trap him than if he spoke English?' Mulvavy reluctantly agreed. Pushed again by the interrogator he admitted that 'there was always a certain amount of difficulty in extracting information from a foreign person'. The questioning continued to produce the reply that foreigners are criminal by 'nature'. This being the case they must be visible and recognizable. The criminal could only be understood, and hence the crime solved, if the true nature of the criminal type was identifiable and known. The Jews are thus perceived and represented here as infinitely mimetic beings, who can disguise their difference and conceal their crimes. Again they emerge as figurations of destabilization.

The chair of the County of London Sessions, Mr McConnel KC, who unremittingly 'laid into' the aliens, gave evidence claiming to show that hundreds of foreigners who landed in the country were organized into 'colonies' and into 'committing depredations'.[35] In addition he suggested that:

> The offences used to be larcenous and generally committed amongst themselves such as goods entrusted for tailoring purposes being stolen or otherwise disposed of. Now, with regard to the offences, the most important one is the increase in burglary and house breaking and stealing from dwelling houses.

Then McConnel was invited or, more accurately, cajoled into identifying more precisely the 'class'of aliens to which he referred. He replied: 'They are all classes together, but the combinations seem to be principally of the German and Yiddish-speaking nationalists.' This shows us yet more confusion, this time of languages, of perceived nationality with nationalism. It is similar to that which existed between language and the 'science' of race. But the distinction he draws enables him to elaborate categories which distinguish between different 'nationalities' and attribute to them different crimes.

The questioning increasingly led McConnel to distinguish between the crimes committed by Germans and by others. He was asked whether German crime was 'scientific'. This term enabled him to identify 'a highly skilled burglary with scientific tools'. An example was produced for examination. From the 'fact' that it had no manufacturer's name on it, it was inferred that it was the tool of a foreign criminal who had brought it into Britain. Further, it was offered as proof that the nature of both crime and the criminal was changing. Crime was now more organized, skilled and clever than hitherto; it was German criminals who were creating a highly specialized 'scientific' form of housebreaking.

The Commission repeatedly provoked assertions that the aliens were not as reputable as the English who previously lived in that district. It was argued that 'the foreigners are so very addicted to gambling'. Mr James Gilmour,[36] formerly Superintendent of B Division, Manchester City Police, who became a sanitary inspector and then returned to the police force, claimed that the lower classes were very fond of gambling and that they gambled in the kitchens and cellars of private houses in the evenings. Often, he said, they started on Friday nights and continued sometimes until Sunday morning, and received payments for the games. Evans Gordon, always at pains to get the witnesses to distinguish between the foreigners and the English, prompted Gilmour to agree that gambling was a foreign vice: 'In all the raids that I have made there have been foreigners caught. In one case there were 22 men caught in one house. All were fined.' At this point in the evidence Evans Gordon abruptly shifted his line of inquiry to question Gilmour about the birthrate and asked: 'Do they increase very rapidly?' Gilmore replied, 'They increase much more rapidly than the English people. They tend to marry young and have large families.'

This about-turn in the questioning – from gambling to the birthrate – sets up a chain of associations suggesting profligacy on the part of the foreigners, leading to a scourge of illegal gambling and potential gamblers throughout the nation. A retired inspector of Criminal Investigation H Division, Stephen White,[37] a Stepney resident, associated the first wave of immigrants with the springing up of hundreds of 'common gaming houses' which, in spite of many convictions, remained 'as rife as ever'.

The illicit manufacture of spirits, and their distribution and sale at restaurants, was yet another cause of concern. Nathaniel J. Highmore,[38] Senior Assistant Solicitor of the Inland Revenue at Somerset House, specialized in frauds in this area. An example of the 'illicit' substance was tasted by Evans Gordon, who himself found it 'tasteless'. He then asked the witness what or whose taste it suited and was told, 'It is entirely consumed by Jews – sold mainly at the big festivals and Passover.' The summing-up confirmed that there was a considerable number of illicit stills in bogus clubs, which sold liquor either without a licence or with a forged one.

Foreigners were also, it was alleged, subject to systematized bankruptcy, the chief offenders being those categorized as Germans, Russians and Russian Poles. During the three years ending March 1903, according to Leadam Hough,[39] Senior Official Receiver in Bankruptcy, attached to the High Court of Justice, of the 289 people who had incurred losses on unsecured loans of upwards of one-and-a-quarter million pounds, 93 were Jews. On the basis of his figures, it was estimated that the proportion of the alien population to the whole population was 2.98 per cent. The orders received against aliens in the metropolis represented 14.5 per cent of the total number issued.

Evidence on the incidence of crime categorized people on the basis of such nationalities as Germans, Russians and Russian Poles and Yiddish-speakers. Volume l of the Commissioners' Report claimed upon the evidence of the Prison Commissioners that over the five years 1899–1903 the number of aliens committed to prison had risen.[40] In that period Americans totalled 23.25 per cent of the prison population, the Germans following with 19 per cent and the Russians and Poles with 17 per cent.

The crimes were categorized as being offences against the person, against property with violence, against property without violence, forgery, drunkenness, disorderly conduct, frequency, hawking without a licence, indecency, keeping a brothel, and obscene language.[41] These were then broken down further to show precisely the increase of foreign criminals and their respective crimes between 1892 and 1902:

Crimes of violence	28 to 56
Larceny and receiving	54 to 86
Night and gaming clubs	20 to 60
Prostitution	150 to 347
Drunkenness	30 to 237
Other offences	94 to 171

In 1892, out of a total of 344 charges, 331 related to British citizens and 13 to foreigners; while in 1902, out of the total of 272 charges, 220 were brought against British citizens and 52 against foreigners. It was argued that the crime rate of the British was diminishing while that of the foreigners was increasing. Indeed Arnold White, much aggrieved that this information had failed to reach the public domain, told the Commission: 'The first evidence that we are importing a criminal Jewish population is shown by the fact that the Government, without mentioning the matter in the House of Commons, are building Synagogues at Wormwood Scrubs, Parkhurst and Pentonville.'[42] The argument that the crime rate was increasing was used to provide the substantive evidence against the unrestricted entry of aliens into Britain, which White, seen and acknowledged as an authority on such matters, explicitly associates with the Jews. These statistics, perceived as 'science', achieved the status of truth.

The 'evils' represented were in fact those associated with social discipline: the problems concerned with the control and direction of people, demography, public health, hygiene and housing conditions. Stedman Jones points out that the 'poor were represented as neglected, perhaps exploited. But more significantly they were generally represented as coarse, brutish, drunken and immoral, another "ominous threat" to civilisation.'[43] In other words, in a more general sense the 'evils' were the issues facing the reorganization of urban life and particularly the regulation of the working class in the late nineteenth and early twentieth century. The institutions in the public sphere worked to transform political exigencies into rational authority in order to guarantee what was understood as the general interest. This was the moment when, as Harold Perkins has argued, the political extension of citizenship to the whole community began the processes of 'differentiating professional society from its predecessors'.[44] These were also the decades of Charles Booth's *Life and Labour of the People of London,* whose work constituted what Stedman Jones has called a 'literature of crisis'.[45] Working-class life was increasingly surveyed and inspected. It was subjected to the scrutiny of the professional classes. The alien issue was both a part of the general question of social reform yet differentiated from it: it was installed as a distinctive category where difference was identified and articulated as an aspect in the maintenance of control.

However, not all the witnesses called before the Commission were hostile to the immigrants. Lord Rothschild presented a case against restricting immigration, but had to do so in terms already established by the pro-restrictionists. Hence his evidence became a series of defensive manoeuvres. The prevailing ideology, which promoted self-help and discouraged any dependency on the state, was itself employed as a defence against the charge that immigrants would be a burden on the rates. Proof that the Jews were increasingly independent was offered by, among others, a Jewish charity represented by Sir Samuel Montague, which was responsible for the issue of free matzo meal before Passover.[46] It produced data, used as a register of poverty, which demonstrated that between the years 1893 and 1902 there had been a steady decline in the numbers of people calling on that form of relief: in 1893, 2414 people accepted free matzo meal but by 1902 only 1725.

William Ward was another witness testifying in defence of immigrant Jews: 'the foreign Jews seem to be moral by nature, their men are thrifty and domesticated and marry freely. This probably is one of the causes of the absence of immorality among women.'[47] Moreover, he suggested that what had been described as their primitive habits should not be interpreted as 'indecent'. This 'primitive' behaviour was defined through yet another opposition: that of the 'mob' – the residuum of the English working class – who by implication frittered away their wages in pubs and were more immoral. Yet another characteristic was thus installed to define the 'bad' (the undeserving) against the 'good' (the deserving) poor.

Diet was used to demonstrate that the aliens were thrifty, hence 'good'. Here morality and food became intertwined. The Jews would spend their money sensibly – on good wholesome food – unlike the 'mob' who dissipated it in pubs. On the evidence of Mrs Amelia Levy:

as to the food of the foreigners, several witnesses have stated that the standard of food is much lower amongst these foreigners than among the natives, and one witness stated that the reason why they could work for less money than the natives was that they could live on a crust of bread and a cup of tea with a piece of dried fish now and then. I can absolutely deny these statements as to the food of the foreigners, and it is a matter of astonishment to me that such statements should have been seriously made. If there is one thing as to which the foreigner is particular it is his food. Firstly he insists on getting the best of everything – e.g. his meat has to pass an official, and no portion of diseased animal will be marked with the necessary seal. The foreign Jew pays more for his meat than the English, and the latter buys largely at the Jewish shops on Saturday night because they know that the meat is good. This is a grievance to the Christian butcher. The foreigners are large fish eaters, and I believe that more fish is consumed in the East End of London than anywhere else in this country.[48]

Further evidence was marshalled to show that an average foreign Jewish family would eat, on an ordinary day, three meals and at least two of these would consist of fish. A good diet enhanced the physical standard of the individual and, it was argued, contributed to the general health of the nation as well as ensuring that the people would not be a burden on the rates: they could be classed as good citizens. It was also argued by Levy that, 'The foreign Jewess of the lower classes is very clever in the preparation of fish and when properly prepared and fresh it is most nutritious.' Food was used to classify people. It was yet another way of articulating their differences and establishing hierarchies between them. Zangwill, in *Children of the Ghetto*, characterized a woman's ability to fry fish properly as a measure of her authenticity as a Jew: 'She [Leah] will marry Sam Levine, though he belongs to a lax English family, and I suspect his mother was a proselyte. She can't fry fish.'[49] According to Zangwill, of all foods, fried fish was sovereign:

> Fried fish binds Anglo-Judea more than all the professors of unity. Its savour is early known in youth, and the divine flavour endured by a thousand childish recollections, entwined with all the most sacred associations, draws back the hoary sinner into the paths of piety.[50]

Fried fish was the binding force which constituted Jewish identity itself. But, as if that was not enough, it becomes a symbol for the superiority of the Jews over the Christians, 'The Christians are ninnies, they can't fry Dutch plaice. Believe me, they can't tell a carp from a dace.'[51]

The defence of the alien recycled a language which assumes identity. The mechanisms of identity formation never operate in a neutral space, but in a domain with its own implicit principles of sifting and selection, through which appropriate forms of behaviour are articulated and forms of domination and insubordination installed. It has been argued, notably by Stedman Jones, that the latter years of the nineteenth century entailed the invention, transformation and remaking of a specific form of English identity and more particularly the 'remaking of the working class'.[52] Stedman Jones maintains:

> The distinctiveness of a working-class way of life was enormously accentuated. Its separateness and impermeability was now reflected in a dense and inward-looking culture, whose effect was both to emphasize the distance of the working classes above it and to articulate its position within an apparently permanent social hierarchy.[53]

But at the same time, as David Feldman suggests, practices that departed from, or did not fit in with, the evolving national pattern and ideas about the nation were construed and represented as alien. The working classes were being addressed as part of the nation more insistently than ever before but the form of this address was circumscribed, creating hierarchies that effected inclusions and exclusions.[54]

The witnesses called before the Royal Commission discussed, in a cursory way, other immigrant groups, including Italians, who were characterized as men of violence, likely to precipitate street brawls, and who wielded knives, while Italian women were likely to be prostitutes. In short, Italians were represented as uncontrollable.[55] Jews, by contrast, were installed as gamblers, as people who courted chance; who transgressed the law in a different way. The fatalism of the gambler is a long way from the much-vaunted ideology of self-help which was thought to be the motive force of the 'respectable' poor. All immigrants were contrasted with the 'good' English workman, constructed as a wholesome John Bull who ate steaks and drank beer. A picture of foreigners as situated at two opposite poles emerges from the evidence. The centre, by inference, was occupied by the British, who were controlled, or at least controllable, so long as the extremes were contained.

A language was being installed to remould, to change people, so that they would fit in with changing ideas of England and Englishness. Philip Dodd argues that this applied to various groups, particularly women, the working classes and the Irish.[56] To this list could be added the Jews. Englishness was being reconstituted both to incorporate and to 'neuter' various groups who had fallen outside the mainstream of political life. But to create the 'one nation' entailed segregation and discrimination.

However, some witnesses, as we have seen, did attempt to defend the Jewish immigrant (Levy and Ward). In their accounts, charity matzo meal and fried fish became emblems of and for Jewish identity. Here, matzo meal was the means by which people were sifted and differentiated: the 'good' Jews, who did not need charity, could be distinguished from the 'bad' ones. Fried fish embodied ideas about health and morality (Levy), and defiance and difference (Zangwill). It was simultaneously celebrated and decried, embracing emotions of pride, shame and fear. But this defence rested always on terms already established for them: on the grounds that they were a people who could be assimilated. Hermann Landau, who had been naturalized for 38 years and worked with the Jews Temporary Shelter, identified and listed characteristics of the 'aliens' that would, in his view, enable them both to assimilate and to be assimilated.[57] For him, they were acceptable because of their sobriety and thrift, which together with their concern for hygiene and morals accounted for their higher standard of living. He praised their loyalty to Britain and argued that second generations had adopted and would continue to adopt English customs.

But even if the financial independence of the Jews could indeed have been proved by statistics, and if it had been shown that they were still a numerically small group and therefore unthreatening, and even more that they were 'good', nonetheless their presence would, it was feared, contaminate London. In this context of an expanding and more visible Jewish community, the established Anglo-Jewry, who had come to think of and represent themselves as Britons of the Jewish faith, created and shaped social institutions such as the Jewish Board of Guardians, the Jews' Free School, the Jews Temporary Shelter, as well as the Board of Deputies of British Jews and the *Jewish Chronicle,* through which to introduce to poor and alien Jews the values of the English middle class.

The worst evils of poverty and slum-dwelling among the East End Jews had to be checked in order to undermine and eliminate the perceived identity of Jew as criminal, insanitary and smelly. However, the better response to the anti-semites would surely not have been to reply, 'the Jews are not really like this', but to have said, as Slavoj Zizek has suggested, 'the anti-semitic idea of the Jew has nothing to do with the Jews: the ideological figure of the Jew is a way of stitching up the inconsistency of [y]our own ideological system.'[58]

Through the 'pastoral' care of its own institutions, Anglo-Jewry participated in the reorganization and stabilization of the ideology of the national culture. Its aim was to re-create Eastern European Jews as British citizens. Assimilation and accommodation with the normative culture, that of the 'host' nation, was the prevailing model for English Jewry. However, amongst the structural difficulties inherent in assimilation, as Zygmund Bauman suggests, were the processes of raising social and political acceptance to levels which, as a consequence of economic depression and deprivation, were impossible for most people to achieve.[59] Assimilation in Bauman's argument was a 'one-way ticket'. Hence the Jews were expected to struggle for assimilation neither for the sake of liberal democratic rights nor even indeed for their rights as Jews, but for the sole purpose of accommodating themselves to the values of the people amongst whom they were to live – the so-called 'host' nation. They were in a 'no-win' situation.

The social insecurity of established Anglo-Jewry was displaced onto the new immigrants, the 'greeners'. Anti-semitism was a force which they believed could only be checked by assimilation. Their fear of anti-semitism was rationalized to justify their support of legislative control on 'alien' immigration. During this period there were between seven and sixteen Jewish Members of Parliament, several of whom, including H. S. Samuel, Conservative MP for Limehouse, were staunch anti-aliens.[60] The Jewish Board of Guardians, whilst helping 'poor' Jews, did everything they could to circumvent the arrival of yet more poor immigrants, including advocating restriction. Indeed, between 1881 and 1906 it facilitated the return to Eastern Europe of over 31,000 Jews.[61]

It was not until after the Bill was passed that Anglo-Jewry started to mount pressure against the restrictions it imposed: these had drastically attenuated the right of political and religious asylum and introduced into Britain a system of administrative justice for the first time. Feldman argues that the Anti-Aliens Act was not a legislative quirk but at the vanguard of a 'transformation of the regulatory ambitions of the British State and a re-orientation of the idea of the nation'.[62] This change was necessitated by the formation of a national and cultural identity to which *Jews* and others gave voice and shape.

Notes

1. Iain Sinclair, *White Chappel: Scarlet Tracings,* Rutland: Goldmark, 1987, p. 63.
2. Todd M. Endelman, *Radical Assimilation in English Jewish History 1656–1945*, Bloomington: Indiana University Press, 1990, p. 3.
3. David Cesarani (ed.), *The Making of Modern Anglo-Jewry,* Oxford: Basil Blackwell, 1990, p. 2.
4. *Ibid.,* p. 5.
5. Leon Poliakof, *The History of Anti-Semitism*, Vol. 3, London: Routledge & Kegan Paul, 1975, p. 324.
6. Endelman, *op. cit.,* p. 3.
7. Hannah Arendt, *The Origins of Totalitarianism*, London: George Allen & Unwin, 1958, p. 169.
8. John A. Garrard, *The English and Immigration*, Oxford: Oxford University Press, 1971, p. 57.
9. Royal Commission (hereafter RC), i, *Report* (1903), p. 14.
10. Zygmunt Bauman, *Modernity and Ambivalence*, Cambridge: Polity Press, 1991, p. 55.
11. *Jewish Chronicle*, 18 September 1888, p. 19, cited in Garrard, *op. cit.,* pp. 49–50.
12. Ilan Halevi, *A History of the Jews*, London: Zed Books, 1987, p. 130.
13. *Jewish Chronicle*, 1 April 1889, p. 19, cited in Garrard, *op. cit.,* p. 65.
14. RC, i, p. 5.
15. *Ibid.*, p. vii.
16. *Ibid.*, Memorandum signed Rothschild, p. 50.
17. *Ibid.*, Warrent v Evils attributed to Alien Immigration, No. 38, pp. 5–6.
18. *House of Commons Select Committee on Alien Immigration*, Vol. 1, SP 1888, ix, p. 92.
19. Theodor Adorno and Max Horkheimer, *Dialectic of Enlightenment*, London: Verso, 1989, p. 192.
20. RC, i, p. 6.
21. Earl of Dudley, Hansard 4S H, (58) 274, 23 May 1898, cited in Garrard, *op. cit.,* footnote 4, p. 53.
22. RC, ii, *Evidence*, George Brown, 2377.
23. *Ibid.*, George Augustus Dix, 5286.
24. *Ibid.*, Revd Ernest Couteney Carter, 10230.
25. Harold Perkins, *The Rise of Professional Society: England since 1880*, London: Routledge, 1990, p. 107.
26. RC, ii, R. Leavis Thomas, 5433.
27. Gareth Stedman Jones, *Outcast London: A Study in the Relationship Between the Classes in Victorian Society,* Harmondsworth: Penguin, 1984, p. 284.
28. Israel Zangwill, *Children of the Ghetto*, London, 1892, p. 58.

29. Perkins, *op. cit.*, p. 28.
30. *Ibid.*, p. 53.
31. RC, ii, 12796.
32. RC, iii, John Mulvavy, 8222.
33. RC, ii, William Walker, 8947.
34. RC, ii, Mulvavy, 8222.
35. RC, ii, McConnel, 12700.
36. RC, ii, James Gilmour, 21195.
37. RC, ii, Stephen White, 7534.
38. RC, ii, Nathaniel J. Highmore, 9857.
39. RC, ii, Leadom Hough, 22760.
40. RC, i, p. 17.
41. *Ibid.*, p. 119.
42. RC, ii, Arnold White, 32989961.
43. Stedman Jones, *op. cit.*, p. 285.
44. Perkins, *op. cit.*, p. 9.
45. Stedman Jones, *op. cit.*, p. 312.
46. RC, ii, Sir Samuel Montague, 16855.
47. RC, ii, William Ward, 18303.
48. RC, ii, Amelia Levy, 17897.
49. Zangwill, *op. cit.*, p. 49.
50. *Ibid.*, p. 45.
51. *Ibid.*, p. 49.
52. Stedman Jones, *op. cit.*, p. 67.
53. *Ibid.*, p. 77.
54. David Feldman, 'The importance of being English, Jewish immigration and the decay of liberal England', in David Feldman and Gareth Stedman Jones (eds), *Metropolis London*, London: Routledge, 1989.
55. RC, ii, *Evidence*, 7735.
56. Philip Dodd, 'Englishness and national culture', in R. Colls and P. Dodd (eds), *Englishness: Politics and Culture*, London: Croom Helm, 1987, p. 1.
57. RC, ii, Hermann Landau, 16266.
58. Slavoj Zizek, *The Sublime Object of Ideology*, London: Verso, 1989, p. 48.
59. Zygmund Bauman, 'Entry tickets and exit visas', *Telos*, no. 77, Fall, 1988.
60. Garrard, *op. cit.*, p. 37.
61. Feldman, *op. cit.*, p. 63.
62. *Ibid.*, p. 79.

5

Cutting the suit to fit the cloth: assimilation in the 1906 Whitechapel Art Gallery exhibition, Jewish Art and Antiquities

> The streets are filled, a river of laughter, lamplight, varnished faces, oaths, the crowd has no thought, where are they going? It doesn't matter. Young girls sauntering on the arms of their men – who strain to catch the eyes of other girls. The doors of public houses open to the street. Song. Carriages. Even men of education, of substance, position, yes, they come here. Their wives allow it, are accomplice to these brutalities. They are serviced; it is done with. This red, this silken, rim of hell.
>
> *Iain Sinclair*[1]

One year after the Anti-Aliens Bill, perhaps as a way of defending themselves from the excesses of anti-alien rhetoric, members of the Anglo-Jewish community staged an exhibition entitled *Jewish Art and Antiquities* at the Whitechapel Art Gallery in East London.[2] The exhibition had two main aims: to uncover Jewish treasures from the past and to display them alongside contemporary artistic achievements. Thus the show attempted to enhance Jewish prestige and status and was designed to represent the cultural achievements of Jews and their place in Western European and particularly English history. The exhibition sought to impart pride and confidence in the value of Jewish existence for the Jews themselves. It offered a unitary concept of *Jew* subsumed under the general category English Jew. On one level we can see it as representing the *Jew* resisting assimilation; on another, it was Jews proclaiming the virtue and achievement of assimilation. This dialectic was played out in an East End that was economically precarious and bristling with social unrest.

The Whitechapel Gallery was a popular venue that attracted a vast number of people to its exhibitions, from both the immediate locality and outside. As an institution it functioned to educate and to civilize the working class of East London. It reinforced the values of the British middle class. Critics took note of its work, which was well regarded in the world of art. Thus, for the Anglo-Jewish community this was an exhibition that might be expected to achieve impact, given its particular timing and its appeal to both Jews and others. Expectations were fulfilled. Between 12 noon and 10 pm for the six weeks between 7 November and 16 December 1906, over 150,000 people visited the exhibition and no fewer than 20,000 of them purchased catalogues.[3] It would be surprising if the show did not affect the views of both Jew and non-Jew.

The Gallery, founded by Canon Barnett and his wife Henrietta, was opened on 12 March 1901 by Lord Rosebery. It was the outcome of twenty years of exhibitions organized by the Barnetts in St Jude's Schools, Whitechapel, where the attendance figures had risen from 10,000 in 1881 to 55,300 in 1886.[4] The success of the venture meant that extra space for exhibitions was desperately needed. In 1897 Canon Barnett decided to purchase land for a 'permanent Picture Gallery scheme'.[5] Within two weeks he had raised the £6,000 necessary for the project and commissioned the architect Charles Harrison Townsend to design the building.

The site chosen for the gallery was next to the Passmore Edwards Library in Whitechapel High Street.[6] The decision to build the gallery next to the library was significant: their social functions were seen as compatible. Both provided the means for the social advancement of the working classes and gave them a respectable and sober form of recreation. Townsend had established a reputation as architect of the Bishopsgate Institute (1894) which provided a library and accommodation for the cultural activities of the working classes.

The architectural style of the Whitechapel Gallery was to be modern – and modern in a particular sense. It was described by the *Studio* as 'a building that attempts to strike its own note, to be personal, and to speak 1897, not 1797 or 1597'.[7] The language of its design had affinities with that of the Arts and Crafts movement. In 1875 Barnett had his church of St Jude's decorated by William Morris. For him:

> The great want of this East End of London is beauty; the streets are ugly, and few signs of taste are anywhere apparent; it is therefore well that it should be possible for both inhabitants and passers-by to enter a building which, by its grace and beauty, should remind them of a world made beautiful by God's Hand.[8]

Furthermore, according to Henrietta Barnett, Canon Barnett believed that 'the social problem is at root an educational problem'.[9] Moreover, Barnett saw 'art as a teacher' and pictures as 'preachers, as voices of God, passing his lessons from age to age'.[10] For Barnett, education, religion and art worked hand in hand to ameliorate social life and resolve social problems.

By the late nineteenth century a transformation of the public and the private spheres was occurring. Education, in a variety of sites, including an art gallery such as the Whitechapel, strove to secure, sustain and legitimate itself as a 'body' and a 'voice' in the public sphere. It sought to inculcate in the population a higher subjectivity which could transcend nature by offering experiences, feelings and pleasures that were beyond what were perceived as the mindless routines of the working-class life. In their first report the Trustees of the Whitechapel stated that its aim was to 'widen the thoughts and the pleasures of East Londoners'.[11] The Report continued:

> There would probably be less poverty, less drunkenness and less vice if the people who have the healthy disciplines of work had also the opportunities of seeing and hearing about things which make life beautiful.[12]

The 'culture' offered by education could, it was argued, control 'nature' by generating a higher form of life.[13] In this context, culture was used to mould people in the reproduction of social roles and in the productive processes. The view expressed in 1885 by Samuel Smiles was typical in this respect:

> I am deeply convinced that the time is approaching when this seething mass of human misery will shake the social fabric, unless we grapple more earnestly with it than we have yet done . . . the proletariat may strangle us unless we teach it the same virtues which have elevated the other classes of society.[14]

Others, like Jack London writing twenty years later, were deeply sceptical of this form of social engineering. He was indeed deeply critical of the form of altruism proposed by earlier Victorian philanthropy:

> I have gone through an exhibition of Japanese art, got up for the poor of Whitechapel with the idea of elevating them, of begetting in them yearnings for the Beautiful and True and Good. Granting (what is not so) that the poor folk are thus taught to know and yearn after the Beautiful and True and Good, the foul facts of their existence and the social law that dooms one in three to a public-charity death, demonstrates that this knowledge and yearning will be only so much of an added curse to them.[15]

London's attack was aimed at those, like Barnett, whom he perceived as do-gooders. His own solution was overtly political and in marked contrast to the paternalistic philosophy espoused by Barnett.[16] Similarly, on 6 January 1906, the *East London Observer* commented,

> East London is nothing; indeed less than nothing – wholly a vile, malodorous, irreclaimable thing, a dumping ground for undesirables, a dustbin, a forgotten garrett, a neglected basement, creepy, smelly, stifling; that superior persons now and then must perforce sniff gingerly at for a short space until they may fly elsewhere to the sham respectables that their souls love, and boast of their daring philanthropic sacrifices.[17]

The role of institutions such as the Whitechapel Gallery, Toynbee Hall (where Barnett was appointed Warden in 1884) and public libraries was that of mediating between the family and the state. However, the historian Gareth Stedman Jones suggests that by the 1890s these institutions were changing in their function:

> They were no longer seen as manor houses from which a new squirearchy would lead the poor to virtue . . . They were now seen as informal social laboratories where future civil servants, social investigators, and established politicians could informally work out new principles of social politics.[18]

As such, a changing attitude to the idea of the responsibilities of the state is indicated. The Whitechapel Art Gallery, which shared a role in elaborating the processes and techniques of social control, saw as its principal audience the urban masses living in and around the Whitechapel district. It had established a tradition, since its inception, of organizing exhibitions which reflected the origins of its local constituents and inflected these in particular ways.

The district of Whitechapel was seen as a foreign continent whose natives had to be observed, educated and tamed – where, it was reputed, only the brave would venture. In the *People of the Abyss*, Jack London dramatizes the difficulties encountered by a person who wished to visit the East End. He compares these difficulties, not without irony, to the trials of an explorer seeking to discover exotic, foreign lands:

> But O Cook, O Thomas Cook & Son, pathfinders and trail clearers, living signposts to all the world, and bestowers of first aid to bewildered travellers – unhesitatingly and instantly, with ease and celebrity, could send me to Darkest Africa or innermost Thibet [*sic*], but to the East End of London, barely a stone's throw distant from Ludgate Circus, you know not the way.[19]

The headquarters of Thomas Cook's travel agency was in Ludgate Circus and provided, as John Pearce maintains, 'the threshold of an ordered universe, offering trips to Europe, the Levant and Egypt'. Cairo was deemed to be 'no more than a winter suburb of London'.[20] According to Pearce, travellers who used the services of Thomas Cook were middle-class tourists for whom Cook's agency substituted regularity and simplicity for confusion and complexity. T. H. Huxley compared East Londoners with primitive tribes, writing that 'the Polynesian savage in his most primitive condition' was not 'so savage, so unclean, so irreclaimable as the tenant of a tenement in an East London slum'.[21] Increasingly, as has already been noted, from the 1880s Jewish immigrants from Eastern Europe had been settling there. Whitechapel conveyed a sense of 'race' as well as class concentration. For many contemporary observers the East End of London meant the *Jewish* East End.[22]

Philip Dodd has argued that between the years 1880 and 1920 specific notions of Englishness were being reconstituted in order 'to incorporate and neuter various groups who threatened the dominant social order'.[23] In addition, Dodd contends, 'the colonization of the other was the necessary complement of the definition of the dominant English.'[24] As we have seen, the making of the English entailed the remaking and incorporation of other identities, including *Jewish*. This process was undertaken in a variety of social locations, e.g., schools, universities, art galleries and museums, and by various professional groups, with the tacit understanding that identity must be secured at the cultural as well as political level. The Whitechapel, by teaching its publics the 'art to live' was part of this larger project of social organiza-tion and control, and one in which identities were at stake and being managed in highly specific ways. The gallery participated in the articulation and negotiation of cultural identity, 'racial' or national.

The exhibition *Jewish Art and Antiquities* was to have been organized by a committee selected from leading Jewish societies. The original intention was to include works by foreign as well as English Jews by inviting the offer of exhibiting objects from 'all countries'. This plan was revised because it was thought that it was too ambitious for the Whitechapel. Thus, it was decided that the authorities of the Gallery should themselves organize the show with support from Jewish societies. The exhibition was funded from individual donations with the support of the *Jewish Chronicle* and the *Jewish World* newspapers. All involved were prominent members of the Anglo-Jewish community.[25]

The catalogue tried to fulfil its educative and social functions in various ways. It made it clear that the initial idea was to mount an exhibition similar in scale to the earlier exhibition of Anglo-Jewish art at the Victoria and Albert Museum.[26] The V&A exhibition took place in 1887, the year before the first Commons Select Committee on Alien Immigration, 1888. The Whitechapel exhibition was originally planned for 1905, the year in which the Anti-Aliens Bill was debated in Parliament. The delay in opening *Jewish Art and Antiquities* meant that it was staged after the Commissioners' recommendations found their way on to the statute books. The proximity of these two exhibitions to political processes and legislation which could directly affect the Jews cannot be mere coincidence and should be understood as part of the subtext of the show.

The objectives of the exhibition according to the catalogue, and I summarize, were

1. To gather together 'the rare, costly, and beautiful Appurtenances from the Synagogues in London'. In addition to these, 'many beautiful exhibits associated with domestic devotion' from private owners would be on view.
2. To show rare Manuscripts and books for the delectation of all but especially for Scholars and Bibliologists.
3. To illustrate by a selection of Portraits and prints the history of the Jews in England since the Protectorate of Cromwell.
4. To exhibit examples of works, mainly by English artists but to include the pictures of some foreigners, 'notably by the Nestor of Dutch Art – the illustrious Jozef Israels'.

The preface to the catalogue sought firmly to establish the notion of Jews with their own history in England. A distinction was made between English and foreign Jews, but whether English or foreign the Jews' participation in European culture was recognized and praised. Religious ritual was celebrated and presented as the bedrock of Judaism. The distinctions between its ritual and ceremonial manifestations and functions were blurred by showing how religious, spiritual and moral values percolated into the secular domain – the home. The version of Jewishness and Jewish identity offered by the exhibition *Jewish Art and Antiquities* or adduced by the catalogue was predicated upon particular notions of high culture, ideas of identity, views of assimilation, middle-class moral values, judgements on class and a need to combat anti-semitism.

I shall proceed with an analysis of the catalogue, the instituting discourse. That discourse is indispensable, for without it there is and was no exhibition. It provided a framework through which the exhibition was supposed to be experienced. As I have already noted, 20,000 visitors to the exhibition purchased catalogues, which sold at the cost of a penny.[27] The catalogue clearly had a didactic function, as the Trustees' Report of 1906 spelled out. Its role and aim were to describe 'the pictures in language which aimed at linking the subject to the experience of the visitors, and at assisting their judgement in appreciating the various merits.'[28] However, it appears from the tone of the Trustees' Report that the value of art and the educative purposes of art exhibitions could not be taken for granted. In fact the text seems to be defensive and an attempt to fend off anticipated criticisms. It suggests that the particular claims it wished to make for the value and uses of art needed to be established, argued and defended. They could not be assumed as uncontroversial. The voice of the Report is assertive, arguing that experience had taught

> that with higher tastes people turn away from the things which make for poverty. A greater love of beauty means, for instance, greater care for cleanliness, a better choice of pleasures, and increased self-respect. The use of the powers of admiration reveals new interests which are not satisfied in a public house but drives their possessors to do something both in their work and their play which adds to the joy of the earth. The sordid character of many national pleasures and the low artistic value of much of the national produce is due to the unused powers of admiration.[29]

The text opposed value to necessity; the need for 'beauty' was set against the need for 'bread'. 'Admiration', which would transform individuals by leading them away from 'base pleasures', was contrasted with 'skill'. Moreover, 'national pleasures' which were characterized as 'sordid' would be transmuted by the 'powers of admiration', as would the 'national produce'. The choice was clear: high culture would rescue the masses from all forms of poverty – social, economic, moral, intellectual and spiritual. It was thought that the acquisition of 'culture' by individuals would lead inevitably to social change and to a better society. These points were reiterated in different ways, with different emphases in the sections of the catalogue that follow.

It starts with the 'Engravings', which were to be found in the lower gallery. This section of the catalogue has no introductory text. It consists of a list of titles, artists' names and ownership, with occasional entries on individual works. The engravings covered a span from the eighteenth century to the contemporary. Judging from the titles, the works replicated the categories established in the preface, ranging from Old Testament subjects, woodcuts from the *Book of Ruth* and the *Book of Esther* by Lucien Pissaro, to local themes like Madame Jacob-Bazin's *Italian Laundress*. A portrait of *Baron Lionel de Rothschild, MP*, by William Richardson, was accompanied by an extended entry:

> b. 1808 in London. Energetic worker for the emancipation of the Jews in this country. Not before the fifth time of his election to Parliament was he permitted to take his seat without taking the oath 'on the true

faith of a Christian'. Philanthropist. Father of Lord Rothschild. d. 1879.[30]

There had been fourteen attempts to remove parliamentary disabilities for both Jews and Catholics. One bill was presented in each of the years 1830, 1833, 1834, 1836, 1847–8, 1849, 1851 and 1856. Four more measures were considered in 1857 and 1858. Lionel de Rothschild was able to take his seat in 1858, when the obligation to take the Christian oath was finally ended. The caption emphasizes the desire and indeed the resilience necessary for an individual Jew to assimilate himself, but at the same time it stresses the difficulties encountered in being assimilated by the 'host' nation. The text gives a double message: it seems to say that assimilation can be achieved, but only by a few and exceptionally able and gifted people. Implicit here is a challenge to the idea that equality of opportunity would lead to an egalitarian society.

With Emancipation the extension of civil rights had encouraged Jews (and others) to fit in with the values of the countries they lived in. In Britain the political integration of Jews into the state was a comparatively minimal process. Since the Resettlement, prompted by Cromwell's Republic of the seventeenth century, any person born there automatically had the right of citizenship. Hence the problem of civil rights technically existed for the first generation alone.[31]

However, while Jews may have been citizens they were in fact only second-class ones. For it was not until 1858, when the obligation to take the Christian oath was ended and Lionel de Rothschild was able to take his seat in the House of Commons, that (male) Jews achieved and received full political emancipation. Jews were a minor aspect of the bigger question of non-conformism and the question 'who could belong?', in the sense of participate in civil society.[32]

Their emancipation followed that of the numerically more powerful Protestant Dissenters and Catholics. The Jews in Britain were small in number – in 1828 it has been estimated that there were about 27,000 and by 1860 circa 60,000 – hence they did not form a critical mass. And their campaigns for political rights relied upon the changes effected by those other more powerful groups.[33]

Little by little throughout the nineteenth century male Jews gained the full rights of citizenship. In 1830 they gained the right to become freemen of the City of London and members of the Livery Companies; in 1833 the right to be called to the Bar; in 1833 the right to vote in parliamentary elections; in 1845 the right to hold municipal office; in 1858 the right to sit in Parliament; the right to take degrees and hold fellowships at Oxford and Cambridge was granted in 1871. These fundamental rights of citizenship were fashioned in the perfect image of the liberal constitution, with its promise to incorporate everyone and make them equal. This was a precarious promise: democratic liberalism assumed the equality of all people united by the idea of the nation. The question put to the Jews was in the form of a demand as to whether they could fit in. Hence assimilation was in the front line of shaping the new order and the identity of the nation itself.

To return to the Whitechapel exhibition, here religious culture appears as contiguous with the secular. For the next section of the exhibition, entitled 'Ecclesiastical Art', the accompanying text was divided into two parts: *Domestic* and *Sabbath Requisites*. The religious Law was at one and the same time contrasted with and linked to the home. The Law was characterized as 'the fountainhead of spiritual consolation'. Home was sanctified and represented as the place where 'sorrows are soothed'.[34] A man's affection for domesticity was combined with 'reverence for *his* faith'. In this regard it is important to note that the exhibition was addressed to the male spectator, as indeed were all the exhibitions in the Gallery. Indeed, Lord Rosebery said, in his speech which inaugurated the Whitechapel in 1901:

> If you offer this civilizing agency, these rooms, this gallery, as a place where a rough fellow who has nothing else to do can spend his time, you offer him an option which he had not had before and which if he avails himself of it cannot fail to have the most favourable results.[35]

This statement both sets up and represents a major opposition between the 'civilized' and 'rough' as well as between male and female.[36] The catalogue to the exhibition addresses the male subject; it is he who needs subjugating. The male Jew is the protagonist, the active subject. Yet he, according to the text, was already civilized in and by a culture which was essentially home-centred. Domesticity is idealized in the bourgeois imaginary. It is a haven which guarantees morality and civilization. The text draws upon and puts into effect a specific notion of Judaism from which it could be inferred that it had a civilizing effect upon its male constituents.

The idea of civilization was dealt with and picked up in the next section, 'Antiquities', where the text maintained that 'scattered throughout all the nations of the *civilized* world the Jews have had points of contact with every nation that has a history'.[37] Thus civilization was defined in terms of a national ideal and the nation state was described in terms similar to those elaborated by Ernest Renan in 'What is a nation?' According to Renan, a nation represented

> a large-scale solidarity, constituted by the feeling of sacrifices that one has made in the past and of those that one is prepared to make in the future. It presupposes a past; it is summarized, however, in the present

by a tangible fact, namely consent, that clearly expressed desire to continue a common life.[38]

In the discourse of the exhibition Jews are shown to have made a contribution to 'civilized' nations in the past. Moreover, it would seem that if a nation is formed out of consent (in the present) then the Jews also have a place. For they are already part of the nation as they share the history of the nation states. Thereby, the Jews are established as civilized and are distinguished from others – non-Europeans – who have not consented to the national ideal and are by inference outside civilization and are 'primitive'.

Four exhibits in particular were used to testify to Jewish presence in England. Aim three of the exhibition was 'To illustrate by a Selection of Portraits and a remarkably interesting series of Prints the history of the Jewish community in England since their re-admission, during the Protectorate of Cromwell.' These were: *An Apology for the Honourable Nation of the Jews* by Edward Nicholas, dating from 1648; *The Restouration of the Jews* (1665); *The Rudiments of the Hebrew Grammar in English* by Hanserd Knollys (1648); and *Narrative of the Late Proceeds at Whitechapel Concerning the Jews* (1656).[39] From these titles it can be deduced that the Jews were associated with a civilized country – England. Their presence, since the seventeenth century, was made manifest in and by the paintings. The Jews were *a priori* cultured.

The display of the precious objects for both synagogue and domestic uses seems to reiterate this point. The text is at pains to point out that the show was not exhaustive or even representative in that it included just a few 'specimens'.[40] The word has scientific connotations and reminded the viewer that, in spite of the miscellaneous collection of objects on view, the items served as evidence of greater truths. The chaos of miscellany was overcome by the display of specimens. The fragments evoked the greater whole from which they had been detached. The display implied an ordered system through which recorded and accumulated facts could be verified. It called for methods of observation and analysis which were seemingly independent of the interests of the observer. Thus an effect of disinterested contemplation was created in which the perceiving subject, the observer, interposed minimally between the objects and their representation. The question how to display the objects – manuscripts, books, inscriptions, seals and rings, coins and medals recording historical and family events of the eighteenth and nineteenth centuries – was in fact the problem of representing historical truth and reality. For the nineteenth-century empirical investigations, the accumulation of 'facts' and 'data' gave to history the status of science and truth. The historian was produced as a disinterested purveyor of this 'truth'.

The catalogue's text also dealt with the objects by evaluating them. According to it, among the best items were ornamented and illuminated prayer books, megillah, Hagadah and Bibles of the fifteenth and sixteenth centuries which vied in elegance and beauty with masterpieces of non-Jewish presses to be found in Spain and Italy. Thus it argued that Jewish craftsmanship was at least as good as that produced in Christendom.

Like all exhibitions, this one at the Whitechapel was partial. It was the culture of Western European Jews which was celebrated. The objects on loan – and most of the organizers themselves – came from the established Anglo-Jewish community, who were by and large from Dutch, German or Sephardic cultures. It omitted large aspects of Jewish cultures, notably those of the Eastern European Jews – those very Jews arriving weekly in the Port of London. Many set up homes and found work in the East End and might indeed have been visitors to the exhibition. The exhibition concealed what were emerging fractures within the Jewish communities themselves – ruptures between the Sephardic and Ashkenazi Jews, among the orthodox, reform and liberal Jews, class differences, and differences between established Anglo-Jewry and 'greeners'. It offered a version of Jewishness which was the Jewishness of the Enlightenment – of a modern English Jewry. Even the expected mode of conduct in synagogue and dress was changing so as to become akin to that of the Anglican High Church.[41] Jewish identity was being produced as an image to which Jews in Britain should aspire rather than perhaps as the conscious expression of what they were – diverse and differentiated.

Jewish art was placed in the Upper Gallery. The text pointed out that the 'Hebrew race' had not been known for fine art culture, although this was not developed as a critical theme. However, a distinction was being made between *Jew* and Hebrew: the former referring to the Jew in the Diaspora, the latter connoting race. Notable exceptions were called upon to disprove the rule, including Meier le Brun, the Jew who in 1270 received a commission from Prince Edward, and Lucas von Leyden (1494–1533), whose real name was Lucas Jacobs and whose art had a debt to Israel van Mecheln, who belonged to the Jewish 'community'. According to the catalogue, if there had in the past been any religious embargoes on painting, nonetheless Jews excelled in decorative arts, graphic arts, line engravings and etching, and special attention was drawn to their contributions in Verona, where Jews were involved in decorative glass.[42]

We are told that it was not until the nineteenth century that the *Jewish* fine artist emerged. Three artists were singled out for attention, thereby showing the range of subjects and treatments of themes embarked upon by Jewish artists. Solomon Hart (1806–81) was described as an history

Figure 12. Solomon Hart, *The Conference between Menasseh Ben Israel and Oliver Cromwell*, 1873, oil on canvas. Photograph with kind permission of the Witt Library, Courtauld Institute of Art, London.

painter of 'essentially Jewish subjects'. *The Conference between Menasseh Ben Israel and Oliver Cromwell* (Figure 12), *The Jews and Their Proposal to Ferdinand and Isabella, Simchatch Torah* and *Elevation of the Law* were cited as examples.[43] These pictures were 'true' history pictures and not 'reconstructed histories like the others'. They are differentiated within the text from 'merely' biblical subjects like the *Prophet Ezekiel* or *Solomon*. 'True' history was defined as the depiction of events which were known to have taken place, in which verifiable facts about a historical milieu were represented.

In addition to historical themes, 'popular' pictures were shown. These 'coincided with the tastes of former generations'. *Waiting for the Verdict* and *Not Guilty* by Abraham Solomon (1824–62) were cited as examples. 'Popular' pictures were differentiated from 'history' pictures and presented as a lesser category of art. In contrast to the popular painters – and of infinitely greater merit as an artist according to the catalogue – was Simeon Solomon (d. 1905), whose work it was claimed, had he lived longer, would have surpassed that of Burne-Jones and

Rossetti. The text celebrated the work of Josef Israels and affirmed him as the 'Jewish Rembrandt' and suggested that little needed to be said about his work. Even though few words were necessary, the language used to speak of it was fulsome and quasi-biblical in tone. Israels did not have to wait for 'his passing for his name to be inscribed on the scroll of the immortals'. He had won 'universal admiration' and the 'applause of every school of artistic thought'. His art was thus represented as reaching beyond the artist's 'origins'.[44] This defensive attempt to establish Jewish artists as equally as good as, if not better than, their Christian counterparts was part of a wider endeavour to assert the intrinsic value of Jewish culture and the benefits that it could bring to the host country.

In the Modern Section, where 'every' school of art was represented – 'Victorian' painters to the 'ultra-impressionists' – it was again claimed that few words were needed to describe the participation of the Jews in contemporary culture.[45] The catalogue text oscillates between different schemata. On the one hand it offers narrative accounts of and explanations for the objects on display and on the other it denies the necessity for such framing discourses. Implicit in this latter schema is the idea that knowledge springs directly from the objects themselves. The text proceeds by making a distinction between British Jews and *foreigners*, here referring to Jews who lived abroad. At that point, however, the text seems to contradict itself by suggesting that some of the figure painters may choose 'to infuse racial passion into their work by the treatment of essentially Jewish subjects, poignant in their significance and profound sincerity'.[46]

According to this discourse, 'essentially Jewish subjects' are those which exhibit particular forms of emotion. The differences between one race and another were considered to be 'essential', that is to say, differences of 'nature' or kind. The techniques of scientific investigation produced empirical and descriptive evidence to define differences between races. Biology, intelligence and physical attributes were made central to definitions of racial identity. Gilman maintains:

> No longer was the perception of the other to be the subject of legend; it had become the focus of a science, with the extraordinary strength that the very word *science* had for the late-nineteenth century mind, supporting its claim for objective status.[47]

The Jews here are represented as emotional by nature. Moreover, emotion had come to be designated as the domain of Woman, whose roles were to care, nurture and feel. Hence the text presents a feminized and castrated image of *Jew*, whose Otherness could be possessed through this image, but for which he could also be reviled. To feminize is to disempower: to control, deny and to disavow. We are back in the world of projection.

Some artists, it was argued, could choose their Jewishness, and their work would be thus infused with 'racial passion' characterized as 'emotionality'. Others, the 'majority', could choose to identify themselves 'entirely' with their 'adopted country' and show no trace of 'distinctive thought or differentiation'.[48] The contradictions continue. Jews are described as a 'race', a 'community', distinctive, yet comparable with and indistinguishable from their various host communities. The neat categories are slipping: if it is race, birthright, biology and inheritance which make a Jew a Jew, what happens to the project of assimilation?

The catalogue provides an example of an apparent paradox which Halevi points out when he argues that definitions of Jewishness proliferated precisely at the moment when the Jews were no longer one thing – were no longer definable as such: 'while there was a sociological splitting up of Jewish social reality into a greater number of very diversified social and cultural situations, the discourse was completely essentialist.'[49] The version of Jewishness identified by the catalogue text as inherent to the Jewish race was that which could be harnessed for the good of the English nation itself, an unstable notion. But, in the claim that Jewish artists were both different from and the same as others, the text demonstrates a capacity for the distinction and incorporation, differentiation *and* assimilation of the Jews.

Three classes of Jewish artists were created in the text: firstly, British Jews who maintained their difference through depicting 'essentially' *Jewish* subjects or themes; secondly, British Jews who assimilated themselves by working within the available artistic traditions and by not referring in any conspicuous or obvious ways to *Jewishness*; and, thirdly, foreign Jews who resided outside Britain. In other words, Jewish identity appears as a choice. But the catalogue concluded with the confident assurance that the course of future development will be 'continual assimilation' with the sole purpose of 'advancing the honour and glory' of the British school. Thus the catalogue proclaimed:

> Young men and women of ability are arising on every side who will certainly remove the reproach of the past, and the graphic arts, like the others, will before long be recognized as equal witness of the emotional and intellectual genius of the House of Israel.[50]

The idea of the nation was, at one and the same time, extended and narrowed. The very construction of the nation was dependent and based upon inclusions and exclusion. It occupied a precarious site spanning potential integration and disintegration. Anglo-Jewry's choice to be 'included' was based on defence and desire. They adopted a utilitarian stance and sought to find a model of Jewish identity and history which could represent the 'good' Jew and the benefits that he could bring to the evolving ideas of the national culture. Anglo-Jewry, it would seem, did not attempt to argue for equal rights.

It is no accident that the Whitechapel Gallery was the initiator of an exhibition which celebrated Jewish cultural achievements and provided the venue for it. As has already been noted, the Whitechapel was located in the heart of the East End of London, where Jewish immigrants were concentrated. Moreover, concurrent with the planning of the exhibition, the Royal Commissioners were taking the evidence which was to lead to the restriction of alien immigration.

If the impression left by the catalogue of the *Jewish Art and Antiquities* exhibition is of the Jews as intellectual, artistic, emotional, socially mobile and capable of being assimilated, this is a far cry from the images created and the pictures drawn by the witnesses to the Royal Commission. The Commission was presented with no evidence about the contribution which the Jews might make to art or culture. It was as though the Whitechapel exhibition and all that was claimed for it was unthinkable. The particular identities constituted for the Jews by and within the exhibition were not those necessarily perceived in the world 'outside', as the evidence presented to the Royal Commission on Alien Immigration showed.

The most powerful image which came from the exhibition was, as we have seen, that Jewish artists could promote 'the power and glory of the British school'. Inherent in this message was again the desire to anticipate and to affirm the dream of assimilation. Political loyalty and trustworthiness were seen as the conditions for granting emancipation and the rights of citizens. These went hand in hand with conforming to predetermined values. Bauman argues: 'Citizenship and cultural conformity seemed to merge; the second was perceived as the condition, but also as the means to attain the first.'[51]

The exhibition *Jewish Art and Antiquities* can be seen as a symptom of a struggle on the cultural plane over the matrix of Jewish identity in England. In the context of the debates of the time, it was an exhibition with a message. Through its address to East End Jews, recent arrivals or 'greeners', it spoke of Jewishness in a way which urged them to assimilate. It proposed a version of Jewishness purged of its own languages, of its Yiddish cultures and also cleansed of a potential class radicalism.[52] Its aim was to encourage the so-called uncivilized, foreign-looking, poor, uneducated peoples to accept the standards set by the English middle classes and to make a version of *Jewishness* which would be compatible with *Englishness*.

The survival of the Jew in Britain was predicated upon imitating the other (the English) in the attempt to become alike. A new identity was established by denying an old one. Odysseus' dilemma provides a metaphor for assimilation itself. Odysseus, when asked his name by his captor Polyphemus, at one and the same time saved and denied himself by giving the name 'Nobody'. Answering to the name and disowning it are one. Odysseus acknowledged himself to himself by denying himself. Thus he made the act of recognition and negation one. He saved his life by losing himself. It is, however, at that very conjuncture that new selves can be born and new identities embraced. We have already seen through the Shackmans' eyes the possible losses and gains projected by assimilation. We have also noted that this may not be a tragic situation, but one of renewal, fashioned in that precarious juncture between identity and non-identity. Nevertheless, this is not simply a question of individual choice but one founded in the constraints provided by social and political exigencies and given particular shape in institutional formations.

Assimilation, argues Bauman, is a particularly modern phenomenon.[53] It derives its form from the modern idea of nationalization in which the state insists upon legal, linguistic, cultural and ideological unification and uniformity. The adaptations and re-interpretations which the processes of assimilation entail provide the unstable conditions in and through which a culture is destroyed and re-made and old traditions are made to assume new forms. These are in themselves shaped in constant recognition of and negotiation with both the 'old' and the 'new' and are always restless, always marked by ambivalence. To turn again to Arendt:

> What non-Jewish society demanded was that the new-comer be as 'educated' as itself, and that, although he did not behave like an 'ordinary Jew', he be and produce something out of the ordinary, since, after all, he was a Jew. All advocates of Emancipation called for assimilation, that is adjustment to and reception by, society, which they considered either a preliminary condition to Jewish Emancipation or its automatic consequences. In other words, whenever those who actually tried to improve Jewish conditions attempted to think of the Jewish question from the point of view of the Jews themselves, they immediately approached it merely in its social aspect. It has been one of the most unfortunate aspects of the history of the Jewish people that only its enemies, and almost never its friends, understood the Jewish question was a political one.[54]

Assimilation, in the sense of acceptance by the non-Jewish society, was granted to some Jews only so long as they were clearly distinguished from the Jewish masses.

Culture is political. Here I follow Efraim Shmueli and take culture to mean a grouping of elements in which inconsistencies have been minimized at the same time as recognizing that incompatibilities never disappear. Efraim Shmueli argues that 'every culture is also a political phenomenon. Human beings forge their life-experiences in the inter-personal realities that activate their economic and political behaviour, and in the prototypes they create for their thoughts and actions.'[55] The fight over culture is a power struggle through which meanings are defined and identities shaped. The exhibition *Jewish Art and Antiquities* shaped an identity which was not solely created by Jews and it was subject to how the Jews were perceived and perceived themselves as *Jews* in their non-Jewish surroundings. This in turn related to the wider issue of the making of that national identity which was in the process of being defined as English. Dodd has argued that its successful creation was both predicated upon and nourished by the illusion that 'everyone had a place . . . and had contributed to the past which had become a settled present'.[56] The Jews of Whitechapel, with all their diverse cultural identities, were invited to become spectators of a culture already complete, presented and represented to them and for them by their trustees. They were given their place in the national culture. They accepted the invitation to assimilate and this came in the form of a contract which had a pre-determined form.

Today I ask what were the options then available to the Jews? In Britain at that moment it could be argued that asserting difference would have amounted to maintaining Jews in an inferior position in relation to the host community. The notion of 'equality in difference' does not hold up. All it would have been was an ideology of domination whose goal was to hide that domination. So perhaps – at the time – assimilation was the inevitable course.

However, the question that still has to be asked is, 'What kind of assimilation and in whose interests?' Like all didactic exhibitions, *Jewish Art and Antiquities* put its message across by trading on a treacherous compromise. If the Jews were respectable and trustworthy, already good citizens – as it seemed to say – it was only at the cost of marginalizing some Jews (to the benefits of others). Thus, the exhibition offered as truth the pretence that what was (and is) in reality an unceasing struggle over identity had already been settled.

Notes

1. Iain Sinclair, *White Chappel: Scarlet Tracings*, Rutland: Goldmark, 1987, p. 83.
2. The organizers included the Rev. Professor H. Gollanz, H.S.Q. Henriques, the Hon. Walter Rothschild, Solomon J. Solomon and the Chief Rabbi.

3. *Trustees Report*, Whitechapel Art Gallery, London, 1906, p. 9 (Whitechapel Art Gallery Archive).
4. Henrietta Barnett, *Canon Barnett: His Life and Work*, Vol. 2, London, 1918, p. 151.
5. *Ibid.*, p. 172.
6. John Passmore Edwards was Liberal MP for Salisbury 1880–85. He gave grants of money to boroughs on the basis that they establish a library.
7. *The Studio*, Vol. 10, 1896, cited in Ribin Roth, *The Whitechapel Art Gallery: Arts and Crafts or Art Nouveau?* Unpublished Open University project (Whitechapel Art Gallery Archive).
8. Barnett, *op. cit.*, Vol. 1, p. 216.
9. *Ibid.*, Vol. 2, p. 154.
10. *Ibid.*, p. 152.
11. *Trustees Report*, Whitechapel Art Gallery, 1906, p. 5.
12. *Ibid.*, p. 14.
13. See Brian Doyle, 'The invention of English', in Robert Colls and Philip Dodd (eds), *Englishness, Politics and Culture: 1880–1920*, London: Croom Helm, 1987, p. 92.
14. Samuel Smiles, 'The industrial training of destitute children', *Contemporary Review*, xvii, January 1885, p. 110; quoted in G. Stedman Jones, *Outcast London: A Study in the Relationship between Classes in Victorian Society*, Harmondsworth: Penguin, 1984, p. 291.
15. Jack London, *People of the Abyss* [1903], London: Journeyman Press, 1977, p. 122.
16. The study of working-class life became a major preoccupation during this period. See, for example, Charles Booth, *Life and Labour of the People of London*, 17 vols, London: Macmillan, 1902.
17. *East London Observer*, January 1906, p. 6, cited in John A. Garrard, *The English and Immigration, 1880–1910*, Oxford: Oxford University Press, p. 49.
18. Stedman Jones, *op. cit.*, p. 328.
19. London, *op. cit.*, p. 11.
20. John Pemble, *The Mediterranean Passion*, Oxford: Oxford University Press, 1988, p. 47.
21. T. H. Huxley, cited by Asa Briggs in *Victorian Cities*, Harmondsworth: Pelican, 1975, p. 315.
22. RC, ii, *Evidence* (1903).
23. Philip Dodd, 'Englishness and national culture', in Colls and Dodd, *op. cit.*, p. 2.
24. *Ibid.*, p. 15.
25. Dr Joseph Jacobs and Lucien Wolf wrote the catalogue text.
26. *Jewish Art and Antiquities*, exhibition catalogue, Whitechapel Art Gallery, London, 1906, Preface.
27. *Trustees Report*, Whitechapel Art Gallery, 1906, p. 9.

28. *Trustees Report*, Whitechapel Art Gallery, 1907, p. 3.
29. *Ibid.*
30. *Jewish Art and Antiquities,* catalogue entry no. 229, p. 18.
31. Todd M. Endelman, *Radical Assimilation in English Jewish History, 1656–1945*, Bloomington: Indiana University Press, 1990, p. 73.
32. David Sorkin, 'What was the Emancipation?' Lecture at the SPIRO Institute, London, 13 August 1990.
33. *Ibid.*
34. *Jewish Art and Antiquities*, p. 18.
35. *East End Observer*, 16 March 1901 (Whitechapel Art Gallery Archive).
36. It is interesting to note that in the 'Modern Section' of the exhibition, one-third of the exhibitors were women.
37. *Jewish Art and Antiquities*, p. 21.
38. Ernest Renan, 'What is a nation?', in Homi K. Bhabha, *Nation and Narration*, London: Routledge, 1990, p. 19.
39. *Jewish Art and Antiquities*, p. 23, 'Preface'.
40. *Ibid.*, p. 21.
41. *Ibid.*, p. 23.
42. *Ibid.*, pp. 84–6.
43. *Ibid.*, p. 84.
44. *Ibid.*, p. 85.
45. *Ibid.*
46. *Ibid.*
47. Sander L. Gilman, *Jewish Self-Hatred: Anti-Semitism and the Hidden Language of the Jews*, Baltimore: Johns Hopkins University Press, 1990, p. 213.
48. *Jewish Art and Antiquities*, p. 85.
49. Ilan Halevi, 'Jewish identity through the ages', *Return*, March 1989, p. 9.
50. *Jewish Art and Antiquities*, p. 85.
51. Zygmunt Bauman, *Modernity and Ambivalence*, Cambridge: Polity Press, 1991, p. 142.
52. William Fishman has written on the socialist and anarchist traditions of East London immigrants in *East End Jewish Radicals 1875–1914*, London: Duckworth, 1975.
53. Bauman, *op. cit.*, p. 141.
54. Hannah Arendt, *The Origins of Totalitarianism*, London: George Allen & Unwin, 1958, p. 56.
55. Efraim Shmueli, *Seven Jewish Cultures*, Cambridge: Cambridge University Press, 1990, pp. 34–5.
56. Dodd, *op. cit.*, p. 22.

6

Yids, mods and foreigners:
the processes of alienization

Could anything spiritual grow on these dung-heaps? These were the
dregs of a society whose champions still claimed that man was made
in God's image, but who evaded meeting that image face to face in the
slums of London.

Rudolf Rocker[1]

In accordance with the deeds of its Trust, the Whitechapel Art Gallery
between 1906 and 1914 – the dates which span the exhibitions *Jewish
Art and Antiquities* and *Twentieth Century Art (A Review of Modern
Movements)*[2] – continued with its civilizing mission. A mixed programme of shows were organized which during this period included:
loans from national museums which were thematized in terms of
historical periods; shows of 'high-class' modern pictures; exhibits of
industry and art; and work by students and school children.[3] All were
conceived of as primarily educational in function. The Trustees' Annual
Report of 1904, commenting on the *Spring Picture Exhibition* which
included works by Rembrandt and Frans Hals, observed:

> The exhibition appealed more than is usually the case at Whitechapel
> to an outside public: but the Committee considered this justifiable,
> seeing that a gallery which relies entirely on loans must make itself
> known to the picture owning class in order to provide its regular visitors
> with fresh entertainment.[4]

Exhibitions were planned, then, to appeal to the Gallery's local
constituents, to be 'popular', and to establish the Whitechapel as a
prestige venue for the showing of art. However, judging from the
annual reports, a tension existed between these propositions which
manifested itself as a schism between high art and exhibitions designed
to be popular. In 1910 it was noted:

The policy of putting artistic interest before popularity cannot, of course, be generally followed, but obviously it is necessary to secure for the gallery a high reputation among the people best qualified to judge and it is the mission of the Trustees gradually to raise the level of the popular.[5]

The perceived breach was to be bridged through education, offered in a variety of forms that are now familiar in public galleries, including catalogues, lectures and guided tours. Indeed, the Trustees claimed, 'There is no limit to that which comes from within a man, when his own mind and interests have been stirred.'[6] The aim of *Twentieth Century Art* was to map out the development of modern art, and in its effects it was to establish the Whitechapel Gallery in the vanguard of contemporary art. Moreover, the exhibition occurred at a moment when, as Charles Harrison has suggested, 'the mainstream practice of modern art was defined and entrenched in England.'[7] To define involves making categories, which entails drawing boundaries and differentiating. Furthermore, definitions themselves create identities and produce hierarchies.

In this chapter, I explore the aesthetic boundaries and hierarchies which were constructed in and by the *Twentieth Century Art* show. I examine the production of the distinctive categories which situated an inside and an outside of and for a mainstream art. In addition, I shall draw attention to the formation of yet another category, which occupied an outside space even when inside – that occupied by the 'alienized'.[8] I shall argue, too, that the ways in which critics represented the exhibition *Twentieth Century Art* not only articulated the dominant definitions of modern art in Britain but also replicated and contributed towards fixing social categories.

In *Twentieth Century Art* a broad range of works, from Impressionist to Cubist and Futurist, were shown. Vanessa Bell, Henry Lamb, Gaudier-Brzska, Stanley Spencer, Paul Nash and Wyndham Lewis were amongst those who had work on view. In addition a large collection from Roger Fry and the Omega Workshop was on display.[9] Separated from the rest and hung together in the Small Gallery, were works by Jewish artists curated by David Bomberg.

Some critics, seemingly blinded by fear, even went so far as to explicitly connect Cubism and Futurism with Jewish artists. Modern art was associated with foreign or malign influences. Furthermore, modern art was seen by some as being part of the occult, irrational and emotive world of the Other. The Other was seen and described as an alien force with an evil influence. The exhibition was to provoke and to create tensions between cultural differentiation and the national culture and between individualism and collective conformity.

The story mounted by the catalogue sought to make connections across a diverse range of art works through identifying their stylistic similarities. A Jewish section within this exhibition did not, and indeed could not, conform to or fit in with the overall theme of the show, with its aim to instate a modernist aesthetic into British art discourses. What bonded this section together were the Jewish origins of the participants. Fifty-three works by fifteen artists were displayed. These included Bomberg, Gertler, Kramer, Modigliani and Pascin.[10] However, before examining the significance of this section, I need to establish the parameters of the exhibition as a whole.

As I mentioned earlier, correspondences between styles formed the basis for categorizing the works and indeed the rationale for the hanging. The show was divided into four main groups. Here, I summarize from the catalogue: the first group showed the influence of Walter Sickert and Lucien Pissarro on modern art and stressed their use of ordinary subjects which, it was argued, were treated in a 'luminous' manner. The second constructed links between Puvis de Chavannes, Alphonse Legros and Augustus John, whose works were characterized by their persistent use of decorative design and linear simplifications in the treatment of human types. The text then argued that a third group had a debt to Impressionist painting and to Cézanne and suggested further that this work differed from the previous group in its use of volumetric drawing and its abandoning of perspective. The final group, characterized as having given up representation almost entirely, had, it was pointed out, recently established a Rebel Art Centre. Though not in this group, the works of Bomberg were mentioned in the catalogue as if hung in this context. His paintings and drawings were to be found in the Small Gallery with the works of other Jewish artists.

As a whole the exhibition was conceived as a follow-on to a show staged in the Whitechapel four years earlier, called *Twenty Years of British Art*.[11] The 1910 exhibition was designed to show the impact on art of French Impressionism, which it considered to have moved art away from naturalism: 'The "Twentieth Century Art" exhibition is concerned with the progress of art since the absorption of the Impressionist teachings, as shown in the work of younger British artists.'[12] According to the 1914 catalogue, the earlier exhibition

> showed that artists had moved away from an academic treatment of history, anecdote, and sentimentality, and had gone in search of a more brilliant treatment of light in landscape, and of more truly decorative treatments of subject, and of a more intimate treatment of human life generally.[13]

Implicit in this statement was the notion of progress, which in art was taken to mean the assertion of the autonomy of aesthetic experience.

Implicit, too, was the association of artistic development with artistic language or style. Moreover, this implied the avoidance of subjects which were morally charged. Additionally, by creating a link between one exhibition and the other, the continuity and evolution of modern art was suggested.

The catalogue accompanying *Twenty Years of British Art* did not have entries on each of the 569 items on display, but it did include short accounts of some of them. A commentary produced for *The Convalescent* by Ambrose McEvoy is typical:

> This modest picture is a remarkable example of the attainment of the harmony necessary to make a painting into a fine work of art. The simple lines of the bare room, the sober colour scheme of ivory and brown and dim red, the quiet light falling on the sofa and its occupant, all combine to carry forward the expression of a gentle, homely beauty.[14]

This commentary shows the shift in critical discourse mediated through particular understandings of French art. The form and the design both articulate 'gentle, homely beauty', which together evoke a scene of calm and simple domesticity. The text links form and content to produce a moral message which celebrates and idealizes the virtues of home. But, above all, it is the achievement of a particular aesthetic quality, 'harmony', which makes this picture work as a successful work of art.

An uncharacteristically lengthy entry on Tonks's *Rosamund and the Purple Jar*, which I quote in full, spells out the ways in which modern art was understood to be superior to nineteenth-century art:

> Fifty years ago the mid-Victorians told the story of Rosamund and her purple jar to children to discourage reckless, unthinking love of beauty. We are now less certain that youth is foolish in grasping the glory of liquid purple, and going barefoot, as long as it does not expect to have boots provided for it, as well as the purple jars of beauty. The painting might almost be taken at first sight as the work of one of the Pre-Raphaelites, every detail rendered with quaint and loving care, yet there is a subtle difference – Rosamund has chosen an Aubusson carpet, not a Brussels, for her room. Behind the work of the artist here one feels a wider culture, a mind that knows childish things for what they are. He can delight in them, and, when his theme, as here, enjoins, revel in their charm, but we feel that he can also put childish things away. He does not labour under the illusion, natural and even praiseworthy as it was in the case of the Pre-Raphaelites, that the only way of art lies in childish methods.[15]

The differences produced by the text between Tonks's actual picture and an imaginary Pre-Raphaelite painting established the ground for judging modern art. The entry started by appearing to affirm the values of narrative painting but it continues by questioning the morality implicit in the work. A modern painting is more knowing, more intelligent, more discerning both in concept and in the handling of paint. Modern art is distinguished, in the text, by its sophistication and its greater understanding of the methods and procedures of art and culture.

The exhibition attracted an attendance of 80,000[16] people in less than six weeks. As the retrospectively produced catalogue commented, 'The East End visitors were numerous and so appreciative that it seemed as if good work was able to interest and attract them by its own merits without the aid of popular subject matter.'[17] The Trustees' Report of the exhibition is explicit in its disassociation of subject matter from popularity. Good art has the power to appeal to the East End visitors. A space was being cleared for artistic judgements in which the ultimate value of art is 'aesthetic'. And aesthetic in a particular sense – one which reified form and divorced it from subject-matter – was in the process of being articulated and made.

Twenty Years of British Art and *Twentieth Century Art* each suggest a change of paradigm for the Whitechapel. Previous exhibitions had been designed to mediate art to its publics in ways which would impart and convey moral lessons. The exhibitions themselves, for example *Jewish Art and Antiquities*, were organized thematically to facilitate this approach. Individual images which were deemed appropriate to instruct were often singled out for attention and comment.

The catalogue which accompanied the exhibition *Twentieth Century Art* began with a short essay through which the show was framed. This introduction was then followed by the list of artists' names, lenders and the title of each work. Authorship and ownership were given priority. There was no additional amplification or elucidation of works. The exhibition employed a modernist approach to art which has now become the familiar discourse of professional art historical management. The form of aesthetic re-evaluation signalled by the exhibitions is significant and made more so given the particular history and ideology of the gallery.[18]

As we have seen, the Whitechapel had been founded by Canon and Henrietta Barnett with the aim of taking high culture to the East End of London. Its programme of exhibitions, lectures and guided tours sought to inculcate in the local population a higher subjectivity which could transcend nature by offering experiences, feelings and pleasures that went beyond what were understood as the mindless routines of working-class lives. The gallery policy was predicated upon the belief that reform through art would lead to the improvement of the 'lower classes'. By teaching them to admire the beautiful, it was thought, they would gain insights and understandings which would enable them to share the values of the classes above them. According to Barnett:

> There can be no real unity so long as people in different parts of a city are prevented from admiring the same things, from taking the same pride in their fathers' great deeds and from sharing the glory of possessing the same great literature.[19]

This commentary established the sketch of a scenario in which culture was used to mould people – both in the reproduction of social roles and in the productive processes. In this context art was used to educate and morally uplift the public.

By 1914, art was no longer to be seen and valued explicitly in terms of its power to morally elevate and set standards for human behaviour. Rather it was now to be judged and assessed in terms of the strength of its appeal to aesthetic categories. In these two exhibitions moral didacticism was being transformed into the progressive imperative. Of increasing importance were ideas about the purity of the aesthetic experience, which were linked with ideas about progress. Art was to be seen and judged in terms of the strength of its appeal to aesthetic emotions and the particular vision of the individual artist. As the catalogue to *Twentieth Century Art* put it:

> A feeling common to the painters, sculptors, and designers represented in the exhibition is that of a compulsion on the artist towards a more personal statement of his relation towards his subject in particular and to life in general than has been expressed in the preceding phases of the development of art.[20]

The exhibitions were part of a process whereby a new theory of art was being formulated, articulated and promoted. In these discourses art's primary concern was understood to be aesthetic and art history and criticism were constructed around artistic or stylistic precedents.

In 1912 contemporary artistic theory had been polarized by the London launch of Post-Impressionism. The Royal Academy, attempting to maintain its prestige and power, closed ranks against the 'new' art. In these debates, Post-Impressionism, with Fry's and Bell's aesthetic theory, was constructed as progressive and defined in opposition to the Royal Academy, which was represented as reactionary.[21]

By pitting the one institution against the other the critics of *The Times* and the *Observer* recreated those polemics in their reviews of *Twentieth Century Art*. *The Times* asserted:

> This exhibition in Whitechapel seems like a challenge to the other in Piccadilly. The Piccadilly artists would say, no doubt, that Whitechapel is the proper place for it and Billingsgate the proper language. Art, like

life, is at any rate more exciting in Whitechapel than in Piccadilly. Something is happening there and nothing at all at Burlington House.[22]

Through the nature of its exhibitions policy, its function and its geography, the Whitechapel presented a challenge to the prestige of the Royal Academy. The values espoused by the Royal Academy served as a negative foil through which 'progressive' or 'advanced' art could be assessed and measured.

For the *Observer* the exclusion of works by Royal Academicians was at least as worthy for comment, as significant, as those works which were included in the show:

> There is scarcely an exhibitor at the Whitechapel who is represented at the Royal Academy. We are thus faced with the remarkable fact that the official guardians of the nation's art, the members of the Royal Academy, refuse to take any account of the vast movement, or succession of movements, which have led twentieth century art into new paths, and, on the other hand what pretends to be a representative exhibition of twentieth century art, organized by laymen who have no axe to grind and who have on previous occasions given proof of their liberal spirit, absolutely ignores the existence of the Royal Academy.[23]

Twentieth Century Art was selected by the Gallery Director, Gilbert Ramsey, with the help of the previous director, Charles Aitken.[24] They had asked William Dawson's permission to dispense with the usual practice of setting up an advisory committee for the exhibition. In a letter dated 5 February 1914 Dawson acceded to this request with the proviso that: 'we shall not have many examples of the "Cubist" and "Futurist" school, though perhaps we should have one or two as an example of what certain members of the public can be induced to tolerate.'[25] To whom was he referring? Whatever may be postulated as an answer to this question, Dawson's fears seem to have been well founded. The *Daily Express* asked what would be the consequences should, 'a whole flood of isms be let loose like a cataract on the unprepared East End?'[26] The Director of the National Gallery, J. B. Manson, had written to Ramsey expressing his disquiet at the decision to include Cubist works in the exhibition.[27] On 15 May, Dawson, in response to a letter from the Chair of Trustees of the Whitechapel, the Hon. Harry Lawson MP, which alerted him to an article in the *Telegraph* from Sir Claude Phillips, agreed with the view that the Trustees 'assume a grave responsibility in opening the doors of such an exhibition without careful preparation and warning to the artistic youth and larger public of East London.'[28] Thus, for the Trustees at least, an educational and

Figure 13. David Bomberg, *Vision of Ezekiel*, 1912, oil on canvas,
114.5 × 137 cm, © Tate Gallery, London.

moral role for art was still of paramount importance. But if this entailed
the 'careful preparation' of the public, many of the critics appear to
have been ill-prepared for the exhibition.

The *Star*[29] began its review with a critique of the very title of the
show. The critic castigated the organizers for creating expectations
which were misleading. Furthermore, the exhibition was 'bewildering'.
The *Standard* saw it as an insane attempt to present a complete review
of the whole evolution of modern art. Bomberg's *The Hold*, *Vision of
Ezekiel* (Figure 13) and *Racehorses* were singled out for comment.[30] A
number of other newspaper reports completely misrepresented the
exhibition. Out of 494 exhibits, a total of 13 – by Nevinson, Roberts,
Wadsworth, Etchells and Wyndham Lewis – could be described as
Cubist or Futurist. Nevertheless, the headline in the *Observer* ran,
'Futurist Art in Whitechapel'[31] and a notice appeared in the *Daily
Express* under the title, 'Futurist Picture Show'. [32]

The *Manchester Guardian* suggested that the nucleus of Jewish art
was Cubist: 'The little gallery at Whitechapel is always made a
particular feature of in these exhibitions. This year it will house the

younger Jewish artists with Mr Bomberg and other cubists as the nucleus.'[33] Yet Bomberg was the only artist in the Jewish section whose work could have been characterized in that manner. The way in which the press dealt with Cubism and Futurism served to associate those forms of modernism with Jewish artists, or if not with the Jews then with foreign or malign influences.

The message of the *Westminster Gazette* was as clear as a bell: modern art was infected by foreign influence. Commenting upon the works of Duncan Grant, the reviewer argued, '[Grant] has surrendered the gift which enabled him to paint a picture so beautiful as the *Lemon Gatherers* for an apprenticeship in cabalistic decoration.'[34]

The force of the reference to the Cabala is to intensify a specifically Jewish connotation and in this context it suggests the idea of an occult, irrational world where reason has been lost. The language is emotive. The idea of Grant 'surrendering' his talent evokes the sense of the artist gradually losing himself to an outside alien force. He is seduced by an evil influence (modern art). The text goes on to argue that Grant could save himself through applying reason.

According to the *Westminster Gazette*, William Roberts was also in grave danger; he had overdosed on modernism. However, the text argued – following the rationale of the catalogue – that if an evolution such as Cubism was legitimately worked out, this evil influence need not be serious. Nonetheless the article continued with further reproaches aimed at modernism:

> and soon the individual artist finds himself out of sympathy with the
> Academy, yet believes that the language of art is a common speech
> based upon representation of reality, will be forced for his own life's
> sake to subscribe to a movement as to a trade union.[35]

Here, progressive art is equated with trade union politics. But the power of this particular association also served to suggest that personal or artistic freedom is at stake. An individual's freedom, under certain political conditions, may be sacrificed for the sake of the collective. Artistic integrity and political conformity were posed against each other.

Whilst the catalogue argued that the development of modern art was evolutionary, the press tended to depict its nature as revolutionary. The term revolutionary had, by this moment, acquired quite particular meanings, in opposition to evolution. The former connoted violent change and the latter a planned or 'natural' transition. Charles Harrison has traced the use of 'revolutionary' in the context of art to an article of 1910 by Frank Rutter, a defence of Post-Impressionism.[36] Certainly by 1914, if the reviews of the *Twentieth Century Art* exhibition are anything to go by, it was seized upon with alacrity. Doubtless, as

Harrison also argues, 'revolutionary art' was not then a term applied casually.

The review in the *Star* displayed anxiety over thinking calmly and constructively about these 'artistic revolutionaries'.[37] Moreover, the *Observer* described the exhibition as representing a revolutionary movement and again, taking up the theme in institutional terms, argued that the exhibition undermined and threatened the position of the Royal Academy.[38] The text continued, commenting on Bomberg's *In the Hold*, in the following terms: 'Here one young fellow with artistic if rebellious instincts exclaimed – I'm going home to buy a penny box of paints and do some of those pictures myself. That's what I'm going to do.' Here two points were made: firstly, it is a rebellious young man who is drawn to modern art; and secondly, modernism invites the uneducated or unsophisticated to experience its pleasures. Rebelliousness and ignorance are represented as if inherent to the comprehension and appreciation of modernism.

The *Morning Post* made an oblique, though immediately recognizable, reference to the Jewish East End: 'The Commercial Road ought to test their appeal to the love of bright colour, an implicit grotesque humour, and the like.'[39] The Commercial Road connoted Jewish in terms of locality and perhaps also through the identification of Jews with commerce. Additionally, the love of bright colour suggested a lack of sophisticated taste and restraint, as indeed did the idea of 'grotesque' humour. This characterization suggests children or 'primitive' peoples and recalls that earlier moment in which a traveller in unknown London, Charles Booth, perceived the working classes as leading lives which were understood as congruent with their physical nature:

> I see nothing improbable in the general view that the simple natural
> lives of working-class people tend to their own and their children's
> happiness more than the artificial complicated existence of the rich.[40]

If working-class life was seen as uncomplicated or simple in contrast with the complexity of the life of the rich, it was also seen as more authentic, as more real. Indeed Mark Gertler, in a letter to Dorothy Brett dated January 1914, appears to have shared this view: 'I was extremely fortunate to live in the East End amongst real people.'[41] A month before, in a letter to Dora Carrington, he had elaborated this notion in aesthetic terms:

> As for realism – my work is real and I wanted it to be real. The more
> I see of life, the more I get to think that realism is necessary . . . I was
> born from a working man. I haven't had a grand education and I don't
> understand all this abstract intellectual nonsense! I am rather in search
> of reality.[42]

His text was both a celebration of the 'authenticity' of Jewish working-class life and a defensive attempt to ward off criticisms of it. However, when he introduced his fashionable friends to the East End, he presented them with an image belonging to the literary imagination. He took them on missions to the cultural haunts. One of these visits with Edward Marsh was described in a letter, again to Brett: 'He [Marsh] loves Jewish theatre and agrees with me that it is far and away more vital than the English, in fact there is no comparison.'[43] In recreating the romance of the ghetto Gertler comes close to George Sims's epic picture book, *Living in London* (1902), in which a contributor, S. Gerlberg, had written of the East End in the following terms:

> Only the superficial think this Jewish colony a mere vale of tears . . .
> Nay! Let no one call the Ghetto melancholy who has not looked in at
> its dancing clubs and watched an old crony at a Hebrew wedding feast
> foot the furious Kosatzli with a gay old dog of ten winters more.[44]

The lives and experiences of East Enders were deemed to be direct, unmediated and natural. Hence, according to the *Morning Post,* they could be expected to find pleasure in an art which was bold, bright in colour, emotionally simple and closer to nature.[45] By inference this was an art devoid of skill, elegance or refinement. It was 'primitive'. And again it was Bomberg's work that was used to exemplify these traits.

The apparently anecdotal account by the *Morning Post* described the gallery as half filled with children, some brought in by parents. 'Stout, foreign mothers and dark sometimes ragged fathers.' These people were not just poor but foreign too. The *Standard* also suggested that children and foreigners could understand these 'puzzle' paintings.[46] Once more, it was Bomberg's works – *In the Hold, Vision of Ezekiel* and *Racehorses* – which served as examples. The *Daily Telegraph* review explicitly mentioned the Jewish section: 'The small room contains a good collection from the brushes of Jewish painters. There are also a great many subjects that will appeal to children.'[47] Again the intention was to associate children and Jews.

The critical reception of the show in the press erected a version of modernism which it explicitly associated with evil. It constructed this modernism as repressive, as working against the freedom of the individual artist. It both linked modernism with revolution and trivialized revolutionary politics by characterizing them as childish and unsophisticated. In short, this identification linked modernism to subversive, foreign, Jewish influences.

It is puzzling, given the anxieties voiced during the planning phase of the exhibition, to consider the motives which led to the creation of a special display of work by Jewish artists. It is even more perplexing since this display did not fit with the overall theme and conception of the show. Its inclusion can be explained in part by local interests, that is to say, the constituency that the Whitechapel sought to serve. However, if the special section of art by Jews had been devised to appeal to East End Jews in order to show to them and others the success story of assimilated Jewry and its cultural achievements, it was a strategy which clearly backfired, as it was bound to do. To hang the works separately, in this context, was a deeply ambiguous act; whilst they were in a position to be celebrated, they were also open to being reviled.

Judgements for art do not exist entirely apart from the normative values of society. For the press – which produces and constructs, as well as mediates, these values – the exhibition served to reinforce the myth of the Jew as a 'stranger in our midst'. The hanging of the exhibition can be read as resonant with Simmel's idea of Jews as the very epitome of strangers – always on the outside even when inside. We have already witnessed this figure in the context of the anti-alien movement. To cite again Zygmunt Bauman's thematization of the stranger, we can go even further and suggest: 'The objects of anti-semitism occupy as a rule the semantically confusing and psychologically unnerving status of foreigners inside.'[48]

Moreover, as the words of Edouard Drumont (a French MP and a noted anti-Semite) propose, the very absence of solid boundaries between hitherto separate groups could in itself be the cause of confusion and lead to fear and resentment. He wrote, 'A Mr. Cohen who goes to synagogue, who keeps kosher is a respectable person. I don't hold anything against him. I do have it in for the Jew who is not obvious.'[49] So even the fact that some Jews assimilated was used against them by anti-semitic theorists. Their presence, now articulated as the not-quite-identical, was a distorted, displaced image of themselves. Ambivalence moves to menace. It is also not in doubt that had the Jews not consented to assimilation they would also have been blamed for anti-semitism.

The liberal compromise had offered emancipation to the Jews in the expectation that they would move closer to British society. In this discourse it was argued that anti-semitism would only end when society tolerated the Jews and this meant their assimilation. But this liberal ideology allowed no place in society for a distinctively Jewish population. Equality of conditions, though certainly a basic requirement for justice, is nevertheless among the greatest and most uncertain ventures of modern society. The more equal conditions are, the less explanation there is for the differences that actually exist between people; and thus all the more unequal do individuals and groups of people become.

The Jews just did not fit in. But, paradoxically that was their place. For although the category Jew was ambivalent there was no escape from it. The Jews filled out and occupied the symbolically important place as Other. This category enabled the re-articulation of a category that escaped articulation. But it had to be there to give sense to the Other. Modernity was, as Bauman argued, simultaneously bringing about the levelling of differences and again creating boundaries and structuring further differences.

> Under conditions of modernity, segregation required a modern method of boundary building. A method able to withstand and neutralise the levelling impact of allegedly infinite powers of educatory and civilising forces; a method capable of designating a 'no-go' area for pedagogy and self-improvement, of drawing an unencroachable limit to the potential of cultivation (a method applied eagerly, though with mixed success, to all groups intended to be kept permanently in a subordinate position – like the working classes or women). If it was to be salvaged from the assault of modern equality, *the distinctiveness of the Jews had to be re-articulated.*[50] [author's emphasis]

Cultural identity is always inseparable from the creation of boundaries. Furthermore, the cultural order is always constituted around the figures at its territorial edge which structure the relationships of superior and inferior. In Britain, the *Jew* as a category was installed at the extreme edge of social relations as Other whereby he occupied both a cognitive and socio-economic position which secured and maintained him as a different, distinctive and inferior class of being. Correspondingly, in the exhibition *Twentieth Century Art* the works by Jewish artists were constructed as other. The terrain they occupied was literally and metaphorically outside the inside of modern art practices as they were being formulated in the exhibition.

In an argument which draws upon the work of Raymond Williams, Peter Stallybrass and Allon White suggest that a culture which is 'inherently dominative' (that is to say, is constructed in a mode inclined towards domination) has access to power and prestige which enable it to create the definitions which come to dominate and form the outside and inside. They continue:

> Bourgeois democracy emerged with a class which, whilst indeed progressive in its best political aspirations, had encoded in its manners, morals and imaginative writings, in its body bearing and taste, a subliminal élitism which was constitutive of its historical being. Whatever the radical nature of its 'universal' democratic demand, it had engraved in its subjective identity all the means by which it felt itself to be a different distinctive and superior class.[51]

The democratic aims associated with the site – the Whitechapel Gallery – and embedded in the particular aims of the *Twentieth Century Art* exhibition were spelled out clearly in the accompanying catalogue, which the authors ended with the following plea:

> They hope that all who are in sympathy with their conscious effort to introduce art to democracy will aid them in their endeavour to show that democratic feeling has been introduced into art.[52]

Now democracy refers to an idea of open argument and equality amongst people who are all deserving of respect. The aspiration to 'equality in difference' cannot stand up. As I argued earlier, it can only serve as an ideology of domination whose goal it is to hide that domination.

European nationalism depended increasingly for its definitions on criteria which were cultural. It was possible to classify national cultures through one culture projecting an image of its difference from another. In this way superiority, which was deemed to be both natural and national, was established. Freud has suggested that

> Closely related races keep one another at arm's length; the South German cannot endure the North German, the Englishman casts every kind of aspersion upon the Scot, the Spaniard despises the Portuguese. We are no longer astonished that greater differences should lead to an almost insuperable repugnance, such as the Gallic people feel for the German, the Aryan for the Semite, and the white races for the coloured . . . In the undisguised antipathies and aversions which people feel towards strangers with whom they have to do we may recognize the expression of self-love – of narcissism.[53]

Here, Freud is referring to a type of narcissism in which a people or a person imagine or are conjured up as what they or he would like to be. When faced with non-British culture (and in particular the work displayed in the exhibition as Jewish art), the press, insensitive to nuances of desire, inevitably re-articulated difference to represent an inferior category: a modernism associated with subversion, foreignness, Jewishness. This could be distinguished in effect from another modernism, a superior modernism, which celebrated the notion of the purity of artistic expression. This was a modernism which could be legitimated as a democratic, progressive form of art. A space was cleared for a version of modernism which sought to banish from the discourses of art all political, symbolic, moral or ideological readings and arguments.

The exhibition was inadvertently part of a larger project and process through which a particular version of modernist theory was being secured. The positioning of the Jewish artists – outside the inside – was important. For in that place, differentiation could occur and hierarchies be negotiated and even enforced. The Other is never exclusively outside: the Other is inside too. Structures of power, forces of domination and resistance, mix and intermingle. The one is implicated with and in the other.

That chimerical place of the alienized was essential for the construction and articulation of the identity of a distinctively British account of modernism. No longer tempted to transgress, the modernism of British culture was rendered safe within such territorial pickets. Little has altered today, perhaps not surprisingly, since the formation of cultural identity is always inseparable from the definition and creation of boundaries.

The exhibition took place in the summer of 1914; Austria-Hungary declared war on Serbia on 18 July 1914. Russia mobilized along the German and Austrian frontiers on 29 July. Germany declared war on Russia on 1 August and on 3 August, on France, invading Belgium on the same day. On 4 August Britain declared war on Germany. Cultural xenophobia was being subsumed by the xenophobia of war.

Notes

1. Rudolf Rocker, *The London Years,* London, 1956, quoted by William Fishman, *East End Jewish Radicals 1875–1914,* London: Duckworth, 1975, p. 235.
2. *Twentieth Century Art (A Review of Modern Movements),* Summer Exhibition, London: Whitechapel Art Gallery, 1914. The exhibition lasted from 8 May to 20 June and was open to visitors each day from 12 noon to 9.30 p.m.
3. *Trustees Report,* Whitechapel Art Gallery, 1901, p. 2.
4. *Trustees Report,* Whitechapel Art Gallery, 1904, p. 5.
5. *Trustees Report,* Whitechapel Art Gallery, 1910, p. 3.
6. *Trustees Report,* Whitechapel Art Gallery, 1902, p. 2.
7. Charles Harrison, 'Critical theories and the practice of art', in Susan Compton (ed.), *British Art in the Twentieth Century,* London: Royal Academy, 1986, p. 55.
8. This term was coined by Tony Skillen (University of Kent) and was suggested to me by David Reason.
9. These works, listed in the catalogue as numbers 36–115, were all on sale. They included furniture and decorative items.
10. Fifty-three works by the following 15 artists were shown: David Bomberg, Moses Kisling, Mark Gertler, Morris Brodsky, Isaac Rosenberg, Bernard Meninsky, Alfred Wolmark, Mark Wiener, Jacob Kramer, Clara Bernberg, Herbert Schloss, Morris Goldstein, Eli Nadelman, Pascin and Modigliani.

11. *Twenty Years of British Art (1890–1910)*, Summer Exhibition, London: Whitechapel Art Gallery, 1910.
12. 'Introduction', *Twentieth Century Art*, p. 3.
13. *Ibid.*
14. *Twenty Years of British Art*, p. 21.
15. *Ibid.*, p. 20.
16. *Ibid.*, p. 6.
17. *Ibid.*
18. See Chapter 5 and also Frances Borzello, *Civilizing Caliban: The Misuse of Art 1875–1980,* London: Routledge, 1987; Linda Hutchinson, 'The Whitechapel Art Gallery 1901–1983', unpublished MA thesis, City University, London, 1983; Ribin Roth, 'The Whitechapel Art Gallery; Arts and Crafts or Art Nouveau? Charles Harrison Townsend (1851–1928)', unpublished Open University project.
19. S. and H. Barnett, 'Class divisions in great cities', in *Towards Social Reform*, London, 1909, cited in Frances Borzello, *Civilizing Caliban: The Misuse of Art 1875–1980*, London: Routledge, 1987, p. 32.
20. *Twentieth Century Art*, p. 4.
21. See Charles Harrison, *English Art and Modernism 1900–1939*, London: Allen Lane, 1987, for a full account of these debates.
22. Anon., 'Challenge of Whitechapel to Piccadilly: an exhibition in the East', *The Times*, 8 May 1914 (Whitechapel Art Gallery Archive). All press clippings have been taken from this archive and are unpaginated.
23. Anon., 'Twentieth century art at Whitechapel', *Observer,* 17 May 1914.
24. Aitken had been appointed Director of the Tate Gallery in 1911.
25. Letter from William Dawson to Gilbert Ramsey, dated 5 February 1914, Whitechapel Art Gallery Archive.
26. P. K. G., 'Side-splitting-art', *Daily Express*, 8 May 1914.
27. J. B. Manson, letter to Gilbert Ramsey, Whitechapel Art Gallery Archive.
28. W. Dawson, letter to the Hon. Harry Lawson, MP, 15 May 1914, Whitechapel Art Gallery Archive.
29. A. J. Finberg, 'The Whitechapel Art Gallery', *Star*, 20 May 1914.
30. Anon., 'Cubists in East-End: picture-puzzles to be seen in Whitechapel', *Standard*, 14 May 1914.
31. 'East End critics: Futurist art in Whitechapel', *Observer*, 10 May 1914.
32. Anon., *Daily Express*, 11 May 1914.
33. 'Post-Impressionists for Whitechapel', *Manchester Guardian*, 9 April 1914.
34. J. M. M., 'Twentieth century art', *Westminster Gazette*, 21 May 1914.
35. *Ibid.*
36. Harrison, *op. cit.*, p. 75.
37. Finberg, *loc. cit.*
38. *Observer*, 10 May 1914.
39. Anon., 'Whitechapel Gallery', *Morning Post*, 11 May 1914.

40. Charles Booth, *The Life and Labour of the People in London*, cited by Philip Dodd in *Englishness: Politics and Culture 1880–1920*, London: Croom Helm, p. 9.
41. Mark Gertler, letter to the Hon. Dorothy Brett, January 1914, in Noel Carrington (ed.), *Mark Gertler: Selected Letters,* London: Rupert Hart-Davis, 1965, p. 63.
42. Mark Gertler, letter to Dora Carrington, Sunday [December 1913], in *ibid.*, p. 60.
43. Mark Gertler, letter to Brett dated January 1914, in *ibid.*, p. 63.
44. S. Gerlberg, 'Jewish London', in George Sims, *Living in London*, Vol. 2, London, 1902, p. 29.
45. *Morning Post*, 11 May 1914.
46. *Standard*, 14 May 1914.
47. '20th century art: Whitechapel exhibition', *Daily Telegraph*, 8 May 1914.
48. Zygmunt Bauman, *Modernity and the Holocaust*, Cambridge: Polity Press, 1989, p. 34.
49. Drumont, cited by Patrick Girard, 'Historical foundations of anti-semitism', in Joel E. Dinsdale (ed.), *Survivors, Victims and Perpetrators: Essays on the Nazi Holocaust*, Washington, DC: Hemisphere, 1980, pp. 70–1. Cited in Bauman, *op. cit.*, p. 58.
50. Bauman, *op. cit.*, p. 59.
51. Peter Stallybrass and Allon White, *The Politics and Poetics of Transgression*, London: Methuen, 1986, p. 202.
52. *Twentieth Century Art*, p. 5.
53. Sigmund Freud, 'Group psychology', in *Civilization, Society and Religion*, Harmondsworth: Penguin, 1986, p. 131.

7

The mythical edges of assimilation: Mark Gertler

This is how one pictures the angel of history. His face is turned toward the past. Where we perceive a chain of events, he sees one catastrophe which keeps piling wreckage upon wreckage and hurls it in front of his feet. The angel would like to stay, awaken the dead, make whole what has been smashed. But a storm is blowing from Paradise; . . . This storm is what we call progress.

Walter Benjamin [1]

The Angel of Death wings its way across the pages of the Gertler literature, which is inexorably haunted by its presence.[2] Knowing that Gertler's life ends in suicide (in 1939), we might be tempted to look at his work as evidence of that fact, seeing it as a witness of that death, interpreting it as something other than that which it was. Powerful explanations perhaps, nevertheless misleading.

Above all, Gertler's work could be revealing of something else. It could be understood, perhaps, as a sign of a struggle between identification with Jewish identity or non-identity or selfhood and alienation from it – described by Shmueli as 'the essence of the Jewish dilemma'[3] – or even as a refutation of that proposition. Or again, perhaps his art could reveal a 'singularity' in tension with the 'universal'. It could provide clues about the ways in which an individual negotiated identities, Jewish and/or English. It could again raise questions about assimilation and indicate just where the limits to that social process lay. Janet Wolff has argued that a reading of Gertler's life and work enables us to understand class and ethnicity at the macro-level of English society between the years 1910 and 1940. It is Gertler's contact with Bloomsbury which proves crucial to this analysis and shows the particular ambivalence of a sector of the upper class to the outsider, the Jew.[4] Re-writing Gertler could begin the unravelling of myth and history.

Born 9 December 1891 in Spitalfields, London. Named Max. In 1899 renamed Mark. Over those eight years Gertler's family returned to Austria and then moved back again to London.[5] His new name signals a change – from foreign to English Jew. It suggests a commitment to stay, to make a home, to assimilate. Gertler was sent to the Deal Street Board School in 1900, where he learnt English. In 1906–7 he attended Regent Street Polytechnic and the following year, with the advice and help of Solomon J. Solomon and William Rothenstein, he went to the Slade School of Art. The Jewish Educational Aid Society gave him a grant which was augmented by donations from Sir Edward Sassoon, Lady Desart and Sefton Sewell and by a Slade Scholarship. In 1912 he left the Slade. Education was for Gertler (and indeed as we have seen for others from immigrant families) the primary means through which he was taught to be English, acquired English middle-class values and began the processes of assimilation.

Being an artist gave Gertler a way out of the East End ghetto and access to an upper-middle-class English form of life. Many letters written by Gertler to friends he made while at the Slade reveal anger and deep ambivalence in relation to his experiences of assimilation.[6] He expressed his unease and disquiet with these middle-class values, often indeed in class terms. For example, writing to Dora Carrington in December 1912, he declared: 'You are the Lady and I am the East End boy,'[7] and 'I feel that I am far too vulgar and rough for you. But I am hoping through my work to reach to your level' (October 1913).[8]

Yet again he confided to Carrington:

> By my ambition I am cut off from my own family and class and by them I have been raised to be equal to a class I hate! They do not understand me nor I them. So I am an outcast (December 1912).[9]

Gertler had become another individual now estranged from his family and his class, as well as from the English middle class.

This déclassé Jew was struggling to find a pictorial language and to structure an artistic identity. In 1911–15 these needed to be compatible with Slade values (and those of his benefactors), responsive to early modernism (and the tastes of his patrons) and true to his changing perceptions of art and artists (Jewish or otherwise). Gertler's artistic debts, like those of most ambitious art students, were many. They were variously to Rothenstein, Steer, Tonks, Epstein, Gauguin, Cézanne and Van Gogh. The latter two became increasingly important to him after visiting Paris in 1911 and 1913.[10] However, his attitude towards his artistic peer group, as displayed in a letter to Carrington dated 24 September 1912, was nothing if not equivocal:

So I went out and saw more unfortunate artists. I looked at them talking art, Ancient art, Modern art, Impressionism, Post-Impressionism, Neo-Impressionism, Cubists, Spottists, Futurists, Cave-dwelling, Wyndham Lewis, Duncan Grant, Etchells, Roger Fry! I looked on and laughed to myself saying, 'Give me the Baker, the Baker,' and I walked home disgusted with them all, was glad to find my dear simple mother waiting for me with a nice roll, that she knows I like, and a cup of hot coffee. Dear mother, the same mother of all my life, twenty years. You, dear mother, I thought, are the only modern artist.[11]

This text can be read as a summary of his search for truth and authenticity in art and life, and suggests that the image of (his, or even the) Mother provided him with such a form. Mother represented for Gertler security and stability. In addition, he contrasts the genuine simple skills of the craftsman, 'the Baker', with the false values of contemporary artists.

Now I shall consider three of the many paintings and drawings of his mother produced by Gertler between 1911 and 1913. They span a range of pictorial languages and show Gertler negotiating different identities, not just for the assumed subject – his mother – but for his art. He is searching for a voice responsive to, yet independent from, available pictorial languages. For Gertler this language had to resonate with honesty and authenticity.

The first picture can be read as a competent Edwardian portrait. Its language owes a debt to Slade School painting. The woman is depicted wearing fine clothes. Her hair is neatly dressed. She has pearls in her ears and rings on her fingers. Her appearance is that of a city woman, middle-class and civilized. Light touches of the brush give her face an animated look. Her eyes, bright and alert, avoid our gaze. They are looking at something outside, beyond the picture frame. Her lively expression masks a tense, haughty mien. Her body, which fills the picture, takes possession of it. Body and face appear at odds with each other. The image connotes, perhaps, a person who is struggling to establish a place – in order to belong – and looking elsewhere. This suggests someone who resents this conflict.

The second painting, which dates from 1913, is part of a bigger change evident overall in Gertler's work. Increasingly from 1912 (the year he left the Slade) his pictures feature images of Jewish or peasant cultures. Here Gertler depicts his mother as a peasant. Her rough hands dominate the image. These are the hands of a worker – a provider. These are the tools which bear the signs of work. Indeed they appear larger than life. She is depicted in a kitchen, the place where food is prepared. The body touches, is connected to, the spoon in the pudding bowl behind her. Her hands are as heavy as the objects. Paint is applied thickly, consonant with the weight of a body, a basin, fruit. Like the objects, the body of the woman is immobile. Its feel is statuesque, a quality accentuated by the fixed set of the eyes, which are less alert than those of the other mother, the one in the earlier painting. This woman is reminiscent of *La Berceuse* by Van Gogh, for whom that painting was to represent not just a woman but someone to comfort and alleviate the pain and sorrow of mankind. Likewise for Gertler his painting was to be understood as symbolic:

> Her large hands are lying heavily and warily on her lap. The whole suggests suffering and a life that has known hardship. It is barbaric and symbolic.[12]

A charcoal drawing dating from 1913 is the third image of *mother* (Figure 14). The sensuality of the lines – the drawing – contrasts with the former portrait, where the paint lies heavy and inert. These lines, which give the shape and the form to the head, also seem to caress it only to possess it, capturing the face, full-lipped, with eyebrows finely arched, beautiful. The pensive eyes suggest a woman of dignity and composure. The drawing shares similarities with works of Jacob Epstein, who in 1912 had taken Gertler to the British Museum and introduced him to the art of ancient cultures.[13]

The languages of the latter drawing and painting are simple, bold and direct, entering the category of primitive. In the art discourses of the time, the idea of the primitive oscillated in its meanings. It was used either to connote closeness to nature, truth and sincerity or to signify the barbaric and uncivilized. Hence the term could be used for praise or abuse. These tensions meet in the archaic forms of the matriarch imaged by Gertler.

Each of these three images traverses a different line from the acceptable mother (civilized and middle-class) to the unacceptable (uncivilized and barbaric). The figure tends to press against the picture plane, placing her close to the spectator. She is larger than life. The images vacillate between comfort and power, love and terror, beauty and ugliness, sensuality and denial. As a whole perhaps these 'matri-archaic'[14] incarnations can stand in all their ambivalence as a metaphor for assimilation, which was for Gertler an experience marked by feelings of deep ambiguity, tension and contradiction. Although they affirm no one thing with certainty, in their wide embrace they deny nothing. His own ambivalence is signalled by a pervasive restlessness in his art, registering perhaps a refusal or even an inability to settle for an all-embracing or indeed a consistent artistic style.

Also the choice of language was acquiring for Gertler the status of a moral imperative. It provided him with a means of disassociating himself from bourgeois art and re-identifying himself with his origins.

Figure 14. Mark Gertler, *Head of the Artist's Mother*, 1913, black chalk on paper, 24 × 21 cm, private collection. With kind permission of Luke Gertler.

In December 1913, writing again to Carrington, he insisted:

> I haven't had a grand education and I don't understand all this abstract intellectual nonsense! I am rather in search of reality, even at the cost of 'pretty decorativeness'. I love natural objects and I love painting them as they are – I use them to help me to express an idea.[15]

A still life dating from 1913 shows Gertler's understanding of realism. Here, as in *Artist's Mother*, the paint is applied thickly, as heavy as the objects in the material world which the artist seeks to transcribe. Realism is concerned with creating a balance between truth to visual experience and its imaginative transformation via the medium (paint). The means of representation do not efface themselves before the scene they represent. It is the logic of the discipline (painting) which dictates the picture. If the painting itself is beautiful so too is that which is portrayed. The picture provides a frame for the real, aestheticizing reality. The still-life images painted by Gertler feature objects of no extrinsic value. They celebrate the simplicity of things perhaps found in the kitchen of the peasant/mother of his imagination. They beautify the commonplace.

Austerity is dignified and aestheticized in Gertler's representations of Jewish people. The cluster of pictures of Jewish themes to which he was devoted during this period may have been a way of asserting and enunciating values which he interpreted as being in conflict with those of the English middle class, represented for and to him by Carrington and her crowd. In July 1912 Gertler had written a letter to Carrington in which he compared her unfavourably with another correspondent, a Jewish girl. He castigated Carrington for being different:

> I have just had a letter from a Jewish girl I once knew. A girl that is simple and beautiful, who is, thank God, not 'arty' and of my own class. She will not torment my life.[16]

Thus he could construct and affirm a version of Otherness or Jewishness in which qualities of sincerity, truth and comfort were vested. His notion of realism provided him with a language through which these values could be articulated.

For Gertler, Jewish men and women, in different ways, were identified by the expression of suffering which he depicted as if incised on their faces. And thus he was able visually to differentiate Jews from others. Here he departed from his erstwhile mentor William Rothenstein who depicted Jews solely in terms of their religious life (Figure 15). But he comes close to the characterization of Jews by the writer S. Gerlberg, who in George Sims's popular book, *Living London*, had described 'beshawled women with their pinched faces [and] long-coated men with two thousand years of persecution stamped in their manners.'[17] Gertler connotes Jews by and through the expression of pained emotion. He situates them within the confines of family relationships.

The sanctification of the family was an important aspect of the bourgeois body politic. Through the family sexuality and social relations were regulated. The successful integration of Jews into English life was dependent upon them fitting in with the evolving values of the bourgeois order. To this end the centrality and importance of the family in Jewish culture was installed both for them and by them in the imagination of

Figure 15. William Rothenstein, *Carrying the Law*, 1907, oil on canvas, 92 × 84.5cm, Bradford City Art Galleries and Museums. © The artist's family.

Jews and others. Gerlberg's essay, 'Jewish London', idealizes Jewish family life, which he argued cut across social classes:

> In essential characteristics they are really one. East-End or West-End, the Jew is still the family man among the nations, delighting keenly in the joys of domesticity.[18]

Jewish family life was reified, and home in this discourse becomes a place of pleasure. There is desperation here registered beyond the genealogy of the plan. For Gertler, moreover, in a picture such as *Family Group* there is no celebration of the family or of home. The people are not located. The picture is devoid of any clues through which we might

Figure 16. Mark Gertler, *The Rabbi and His Grandchild*, 1913, oil on
canvas, 50.8 × 45.9 cm, Southampton City Art
Gallery/Bridgeman Art Library, London and New York.
With kind permission of Luke Gertler.

become familiar with and identify with the family or recognize home.
It is an image which denotes barrenness. The picture is absolutely still
save the movement of the child who is constrained by the mother. There
is no connection between the adults. The man's gesture is vague. Is he
pointing? Is he supplicating? In Gertler's image contact or relationship
appears as failure and as a possession, a synonym of power.

Again, repression and suffering are the dominant themes in the
relationship connoted by *The Rabbi and His Grandchild*, dating from

May 1913 (Figure 16). The Rabbi – wearing a skull-cap – is represented as long-suffering. The expression on his face, the look in his eyes, register the tribulations of life. The child's face is reminiscent of a cherub. Yet her lips are ripe and sensual and she is decorated with earrings. She is presented to us – displayed for us – through the gesture of the old man's hand. His middle finger delicately touches her chin, raising it slightly. Its effect is to liken her face to that of a precious object. This is an image full of erotic ambiguity. Indeed the child's burgeoning sexuality, both enticing and rejecting, makes this more than a picture of old age and youth. Rather it becomes a site of repressed desire.

The old man reappears in *A Jewish Family* (1913). He props himself up with the aid of a stick. He is creased with sorrow and could be in mourning – perhaps for the child? Her dress could be a shroud. But she is also like a carved doll and a small adult. Playfulness is kept under wraps, in check, signifying perhaps the tight culture for which she is being prepared. The adults are her future. They are what she will become. The bodies of the two women are joined together. The one in profile is dressed as a peasant with her head covered in a scarf. The other woman confronts us. Her hair resembles a halo. Are we again facing the 'good' and 'bad', the 'ugly' and the 'beautiful' Mother?

Poverty and sadness, sexuality and repression, tensions between men and women, young and old, are witnessed in these images. They escape the notion of the happy family constructed by and in bourgeois texts (such as Gerlberg's) which revere domesticity, home life and the family. As such, Gertler's pictures may be understood in contrast to them as more real and genuine. But paradoxically they too are mythical. To venerate low life can also have the effect of celebrating it. Moreover, by representing this other side of life, the images serve to reaffirm the position of the Jew-as-Other.

A Jewish Family was included in the exhibition *Twentieth Century Art (A Review of the Modern Movement)*, which, as we have seen, was held at the Whitechapel Art Gallery in the summer of 1914. As has already been noted, this show had a special section of works by Jewish artists, curated by David Bomberg. Out of the fifty-three works displayed from a broad range of Jewish artists, Gertler showed seven.[19] Bomberg himself exhibited five works. The other artists, including Modigliani, Jacob Kramer, Isaac Rosenberg and Jules Pascin, had no more than two or three works each. Gertler's *Jewish Family* was appraised by the critic of the *Star* newspaper, A. J. Finberg, in the following terms,

In Mr Mark Gertler's 'Jewish Family' so much emphasis is placed upon certain characteristics of the sitters that presentation is occasionally pushed to the point of caricature. The seated old man in the picture is as monstrously grotesque as a gargoyle or some of the figures in medieval wood-carvings. But this kind of wilful exaggeration and emphasis belongs to a different world from that of abstract geometrical diagrams. It belongs to the world of flesh and blood, and therefore stirs our imagination and our sympathies. It seems on the whole the only proper development of the realist art of the nineteenth century, as it brings back vitality and vivid personal expression and interest to an art which had become too scientific and impersonal.[20]

The picture was used by Finberg along with those of Henry Lamb, R. Ihlee, John Curry and Stanley Spencer to create a category of modern art, which was imaginative, personal, expressive and humanist against the Cubo-Futurist works on show, particularly those by Bomberg, Wyndham Lewis and Frederick Etchell. Finberg, by placing Gertler and Bomberg in contexts outside Jewish art, confounded the category as established in the exhibition. However, as I argued earlier, the effect of the critical reception of the show replicated prevailing social categories.

The exhibition, by creating a special section for Jewish artists, recreated the place occupied by the 'alienized'. This was a space outside the mainstream of modern art even when apparently inside it. It was there that differentiation occurred and hierarchies within modernist art practices were installed. Difference was re-articulated to establish an inferior category of modernism. In spite of the attempt of the critic of the *Star* to rescue his art – and by implication all Jewish art – from this lower class, Gertler was nonetheless entrenched there. Jewishness was unnegotiable. It was unequivocally Other.

This Otherness and Jewishness was an endless source of fascination for Gertler's friends (some of whom possessed his works on low-life themes).[21] Again, as seen in the previous chapter, Gertler used to take them to the East End. He describes one such visit with Edward Cannan in a letter to Dorothy Brett written in January 1914: 'Cannan thought I was extremely fortunate to live in the East End amongst real people.'[22] For them it was a journey to an unknown London,[23] and represented a transgression. In their imagination the East End was simultaneously hallowed and reviled. To cite Gerlberg again,

> The ghetto was not all poor. It is really homespun lined with ermine, Dives cheek by jowl with Lazarus. These industrious female costers, for instance, arguing volubly with reluctant customers, have left a husband – working in a factory – who is preparing to blossom into an employer, a son retailing jewellery in a second street, and a daughter selling hosiery in a third.[24]

The low domain – the forest, the fair, the theatre, the slum, the circus, the seaside resort, or the savage – as Stallybrass and White suggest, are placed at the outer limits of civilized life and become the symbolic contents of bourgeois desire.[25] The East End slum or ghetto is a site/sight which is simultaneously coveted and denied.

By 1915 Gertler felt impelled too to break free from the East End, from the slum, from his family and move to Hampstead, which, in part at least, suggests that he was attempting to revoke a fixed Jewish and/or class identity. In a letter to Carrington, of January 1915, he explained his feelings about leaving and set out his reasons for doing so:

> I am immensely relieved to leave it and even my parents, although I like them. There, I shall be free and detached – shall belong to no class . . . I shall be just myself . . . I was beginning to feel stifled by everything here in the East End, worried by the sordidness of my family, their aimlessness, their poverty and their general wretchedness. I used to get terribly depressed also by my father, in whose face there is always an expression of the suffering and disappointments he has gone through. I keep wondering why they are alive and why they want to live and why nature treated them so cruelly.[26]

However, this geographical relocation could not suffice. It could offer him no guarantee of the detachment that he sought. Although assimilation had alienated Gertler from his family, it did not, nor could not, lead him to the full and unconditional acceptance of the world outside.

The year after his move, Gertler painted *Merry-Go-Round* (Figure 17), about which D. H. Lawrence wrote an effusive, while at the same time somewhat equivocal, letter to Gertler. For Lawrence it could only be a Jew who could paint such a picture. He described the painting as 'horrifying', as 'terrifying', and as 'obscene':

> It would need your national history to get you here, without disintegrating you first. You are of an older race than I, and in these ultimate processes, you are beyond me, older than I am. But I think I am sufficiently the same, to be able to understand.[27]

Lawrence claims that both he and Gertler are outsiders. They share the experience of a class to which they do not belong by birth. Lawrence identifies himself with the Jew but at one and the same time he differentiates himself. He claims that the Christian (Lawrence) is three thousand years behind the Jew (Gertler). The Jew is more ancient, more 'primitive'. Yet again Gertler is produced as fundamentally different in kind. Race was produced to explain his art, and indeed in its effects served to overdetermine the interpretations of it. Lawrence was keen that another Jew, Jacob Epstein, should evaluate this painting. Explicit here is the idea that the image needed a Jew to provide proper critical insights. Lawrence would seem to be saying that his own

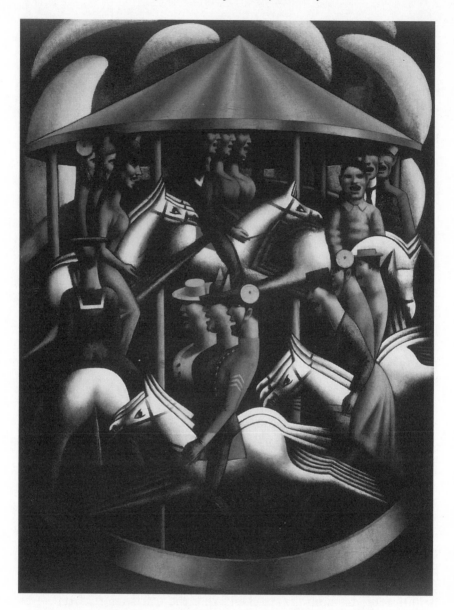

Figure 17. Mark Gertler, *Merry-Go-Round*, 1916, oil on canvas, 189.2 × 142.2 cm, Tate Gallery, London. With kind permission of Luke Gertler.

judgement was finally dependent upon the unconditional support of another, a Jew: authentic judgement could only be provided by the same.

Of course Gertler's experiences of assimilation were not unique. Indeed, in general terms cultural assimilation was experienced as an individual choice. This was mediated in such a way as to foreclose and lock the individual in an ambivalent mode from which it must have appeared impossible to flee. Breaking away from 'home' did not provide an escape from the predicament.

Gerlberg had earlier described the East End as 'cosmopolitan' and 'symbolic of the vagabondage of the race'.[28] This imagery percolated into the very representations of Gertler himself. He becomes inscribed as both subject and object of romantic fictions. Subsequent writing on Gertler reeks of exotic and hardly repressed erotic images. He was himself a 'gypsy', a 'vagabond'.[29] More, 'this gypsy gaudiness and vehemence were part of his instinctive nature not a deliberate taste'.[30] And again: 'There was about him an attractive vagabond gaudiness, a member of an oppressed race.'[31]

In the amorphous world of projection the gypsy, along with the Jew, has been installed as the Other. The gypsy Carmen is described by Sander Gilman as the 'quintessential Other . . . possessing all languages and yet native only in her hidden tongue, proletarian, and black'.[32] The gypsy is yet another unfathomable mixture, another disorder. If Gertler was not to be named as a Jew, then he was identified as gypsy. Whatever – gypsy or Jew – Gertler was never enabled or able to transcend a pre-given identity – that of an Other.

The search for the essence of Gertler's work prescribed by and through ascribing an identity for Gertler continues even today in the reviews which followed the retrospective exhibition held at Camden Arts Centre, London, in 1992.[33] Tim Hilton in the *Guardian* affirms and reiterates the image of Gertler as a gypsy: 'a certain gypsy gaudiness is what they said about Gertler at the time, and this is a good description of the way he inclined towards garish effects.' Hilton asks, 'Is Gertler's colour sense, his liking for interiors and rich patterns, part of a Jewish identity that he was determined to preserve?' What Hilton identifies as the extremes or the excesses of his art provide him with his definition of Gertler and allow him to contain Gertler's art. It is always in opposition to what he characterizes as 'English' painting. Indeed, Hilton claimed, 'Gertler is at his best when he is least like an English painter.' By English, Hilton here means Bloomsbury and 'good' taste. For him, Gertler is only a good artist when he enters a 'heated and blowsy realm in which taste is pushed beyond English bounds'.[34]

Again the theme of gypsy is invoked by Mary Rose Beaumont, who in *Arts Review* suggests, 'The post-war influence of Renoir suits Gertler's natural bent for what one critic termed "this gypsy gaudiness".' She continues by quoting an article by Anthony Blunt from 1932: 'In general, borrowings in painting merely turn out duller than the originals, but Mr Gertler manages to make his definitely more unpleasant.' Following Blunt, Beaumont explains that this is due to a quality rare in English painting, 'namely vulgarity'. But then, as she reminds us, Gertler was not 'after all English' and although 'he conformed in his early Slade days, he could never be assimilated'.[35]

The critic of the *Economist* would seem to agree with Beaumont:

> This gypsy gaudiness did not suit English tastes, and sometimes Gertler's obsession with surface sumptuousness can alienate any viewer; but they show his joy in nature's abundance, made more acute by his early privation.[36]

Similarly, John McEwen in the *Sunday Telegraph* picks up on the excesses of the work, which he then goes on to explain in culinary (cultural) terms: 'In combination it is a richness which like Jewish pastries can prove too much for English tastes.'[37] He continues with the suggestion that Gertler is 'quintessentially Jewish by nature and therefore beyond the pale of any English comparison'. The same critic, reviewing the show in the *Independent Magazine* under the title 'The Outsider', perpetuates the image of Gertler as a gypsy, 'not least for the gaudiness of his painting'. He goes on to describe Gertler as 'a dandy in dress, with wit and looks to match'.[38]

Meanwhile in *Vogue* William Feaver installs another familiar characterization of the Jew as neurotic and by so doing identifies Gertler's depression with his social disadvantage as a Jew. He ends his piece by repeating the anecdote about Gertler and Charlie Chaplin with which he had introduced it: 'He met Chaplin, danced a little and despaired.' Feaver psychopathologizes the artist and trivializes his art.[39]

Linda Talbot in the *Ham and High* bemoaned the lack of consistency in Gertler's work: 'Had he lived longer, a more consistent identity might have emerged.'[40] Two weeks later the same paper announced, 'Do go and see the return of Mark Gertler and celebrate the fact that the outsider has come home in belated triumph.'[41]

'Gertler: a story of doubt' is the title of William Packer's article in the *Financial Times* where he writes,

> I said, of the Ben Uri show in 1982, that it was easy to see how convincing he must have seemed in his early days, and equally easy to understand how desperate his sense of his own subsequent failure must have been. I thought those later paintings extraordinary, flailing

exercises in pastiche, but not in any knowing or cynical way. Rather more poignant than that, they suggested a repeated and despairing effort to catch the secret of another's authentic vision. In this he inevitably failed, and stood revealed as a truly tragic, unenviable figure.[42]

What has been taken as Gertler's (stylistic) inconsistency (unreliability or neurotic symptoms and his suicidal tendencies) seems to have been the cause of the critics' dilemmas. All have offered explanations of his work on the basis of his being an outsider, a Jew who is already assumed disordered. In each review emotion, sensuousness and sensuality are highlighted and then used to denote excess in a scoffing way. In all, these features become the way of differentiating, identifying and classifying Gertler, the Jew and his art. His art is always viewed as a direct product of his Otherness. His work is scrutinized to reveal a true and essential identity as Jew: emotional, sensual, out of order. Excess. It is always characterized as un-English, that is to say, his art is not understated or urbane. Earlier, Anthony Blunt not only accused Gertler of 'vulgarity' and 'plagiarism', but also he opined:

On the whole our painting lacks inventiveness, and perhaps life, but it is usually restrained by a certain taste, in itself a pleasant quality though it may be to some extent inseparable from the lack of vitality from which contemporary English painting seems to be suffering.[43]

For Blunt it would seem that Gertler's work was irredeemable, that English restraint or good taste could not rescue it, and it could not be saved from itself. After all, it was not 'our' art. Bad taste, over-the-top, excessive, gaudy, gypsy or Jew are the categories which have been installed to celebrate and/or deride Gertler's work.

In an unpublished lecture on Gertler, Sarat Maharaj discussed the issue of his 'identity' in rather different terms when he argued that it is impossible to say whether Gertler's work is English or Jewish.[44] For him, Gertler's art represents an unceasing restless shuttle between these two poles. It puts both those worlds into equal question: *The Pond, Garsington*, is for Maharaj a metaphor for England, that privileged England occupied by Bloomsbury, while the images of Jewish life reaffirm Gertler's origins – the world of the barbaric, of the primitive, of the exotic and of excess. It was the confrontation of those two worlds that was condemned by critics and provided the grounds upon which Gertler's art was (and is) still challenged.

Maharaj, in contrast with Packer as cited above, celebrates and affirms Gertler's work precisely as pastiche. Furthermore he situates it within, not outside, British modernism. It shares, for example, 'vulgarity' with the Futurism of *Blast*. Moreover, for Maharaj, Gertler's

Figure 18. Mark Gertler, *Still-Life with Benin Head*, 1937, oil on canvas, 74 × 94 cm, private collection. With kind permission of Luke Gertler.

still-life paintings are deliberately and unequivocally kitsch. The objects he selects are from the minutiae of the marginal, the excremental. *Still Life with Aspidistra*, which dates from 1926, is described and praised by Maharaj as an example of a severe and knowing pastiche of middle-class respectability. The aspidistra is, after all, the ultimate sign of proper Englishness.

All of Gertler's still-life images are loaded, perhaps with boxes, with wicker work, with samplers, with toys, with richly coloured textiles and with ornaments. Like the *Basket of Fruit*, they are packed with things; exaggerated, exotic, excessive and charged with desire. Everything is heightened as if on parade. Each object within becomes spotlighted. These images are described by the critics as vulgar, and it is this very vulgarity that makes them transgressive. Taking *Still-Life with Benin Head* (1937), Maharaj suggests that it is firstly a representation of a Benin sculpture (Figure 18). Then it is a remaking

Figure 19. Mark Gertler, *Coster Family on Hampstead Heath*, 1924, oil
on canvas, 141 × 197 cm, Tel-Aviv Museum of Art, Israel.
With kind permission of Luke Gertler.

of it, as a deliberate citation of Picasso. And it is in that space between
the two that the going-beyond of identity is marked. To simply
designate the works as either English or traditional Jewish is precisely
to miss the point. In his reinterpretation of Gertler's still-life paintings,
Maharaj begins to map out a discourse through and in which the logic
of identity thinking can be re-thought and challenged. Identity is never
a simple either/or but a complex realm of endless negotiation and re-
negotiation.

Coster Family on Hampstead Heath, which dates from 1924, is an
image connoting alienation and separation but in the guise of reparation
(Figure 19). Here, the family group, which I take to be a mother, two
daughters and a son, are shown picnicking on Hampstead Heath. The
painting has been said to ape the conventions of eighteenth-century
portraits, conversation pieces or set pieces, where the portrait situates
the sitters surveying their land.[45] But Hampstead Heath is common

land. A coster family is likely to have gone there from East London. Indeed, a railway connection operated which was frequently used by East Enders to take them there for work and/or leisure. Maybe it refers to the *Déjeuner sur l'herbe* of the nineteenth century. Hence, it can be seen as a celebration of leisure (free) time.

At the centre is the mother, another great matriarch, this one reminiscent perhaps of Giotto's *Ognissanti Madonna*. She is dressed in blue and red, the characteristic colours of the Madonna's clothes, and at the heart of the image is her right hand, which points to her sex. In her left hand, the place occupied by the child Jesus in traditional paintings of the Madonna and Child, the woman holds a mug of tea. Beside her, on the ground, is an English teapot. Here an association with the Empire is invoked through that most quintessential of English beverages, Indian tea. The still life of food consists of apples, cherries, bread, a pear. Each resonates with Christian symbolism: the apple refers to the Tree of Knowledge; the cherries to the fruit of Paradise; the pear to the Church; the bread to the Communion. But it would be a mistake to read each as simply standing in for any one or all of those meanings. The imagery is not quite 'English' and defiantly not 'Jewish' in the normative sense of those terms.

The matriarch is flanked by two girls, one of whom holds a basket of flowers. At her feet lies a languid youth reminiscent of a *pietà*, who holds a flower. These solid figures are placed in a landscape with little depth, which has the effect – as in the earlier images of Gertler's mother – of pushing the figures towards the viewer. The middle ground is compressed, so that the space of the picture is oppressive. Colour further articulates this spatial compression. Blues are immediately countered by reds to offset any possibility of deep recession; distance is given by the spire of an English church. The hat of the coster is blue and red, as is the dress of the girl on her left. The sky is gloomy, as indeed is the landscape. Each individual is clearly defined, outlined, distinctive and separate from each other. No one touches here. Even the gazes of their eyes have been carefully orchestrated to avoid each other. The boy and girl on the left look to the right, while the girl on the right looks to the left. The Great Mother, head on, faces us but also deflects our gaze. There is no contact articulated either within or outside the frame. She is implacable, untouchable, distant in demeanour. Each figure looks beyond the picture. They are locked in their own worlds beyond each other and beyond the frame. They are on display, like the still-life objects on parade. This ordering (in excess) paradoxically signals disorder, the out-of-the-ordinary. Like a frieze or a tableau, it seems as if a drama is taking place. It is situated in the rare space of common land. It belongs to everyone and no one. Everyone has a place but no one belongs.

This 'quintessential' English pastoral scene is overlaid with arcane signs and symbols. It is neither English, nor Christian, nor Jewish, but it disquietingly articulates the disintegration and re-integration of all. It is not reducible.

The romanticization and myths of the Jew and the East End were to haunt and remain haunting. Difference, Otherness, Jewishness are maintained and diffused throughout the texts (both past and present) which have sought to describe Gertler and explain his art. His work and his biography are considered to be one but have failed to re-engage that individual with Life. In these accounts fables predominate. The place secured for his art has been outside the mainstream of British culture. When installed it is always the art of the Other. *Jew* is inscribed before the work, which is then read through that discourse. Gertler takes us to the very edges of assimilation. These limits may be social and economic, but they are also fantastic and mythical. And as such they lie beyond the winds of history and the wings of fate. Here I refer again to Walter Benjamin's essay 'Theses on the philosophy of history', in which the image of the angel alludes to our ability to understand our contemporary situation in the context of the headlong flight into modernity:

> A storm is blowing from Paradise; it has got caught in his wings with such violence that the angel can no longer close them. This storm irresistibly propels him into the future to which his back is turned, while the pile of debris before him grows skyward. [46]

Benjamin's allegory can be seen to figure the instability of the discourses of *identity* which are also figured in Gertler's troubling art.

Notes

1. Walter Benjamin, *Illuminations*, London: Fontana, 1973, p. 259.
2. See, for examples, Quentin Bell's 'Introduction' to Noel Carrington (ed.), *Mark Gertler: Selected Letters*, London: Rupert Hart-Davis, 1965, and John Woodeson, *Mark Gertler, Biography of a Painter 1891–1939*, London: Sidgwick & Jackson, 1972.
3. E. Sumueli, *Seven Jewish Cultures*, Cambridge: Cambridge University Press, 1990, p. 7.
4. Janet Wolff, 'The failure of a hard sponge: class, ethnicity and the art of Mark Gertler', *New Formations,* no. 28, Spring 1996, pp. 46–64.
5. Biographical information in this chapter comes from Woodeson, *op. cit.*, pp. 353–6.
6. *Mark Gertler: Selected Letters* includes letters from Gertler to his friends Dora Carrington, Edward Marsh and the Hon. Dorothy Brett.
7. *Ibid.*, p. 47.

8. *Ibid.*, p. 57.
9. *Ibid.*, p. 49.
10. Gertler's trips to Paris were paid for by the Jewish Educational Aid Society. John Woodeson, *Mark Gertler*, exhibition catalogue, Colchester: The Minories, 1971.
11. *Mark Gertler: Selected Letters*, p. 47.
12. *Ibid.*, p. 55.
13. Gertler described this visit in a letter to Carrington, July 1912, *Mark Gertler: Selected Letters*, p. 43.
14. David Reason suggested this term to convey the idea of archetype/archaic/matriarch.
15. *Mark Gertler: Selected Letters*, p. 60.
16. *Ibid.*, p. 37.
17. S. Gerlberg, 'Jewish London', in George Sims, *Living London*, Vol. 2, London, 1902, p. 29.
18. *Ibid.*
19. Gertler exhibited *My Mother, Mother and Babe, Jewish Family, Gt. Grandmother's Dress* and three unidentified still-life paintings.
20. *Star*, 20 May 1914.
21. Edward Marsh was a major collector of Gertler's work at this time. Professor F. Brown and Mrs Blundell figure amongst others. See the catalogue of works in Woodeson, *op. cit.*, pp. 357–91.
22. Letter from Gertler to Carrington, *Mark Gertler: Selected Letters*, p. 63.
23. Numerous contemporary texts sought to understand and to capture East London. See, for example, Charles Booth's *The Life and Labour of the People of London 1883–1903*, London: Macmillan, 1896; Jack London, *The People of the Abyss,* London, 1903; George Sims, *Living London*, London, 1902–3.
24. Gerlberg, *op. cit.*, p. 29.
25. P. Stallybrass and A. White, *The Politics and Poetics of Transgression*, London: Methuen, 1986, pp. 18–20.
26. Letter to Carrington, *Mark Gertler: Selected Letters,* pp. 80–1.
27. Letter, D. H. Lawrence to Mark Gertler, 9 October 1916, in *Mark Gertler: Paintings and Drawings*, London: Camden Arts Centre, 1992, p. 40.
28. Gerlberg, *op. cit.*, p. 29.
29. Sylvia Lynd, 'Introduction', *Mark Gertler Memorial Exhibition*, London: Leicester Galleries, May 1941.
30. *Mark Gertler*, London: Ben Uri Gallery, 1944.
31. Woodeson, *op. cit.*, p. 7.
32. Sander Gilman, *Jewish Self-Hatred: Anti-Semitism and the Hidden Language of the Jews*, Baltimore: Johns Hopkins University Press, 1990, p. 6.

33. *Mark Gertler: Paintings and Drawings*, Camden Arts Centre, London, 17 January–8 March 1992 (and touring).
34. Tim Hilton, 'A brush with Bloomsbury', *Guardian*, 19 January 1992, Camden Arts Centre Archive. All reviews are taken from the press cuttings book and are unpaginated.
35. Mary Rose Beaumont, 'Mark Gertler', *Arts Review*, April 1992.
36. 'Rich little poor boy', *Economist*, 8 February 1992.
37. John McEwen, 'Outcast brought in from the cold', *Sunday Telegraph*, 2 February 1992.
38. John McEwen, 'The outsider', *Independent Magazine*, 18 January 1992.
39. William Feaver, 'Art war and roses', *Vogue*, January 1992.
40. Linda Talbot, 'Mark Gertler', *Ham and High*, 24 January 1992.
41. Anon., 'The return', *Ham and High*, 7 February 1992.
42. William Packer, 'Gertler: a story of doubt', *Financial Times*, 4 February 1992.
43. Anthony Blunt, 'Art: plagiarism and vulgarity', *Spectator*, 15 October 1932, p. 478. Cited in Andrew Causey, 'A certain gypsy gaudiness', *Mark Gertler: Paintings and Drawings,* Camden Arts Centre, 1992, p. 32.
44. Sarat Maharaj delivered this paper at a symposium on the subject of cultural identity held at the Camden Arts Centre, London, in March 1992, to coincide with the Gertler exhibition.
45. Causey, *op. cit.*, p. 24.
46. Benjamin, *op. cit.*, p. 259.

8

The subliminal Greenberg:
assimilation and the ideal other

What I want to be able to do is accept my Jewishness more implicitly, so implicitly that I can use it to realize myself as a human-being in my own right *and as a Jew in my own right*. I want to be free to be what I need to be and delight in being, as a personality without being typed and prescribed to as a Jew or, for that matter, as an American.

Clement Greenberg[1]

The American art critic Clement Greenberg (1909–94) was a first-generation Jew, born in the Bronx. His parents came from Lithuania and were, as he put it, 'free-thinking socialists'. He himself was a fellow traveller: his mode of thinking was formed by Marxism but it was also indebted to the philosopher Immanuel Kant's formulations about intuitive experience and aesthetic judgement. His work, it can be argued, laid the foundations of aesthetic theory in the post-war West and was instrumental in the legitimization of American Abstract Expressionism.

Greenberg perceived the essence of modernism to be the reflexive criticism of a discipline – painting, sculpture, literature – from within itself, in order to save art and culture from disintegration. Enlightenment, which was for him synonymous with high culture, is defined as always in jeopardy and under threat. His work was thus a redemptive act.

In this episode, I consider some of his ideas concerning *Jewishness,* and I suggest that his notion of *Jewish* identity parallels those he held about modernist art: Jews and art are perpetually endangered, hence the analogy. His project is fraught with ambiguities which, both through his own attempts to iron them out and the tendency of other writers to banish them to the margins of his work (if not to ignore them), have led to a diminished understanding of the scope of Greenberg's own work and by extension to a further diminution of the questions posed by art criticism in modernity. Moreover, by considering Greenberg's attitude towards *Jewishness* in the post-war period, some light is shed on his solution to one of the problems inherent in modernist aesthetics, the conflicting demands of the 'particular' and the 'universal', in his case being a Jew and an American. This contributes to a broader reappraisal of the aesthetics and politics of social democracy.

In an article published in 1950, entitled 'Self hatred and Jewish chauvinism: some reflections on positive Jewishness', he lamented, 'What I want to be able to do is accept my Jewishness more implicitly, so implicitly that I can use it to realize myself as a human-being in my own right *and as a Jew in my own right.*' Here Greenberg describes a desire. Like all desire it is bound to paradox. Whilst he espouses uncategorizable *identity* to achieve this end – in itself an impossible and probably a tainted desire – the particular must be subsumed by homogeneity. So it was that Greenberg, driven by the logic of assimilation, falls prey to the American dream and probably in spite of himself resolves the paradox.

In the late 1940s and 1950s, questions of Jewish identity and the formation of an American national culture were on the cultural and political agendas. Before the war, as Irving Howe points out in his autobiography, his generation felt that their position as Jews was largely subordinated to commitments to cosmopolitan culture and socialist politics on an international scale:

> The fact of Jewishness figured much more strongly than we acknowledged in public. We still didn't identify with a Jewish tradition, yet in practice we grew increasingly concerned with Jewish themes. There was a kind of cultural lag: a recognition behind reality.[2]

Indeed, Greenberg's own contributions to the journal *Partisan Review* between 1936 and 1940 show his negotiations with a Marxism distinct from Stalinism in the wake of the Popular Front (1935) and the Moscow Trials (1940).[3] It was in 'Avant-garde and kitsch' that he developed his most sustained critique of capitalism.[4] In this seminal essay, Greenberg positions High Culture (reflexive, critical and demanding) against Kitsch (easy enjoyment and passive consumption). The methods of the avant-garde are justified by him as enabling culture to progress. Progress is productive of its own forms of violence. Greenberg's affirmation of modern (abstract) art was a complex cultural–political strategy which entailed building boundaries that inevitably precipitated exclusions. The subsequent de-politicization of his aesthetic theory has been explained by Serge Guilbaut as part of the move towards the de-Marxification of American culture after the

Second World War.[5] But this is not the whole story. I would add that the impact of the Jewish Question on American cultural politics cannot be overlooked at a moment so marked by the Shoah. Excavating Jewish identity in this period was painful, troubling, and for some traumatic. Greenberg himself cautioned:

> No matter how necessary it may be to indulge our feelings about Auschwitz, we can do so only temporarily and privately; we certainly cannot let them determine Jewish policy either in Israel or outside it.[6]

In New York, the focus for intellectual debate on the theme of Jewish identity turned on Jean-Paul Sartre's 'Reflections on the Jewish question', published in *Commentary* in 1948.[7] Greenberg was an associate editor at the time. In these essays, serialized in three parts from his book *Réflexions sur la question juive* (1946), Sartre revealed the basic deception played out in democratic liberalism: on the one hand, individual rights are advocated, and on the other, the limits to those very rights are hidden. Sartre argued:

> The Jews nevertheless have a friend: the democrat. But in practice this friend offers only the most pitiful protection. Of course he will proclaim that all men have equal rights and of course he founded the League of the Rights of Man. But his very pronouncements reveal the weakness of his position. In the 17th century he chose, once and for all, the concept of analysis. The only thing which matters for him are concrete syntheses offered to him by history. He knows neither Jews, Arabs, Blacks, the bourgeois or the worker, but only man unchanged everywhere and in all periods. By a process of reduction each collective grouping is conceptualized by him as an accumulation of molecules: a social body in a similar garb as one of individuals.[8]

Liberal democracy has been predicated upon the principle that all people are equal and alike. Despite their magnanimity, suggests Sartre, the democrats are close to the anti-Semites insofar as they end up wanting to destroy the *Jews*, leaving only their 'humanity'. These 'friends', as Sartre ironically calls the democrats, 'construe everything as a singular incarnation of those universal traits which, according to him, make up human nature'.[9] The process of synthesis, which is the predominant configuration of Western thought, assimilates everything to the same. The Jews could belong only as long as they suppressed themselves as *Jews* – thereby difference is subordinated to identity and to the universal. The liberal enterprise, Sartre explained, is blind to relationships of power. In his study of anti-semitism, Sartre demonstrates the limits to the practices of liberal democratic ideology and to philosophy which posits equality with the effect of veiling substantial inequality.

It is also worth noting that similar reflections on the Jewish question did not lead him, as they had led Marx, to subordinate Jewish particularity to the universalism of a communist project. In 'On the Jewish question', written in 1844, initially as a critique of Bruno Bauer's two essays on the same theme, Marx set out his fundamental critique of the political principles of liberalism. He began with an analysis of (speculative) philosophy, which was for him a form of alienation that he compared with religion. Speculative philosophy and religion, Marx argued, must be rejected. His goal was the transformation of the state into human society in which class conflict would be eradicated, or at least transformed through a dialectical progression. Just as the state would wither away, so too would religion, so too the Christian and the Jew. Marx proposed that the 'secret' of the Jew was not to be found in his religion, but that the secret of his religion was to be discovered in economic and social life in which 'the contradiction of the State with a specific religion like Judaism, into the contradiction of the State with specific elements' would be exposed. Marx's project subjugated all difference to the ideals of the universal and the laws of economic necessity.[10]

Of course Sartre, writing immediately after the Shoah, was particularly sensitive to the plight of the Jews, and was also aware of the dangerous effects of the universalizing imperatives embedded within the democratic logic of identity by then clearly witnessed in the ideology and practices of totalitarian regimes. Accordingly, he argued for 'the specific nature of the Jewish fact and of the necessity for giving the Jews particular rights', which he later incorporated into a draft constitution written in the 1950s.[11] Sartre's analysis of the Jewish question was not in itself a history of the Jews; rather it was a study of anti-semitism and of the Jewish predicament as Other in the European imaginary and body politic.

When first published and indeed since, Sartre's work has been both celebrated and condemned, as Susan Rubin Suleiman points out in her careful criticism of *Anti-Semite and Jew*, attesting to the problematics of representation.[12] However, her overall inquiry is bolder and has a different agenda from that implied by my comment. Suleiman asks if the same book can now be read 'as an example of anti-semitism *malgré soi?*' She concludes, particularly as a consequence of the chapter 'Portrait of the Jew', that the effects of the text, if not its intentions, are indeed anti-semitic insofar as Sartre repeats the tropes of anti-semitic discourses. We know in dialectical terms that each category, anti-Semite and Jew, is necessary and dependent on the other to give each its own identity. Moreover, as we have seen throughout my text, this double bind is a consequence of fixing and representing an identity. Sartre in his characterizations of both anti-Semite and Jew almost inevitably repeats the trap of identity thinking and his thoughts get locked into the inexorable processes of identity production. Sartre's text displays 'anti-semitic' inclinations to the extent that it is shackled by the logic of identity. Nevertheless Suleiman is perhaps too quick to judge, and the demand may be after all not about judgement but rather a stricture about what is entailed in making judgements. Sartre's intelligence was generous and his work above all shows how ethical life is constrained in ways which undermine its promises. However it is not my purpose here to take up this argument *per se*, rather my concern is to consider Greenberg's and to a lesser extent Harold Rosenberg's responses to this work.

Each critic provided major and very different rejoinders to Sartre in *Commentary*, which were also a reaction on their part to criticism from orthodox Jewry. Greenberg, in an ascerbic footnote, castigates a Rabbi Silver who in *The Day* (16 July 1950) had used the term 'uprooted intellectuals' to criticize secular Jewish intellectuals. Greenberg reminded him that the 'uprooted intellectual' had been and continues to be 'a favourite in the totalitarian (and anti-semitic) lexicon of abuse, from Mussolini and Hitler to Stalin'. Harold Rosenberg, in 'Jewish identity in a free society', is also critical of the 'rootless' metaphor and argues against the affirmative stance of those he calls the twentieth-century Sadducees who desire absolute and exclusive commitment from other Jews.[13]

In 'Self-hatred and Jewish chauvinism: some reflections on positive Jewishness', Greenberg seems to accept and expand upon Sartre's definition of the 'inauthentic Jew' as one who regards his Jewishness as a 'psychological handicap' in seeking acceptance in the Gentile world, and calls him the 'negative Jew':

> The 'negative Jew', fleeing his Jewishness, expresses his self-hatred directly, even if he rationalizes it in some cases by maintaining that there is really no other difference than that of religion between himself and the Gentiles.[14]

For Sartre the Jew must assume responsibility for Jewishness and not try to conceal or disavow it. Similarly, Greenberg argues:

> The ultra-assimilationist Jew does violence to himself as a human-being pure and simple, as well as Jew because he tries to make himself more typically English, French or German than any Anglo-Saxon, Gaul or Teuton ever is. He over-defines himself . . . The nationalist Jew, too, always acts with reference to his Jewishness. But even though it is an ostensibly political reference, by the too great strenuousness of his effort to assert his Jewishness he likewise over-defines himself.[15]

Both Sartre and Greenberg are involved in category building: the former, the 'inauthentic' or 'authentic' Jew; the latter, the 'negative' or 'positive' Jew. Greenberg identifies both these tendencies as symptomatic of Jewish self-hatred, which is also inclined towards chauvinism. Greenberg's text, enunciated in an autobiographical voice and in a confessional tone, is marked by dilemmas which reveal the paradoxes and complexities of his own position.

Rosenberg's writing shows less incongruity and is less introspective than Greenberg's. On the one hand he applauds Sartre's bravery for writing 'Reflections on the Jewish question', at a 'moment of intense confusion', but on the other hand he goes on to criticize Sartre's 'Portrait of the Jew' for reiterating anti-semitic ideology, arguing that 'on the basis of his authentic–inauthentic conception, Sartre has consciously permitted himself to accept the anti-Semite's stereotype of the Jew'. His critique focused on what he takes to be Sartre's no-history thesis of the Jew: Sartre represents the Jews as having, 'no-history and [being] but the wretched creatures of anti-semitism'.[16] The Jew always remains an outsider defined by the anti-Semite:

> Here in America where Jews are not the only 'foreigners', nor the only target of racialism, it should be clear that being singled out by the enemy is not the cause of our difference from others, is not what makes us Jews.[17]

Rosenberg insisted that Jews have their own history and tradition which is maintained by Talmudic scholarship:

> The continuity of the modern Jew with Jews of the Old Testament is established by those acts which arise from his internal cohesion with his ultimate beginnings, in which his future is contained as possible destiny – the acts of turning towards the Promised Land in his crisis. And these acts, not deducible from his surroundings, mark the Jew's situation and reveal who the Jew is.[18]

Jewish identity in the modern era was for Rosenberg a question of will based on memory – the Midrashic ideas of remembrance, the recreation of the past for the present, 'a net of memory and expectation'. In addition Rosenberg was concerned to show what was for him the incontestable difference between being a Jew in America, a 'free society', and being a Jew in Europe.

Whilst for Sartre the Jewish question is posed as a question around citizenship in liberal democracies, for Rosenberg and Greenberg this question does not arise: they are both Jews and Americans and, as Greenberg stressed, 'naturally'. The issue of Jewish identity was, for Greenberg, less to do with questions of history in the sense that Rosenberg understands it, and more to do with overcoming Jewish self-hatred – including his own, itself of course a historical legacy. Above all, his problem – as the opening quotation of this chapter suggests – was how to live as both an American and a Jew without giving the lie to either. The main struggle he maintained 'still has to be fought inside ourselves', and he concluded that 'the problem has to be focused directly in the individual Jew and discussed in personal, not communal terms'. Hence, 'Jewishness, in so far as it has to be asserted in a predominantly Gentile world should be a personal rather than a mass manifestation, and more a matter of individual self-reliance.'[19] The 'negative' and 'positive' Jew cancel each other out. Through this move Greenberg creates a space in which Jewish identity can be embraced willingly and spontaneously on an individual basis. The Jew in this discourse is a free subject of history – free to make his destiny.

Greenberg here adopts a position that is similar to his aesthetics, in which notions of the artist are predicated upon concepts of individual freedom. We are here in the Cold War, where freedom is taken up as the *leitmotif* of the West and opposed to equality which is taken as the repressive ideology of the communist Eastern bloc. Serge Guilbaut argues that the cultural fate of the West in the post-war period was sealed through the protracted cultural and political debates that took place in New York during and after the Second World War. The origins of these debates lay in the 1930s, but as far as their effects on culture were concerned it was the hysterical anti-Communist dialogues of 1946–7 that were to prove critical. The outcome was that Abstract Expressionism achieved its success, so Guilbaut claims, not solely on aesthetic grounds but because of the ideological uses to which it was put. Thus it was that the 'drip' of Jackson Pollock's paintings, no less than Bendix washing machines and Lucky Strike cigarettes, came to be symbols of the Great American Dream.

The discourses of Abstract Expressionism, as adjuncts to individualism and to consumerism, quickly appropriated and redefined the concept of freedom. Guilbaut argues that the new definitions of freedom at the centre of liberalism in America were set out by Arthur Schlesinger in *The Vital Centre*, published in 1949.[20] In Britain these ideas were elaborated by F. A. Hayek, who argued that socialism is synonymous with repression of the individual. In *The Road to Serfdom* he maintained:

> There can be no doubt that the promise of greater freedom has become one of the most effective weapons of socialist propaganda and that the belief that socialism would bring freedom is genuine and sincere. But this would only heighten the tragedy if it should prove that what was promised to us as the Road to Freedom was in fact the High Road to Servitude.[21]

Freedom here becomes indistinguishable from the ability to buy goods and services. The freedom to choose, first enshrined in the ideas of Adam Smith in the eighteenth century, became the dominant definition of freedom. The defence of liberty superseded the notion of individual rights. There was a crossing of discourse in which free choice, in the sense of consumerism, became linked with notions of individual freedom. These affected ideas of artistic freedom and were used to supply the West with the very images of freedom. At his speech at the twenty-fifth anniversary of the Museum of Modern Art, New York, President Eisenhower declared:

> Freedom of the Arts is a basic freedom, one of the pillars of liberty in our land. For our Republic to stay free, those among us with a rare gift of artistry must be able to use their talent . . . How different is tyranny. When artists are made the slaves and the tools of the state; when artists become chief propagandists of a cause, progress is arrested and creation and genius are destroyed . . . Let us resolve that this precious freedom of America will, day by day, year by year become even stronger, ever brighter in our land.[22]

The idea of the free individual in a free society was thus associated with the condition and the form of modern art. The idea of liberty is presented without any discussion of sovereignty, inequality or power and is completed in the image of America. The West affirmed individual freedom over and above the equality that was proclaimed in the East. Freedom is defined in terms of the individual's right of expression, as Chaim Potok makes plain in his novel, *My Name Is Ascher Lev*. The art teacher describes the dilemma of the young Jewish boy of the title, who wishes to become an artist against the values of his family and his religious community. He offered him the following advice:

> Listen to me Ascher Lev, as an artist you are responsible to no-one and to nothing, except to yourself and to the truth, as you see it. An artist is responsible to his art. Anything else is propaganda. Anything else is what the Communists in Russia call art. I will teach you responsibility to art. Let your Hasidim teach you responsibility to Jews.[23]

Thus the protagonist is saved from his dilemma and becomes a famous artist. Free expression and responsibility to the self work here to sever art from social identity, in this case Jewish, and function at the same time to shape the identity of American art, which is *a priori* free and separate from ideology. Hence truly modern art was understood to be the free art of a free society. It was represented by Greenberg as pure, non-ideological and signifying the absolute freedom of the artist.

Greenberg had elaborated in 'Towards a newer Laocoon' (1940) his defence of 'abstract purism' and 'non-objective art'. He argued that the duty of art in modernity was to test the adequacy of its own resources. Accordingly, each form of art must determine the effects special to itself and by so doing achieve autonomy: 'The avant-garde arts have in the last fifty years achieved a "purity" and a radical delimitation of their fields of activities for which there is no previous example in the history of culture.'[24] Greenberg rejected 'subject-matter', which he described as a diversion from the purity and specificity of the medium of art itself. Barnett Newman's work was for him the perfect demonstration of his argument that modern art was inevitably and necessarily engaged with the purification of its medium.

In *Art Chronicle*, Greenberg championed Newman as a major painter who displayed 'both nerve and conviction'. He continued, '[Newman] keeps within the tacit and evolving limits of the Western tradition of painting.'[25] The force of his argument led Greenberg to suppress any notions extrinsic to the workings of the work of art itself. To restore the identity of painting, 'the opacity of its medium must be emphasized. For the visual arts the medium is discovered to be physical',[26] in other words, the flat surface, the shape of the support and the properties of pigment. The quality of the work is to be measured in terms of its ability to demonstrate what is valuable in its own right and which cannot be attained from any other kind of activity. What Greenberg evaluated as 'good' was that which makes explicit what is unique or irreducible in art in general and also in each particular art. Such judgement is 'disinterested': it is not a matter of individual taste or preference, or even historically produced knowledge. It is universal.

The 'Sublime' is the category invoked by Newman himself to describe the aim of his work, which is to reach for the absolute. He declared:

> We are freeing ourselves from the impediments of associations, nostalgia, legends, myth, or what have you that have been the devices of Western European painting. Instead of making cathedrals out of Christ, man or 'life', we are making it out of ourselves, out of revelation real and concrete, that can be understood by anyone who will look at it without the nostalgic glasses of history.[27]

This quotation can be understood, perhaps, as the avant-garde artist overthrowing tradition in order to create anew, and as a categorical negation of such. Or, perhaps, as the assertion of difference from the tradition of oil painting, and of humanist man. Or again, perhaps, as an assertion of his identity as a second-generation Jew in America: a purgative act of regeneration. In this latter sense Newman's work can be seen as an articulation of 'particularism' in *tension* with 'universalism' – the implications of which will be discussed later in this chapter.

Rosenberg believed that the work of Newman confronted the problem of Jewish identity in an especially profound and immediate way. Yet he also argues that Newman's work escapes the strictures of identity to create a universal aesthetic filled with meaning for all people of all eras. Arguably, in Newman's own account, as well as in Rosenberg's and Greenberg's, the tension between the 'particular' and the 'universal' is eradicated. The rhetoric of the universal, with its appeal to the sublime, effectively conceals its own contradictions. Art is not concerned with representation but is conceived of as presenting the unpresentable: the image impresses its immediate presence but not the meaning of the instance of its appearance. Furthermore, the eradication of the subject in purified abstraction answers aesthetically to Greenberg's thinking on the question of 'authentic' Jewish identity. Both are reduced to a universalist category of formal adequacy and competence. As an effect of this reasoning the erosion of the 'political' in Greenberg's writing is further espoused and legitimated.

The question of Jewish identity was directly confronted by Greenberg, if only to be subsumed by his overarching desire to reinvent the universal, in his essay on Franz Kafka published in 1956.[28] An earlier version, 'The Jewishness of Franz Kafka: some sources of his particular vision', appeared the year before in *Commentary* (April) and provoked an intriguing correspondence between Greenberg and the Cambridge literary critic, F. R. Leavis.[29]

In summary, Leavis's main points of contention are with Greenberg's characterization of his own critical judgements as resting on moral grounds, questions of taste, Kafka's literary standing in the canon and, most importantly for my purposes here, the significance of Kafka's *Jewishness* for the interpretation and appreciation of his work.[30]

Leavis notes that Greenberg accounts for Kafka's literary expression in terms of its adaptation of 'traditional theologico-legalist "logic"', *Halachah* (Law), which he also suggests is of 'special interest for those familiar with Jewish culture and tradition'. He criticizes Greenberg's article for overdetermining the reading of Kafka and further undermines Greenberg's position by situating himself as neither Christian nor Jew, yet able to evaluate Kafka's literature. He accuses Greenberg of critical confusion, and for overestimating both the importance of the Jewish sources as well as the originality and achievement of Kafka's work.[31] Greenberg replies:

> What I cannot see at all is why the resemblances I find between the method of Kafka's imagination and the Halachah logic should have any more *special* – that is, exclusive – an interest for 'those familiar

with Jewish culture and tradition' than Shakespeare's echoes of Montaigne have for experts in 16th century French literature . . . I hoped I was explaining the cause of an effect in Kafka's writing . . . nor was the Jewishness of Kafka's art expected to recommend it in any way that it could not recommend itself at first hand to any reader, Gentile or Jew.[32]

The significant revisions he made to the second version of 'Kafka's Jewishness' took this line on board and indeed go some way to describing, as he puts it, 'the cause of an effect' and might be explained as a further response to Leavis's original comments. Reading this text gives an additional twist to Greenberg's proposed desire and to his own projections concerning the identity of the Jew.

Greenberg had started his first essay by establishing Kafka's writing as 'strange'. He attributes this quality to the writer's neurosis, which he presents as the likely consequence of Kafka's state: a Jew in the Diaspora, a writer, writing in German, living in Prague, ill at ease, not at home in Western culture. Leavis admonishes Greenberg for making these particular points and insists that if the novel succeeds it does so only insofar as it triumphs as the expression of neurosis and writes: 'We walk the neurotic treadmill, we suffer the claustrophobia, and we share the life-frustration in so far as we respond to Kafka's art.'[33] Hence, it speaks to Everyman and is thus universal.

Greenberg's revised article underplays the theme of neurosis. It opens dramatically and differently from hitherto with the assertion that 'Kafka the *writer* could do with a little more placing. And to this end it would be useful to inquire a good deal further into his Jewishness, but as it relates to his writing alone rather than his personality or neurosis.'[34] Whilst pursuing his earlier claim that Kafka's writing can be understood as a consequence of his Jewishness, he now adds the significant caveat that the personality or the neurosis of the writer is not to be confused with his work:

> Jewishness becomes the condition of Kafka's art mainly to the extent that it emerges as its subject, it informs its forms – becomes indwelling form. Through his *Dichtung* – literally, his imaginings and musings – Kafka wins through to an intuition of the Jewish condition in the Diaspora so vivid as to convert to expression of itself into an integral part of itself: so complete, that is, that the intuition becomes Jewish in style as well as in sense.[35]

Accordingly, Kafka's work achieves its identity through the subject: the subject defines itself and is itself inscribed in and by its form. There can be no separation between the form and subject of Kafka's art. Jewishness is integral to the content of the work, which is itself the result of the effect of a work of art. Thus Greenberg tempers Leavis's criticism and is able to name, and to accommodate and absorb, the particularity of Kafka's *Jewishness.*

Greenberg goes on to describe Kafka as an 'emancipated and enlightened Jew'[36] and 'among the great Modern writers'.[37] He argues that the enlightened Jew in the Diaspora, in contrast to the traditional Jew, assimilates himself into the mainstream of modern life. As a consequence he is forced to create or invent for himself a new *Halachah.* The modern Jew breaks with tradition and immerses himself in a present, severed from the past and uncertain about the future. His position resembles that of the modern artist – insofar as he is also involved in rejecting tradition.

Through a series of elaborate twists, the position of Kafka-the-Jew becomes identified by Greenberg with the condition of Modernity itself: the circumstance of Kafka's very *Jewishness* is itself identified as the predicament of Modernity. His writing is *Jewish,* not in the sense that Kafka represents *Jewish* themes but in that its precedent comes from the tradition of the *Halachah.* However, and more important, it is modern in its effect, exemplified and conveyed in its form. The issue of the *Jewishness* of Kafka is subordinated to an interrogation of Modernity. Greenberg regards *Jewishness* and Modernism as synonymous and by his so doing the 'particular', or the singularity of Kafka's writing, is subsumed by the 'universal'.

Struggle as Greenberg did with criticality, it is perhaps the nature of the universal to evade criticism. Purity is connected through a chain of associations to the universal and is the defence of progress and modernity. Through Greenberg's pursuit of the universal, tension is wiped out. Difficulty turns to certainty. The purification of the medium becomes a way of defending art against its own potential dissolution and of founding a new certainty. However, it is the very articulation in *tension* between universalism (homogeneity, identity) and the demands of the particular (heterogeneity, pluralism) which must, I think, be the precondition of aesthetic judgement, and allow the singular to be disclosed, and by extension to provide a precondition of a modern liberal and democratic society.

In an argument presented by Chantal Mouffe, the importance of differentiating between the democratic logic of identity (universalism) and the liberal logic of pluralism (particularism) is stressed. These two logics, she argues, must never be reconciled or resolved, for without the tension between them either totalitarianism or unfettered individualism emerges.[38]

To develop her critique of liberal democracy Mouffe draws upon the work of Carl Schmitt whose writings, which eventually led him to embrace and produce apologetics for the Nazi régime, explored the logic of democratic liberalism and the meaning of citizenship. His work enables us to grasp the two logics of liberal democracy: the democratic logic of identity and the liberal logic of pluralism. Schmitt's work reveals the distinctions between government and governed, the law and popular will. For him the problem was how to achieve political unity around the state. His critique led him to espouse a notion of democracy without liberalism. He conceived true democracy as being based on homogeneity.

While we might, as Mouffe suggests, accept the need for homo-geneity – insofar as it can be interpreted as finding agreement and identifying with a certain number of political principles that after all provide the common substance required for democratic citizenship – the problem is that of relating the particular to the general will. Moreover, there can be no collective will, no homogeneity, no 'us' without the designation of a 'them'. Thus at any moment antagonism is bound to be ushered in, with the 'them' connoting the enemy. Politics cannot be 'known' without knowing what or who the enemy is.

The 'friend' and 'enemy' dichotomy comes from Mouffe's reading of Schmitt, who had deployed it as a means of articulating the idea of the collective 'body', which is to say the 'we' of the political.[39] Schmitt himself had witnessed the precarious collapsing of order and boundaries, the disorder that presaged Hitler's coming to power, and wished to protect and conserve order at all costs. However, the political always has to do with conflict and antagonisms. So the democratic logic of identity of government and governed cannot alone guarantee respect for human rights. In conditions where one can no longer speak of the people as if it were a unified and homogeneous entity with a single general will, it is only by virtue of political liberalism that the logic of popular sovereignty can avoid descending into tyranny. It is the very loss of pluralism that paves the way for totalitarianism.

Mouffe believes that liberal rationalism can accommodate and contain conflict since it is precisely the case that it indicates the limits to any radical consensus and reveals that any consensus is based on acts of exclusion. It is the concept of individual freedom which saves democracy from authoritarianism. Democracy in its pure form must itself be constituted by the logic of identity and equivalence and is impossible if pluralism is admitted. Pluralism prevents complete identification and totalization: hence it prevents 'pure' democracy and saves it from its own logic.

However, pluralism itself cannot be an absolute value, and respect for heterogeneity alone does not deal with the problems of pluralism. Any thinking of the political, Mouffe maintains, must recognize also that the limits of pluralism are not simply empirical: some models of life and some values are by definition incompatible and, as Mouffe puts it, that 'is the very condition which constitutes them'.[40] Above all, she declares, if the aim is to provide a liberal democratic regime with an ethical and political content, then it is important and necessary to examine the liberal problematic to determine which of its different elements are to be defended or rejected. Not all differences can be accepted and protected. Accordingly, the state must judge: 'It must promote some forms and forbid others.' Thus, the state cannot be neutral. It must take on the character of an 'ethical state'. Here Mouffe is following Joseph Raz, who in *Morality and Freedom*, while defending the fundamental contribution of liberalism (the defence of pluralism and individual freedom), adds to it a concept of the subject as the product of specific institutions and practices. This notion of a socially instituted subject avoids the dangers of unfettered individualism.[41]

Equivalence without difference or difference without democracy are tensions which can never, indeed should never, be attempted or resolved. It is the existence of this tension, as Mouffe explains, that must be defended, not eliminated. It is this tension, in fact, which also shows up as a tension between our identities as individuals and as citizens or between the principles of freedom and equality which constitute the best guarantee that the project of modern democracy is alive and occupied by pluralism. The desire to resolve it could lead only to the elimination of the political and the destruction of democracy.

Paradoxically, democracy is only possible precisely because the universal has no definite body and because the institutions are themselves fallible. The solution of this paradox, in an argument presented by Ernesto Laclau, 'would imply that a particular body had been found that was the *true* body of the universal. But in that case, the universal would have found its necessary location, and democracy would be impossible.'[42] The unbridgeable distance between the universal and the particular is the precondition of democracy. Thus the very 'failure' or impossibility of society to constitute itself *as* a body makes democratic interaction achievable. A radical democracy can only be alive and achieve effective pluralism if it is recognized that it is impossible to accomplish. It is always and perpetually to come. Hence, perhaps, the shape of modern anxiety, marked by the difficulty of conceptualizing the mix of freedom and unfreedom which continues to mould our subjectivities.

Greenberg ended 'Kafka's Jewishness' with the declaration, 'Kafka's Jewish self asks this question and in asking it, tests the limits of art.' Perhaps we could reformulate this remark to suggest that 'Kafka's Jewish self' yet again tests the limits and ethics of liberal democracy.[43] Greenberg participated in formulating an aesthetic in which the tension between the universal and the particular was eradicated. This very tension must be maintained to save democracy from sliding into totalitarianism. It is the abandonment of this tension, if we follow Mouffe's logic, which makes Greenberg's writings open to charges of authoritarianism. The certainty of judgement for which he strove, subjugates. This is not to suggest that judgement should be eschewed. It is rather to advocate that its precondition should be doubt and uncertainty. Above all, against Greenberg's logic, art criticism should be prepared for surprises precisely because meanings are both structured and changeable. His work was a desperate attempt to defend art against the uncertainties of meaning in capitalist society and hence to make culture more secure.

Greenberg's project was to affirm the universal emancipatory possibilities of modernity but it also could be mobilized to negate anything which transgressed the rites of purification he considered necessary to preserve them. He creates an unassimilable vision of liberty and authoritarianism. Greenberg's account of modernity requires a narrowing of the focus of art and mutates into a dogma of closedness. It is as Andrew Brighton has noted, 'neither an accurate nor an encompassing description of the plurality of serious art'.[44] Such was the risk he took in his desire to complete the project of modernity, and by so doing he irons out difficulty in favour of purity.

Writing his 'desire', Greenberg creates history as the possible reconciliation of the universal and the particular, between American and Jew. His work can be read as a testimony to that desire. To attain the universal, conflict must be suppressed and assimilated to identity. His crisis is one of identity and lack of identity. The spirit of authoritarianism presides in order to guarantee him the ethic of liberty and to allow Greenberg himself to 'delight in being'. The whole presented as the universal gives evidence of anxiety posed by the conflict between inner autonomy and outer heteronomy. In order for him to write his way out of this dilemma, his work became a sacrifice to an ideal. The Americanization of aesthetic identity is hence paradoxically secured, and Greenberg's American and Jewish dilemma is sublimated and thereby apparently resolved.

Notes

1. Clement Greenberg, 'Self-hatred and Jewish chauvinism: some reflections on "positive Jewishness"', *Commentary*, November 1950, p. 434. Republished in Volume 3 of *Clement Greenberg: The Collected Essays and Criticism,* ed. John O'Brian, Chicago: University of Chicago Press, p. 56. The citations which follow come from this.

2. Irving Howe, *Margins of Hope*, London: Secker & Warburg, 1981. I am grateful to Katy Deepwell for this reference.

3. Fred Orton and Griselda Pollock, 'Avant-garde and *Partisan Review*', *Art History*, Vol. 4, no. 3, pp. 305–27.

4. Clement Greenberg, 'Avant-garde and kitsch', *Partisan Review*, Vol. 6, no. 5, Fall 1939, pp. 3–39. Republished in Clement Greenberg, *Art and Culture*, Boston: Beacon Press, 1961, pp. 3–22.

5. Serge Guilbaut, *How New York Stole the Idea of Modern Art: Abstract Expressionism, Freedom and the Cold War*, Chicago: Chicago University Press, 1983.

6. Greenberg, 'Self-hatred and Jewish chauvinism', p. 51.

7. Jean-Paul Sartre, 'Reflections on the Jewish question', *Commentary*, April, May and June, 1948. Translated from *Réflexions sur la question juive*, Paris: Gallimard, 1946, later published as *Anti-Semite and Jew*, New York: Schocken Books, 1949.

8. *Ibid.*, p. 65–6 (my translation).

9. *Ibid.*, p. 66.

10. Karl Marx, 'On the Jewish question', in David McLellan (ed.), *Early Texts*, Oxford: Basil Blackwell, 1972, pp. 85–115.

11. Simone de Beauvoir, 'Conversations with Jean-Paul Sartre', in *Adieux: A Farewell to Sartre*, trans. Patrick O'Brian, London: André Deutsch and Weidenfeld & Nicolson, 1984, p. 393.

12. Susan Rubin Suleiman, 'The Jews in Sartre's Réflexions – an exercise in historic reading', in Linda Nochlin and Tamar Garb (eds), *The Jew in the Text: Modernity and the Construction of Identity*, London: Thames & Hudson, 1995, pp. 201–18.

13. Greenberg, 'Self-hatred and Jewish chauvinism', p. 431; Harold Rosenberg, 'Jewish identity in a free society', *Commentary*, June 1950, p. 510.

14. Greenberg, *op. cit.*, p. 46.

15. *Ibid.*, p. 56.

16. H. Rosenberg, 'Does the Jew exist? Sartre's morality play about anti-semitism', *Commentary*, January 1949, p. 9.

17. Rosenberg, 'Jewish identity', p. 18.

18. *Ibid.*, p. 12.

19. Greenberg, 'Self-hatred and Jewish chauvinism', p. 53.

20. Guilbaut, *op. cit.*, p. 198.

21. F. A. Hayek, *The Road to Serfdom*, London: Routledge, 1944, p. 40.

22. Dwight Eisenhower, speech printed in *Bulletin of the Museum of Modern Art*, 1954–8. Cited in John Hyatt, *Art Wars*, Rochdale: Rochdale Art Gallery, 1984.

23. Chaim Potok, *My Name Is Asher Lev*, Harmondsworth: Penguin, 1977, p. 191.

24. Clement Greenberg, 'Towards a newer Laocoon', *Partisan Review*, July/August 1940, in Francis Frascina and Charles Harrison (eds), *Pollock and After: A Critical Debate,* New York: Harper & Row, 1989, p. 41.

25. Clement Greenberg, 'Art Chronicle: 1952', in *Art and Culture*, Boston: Beacon Press, 1961, p. 150.

26. Greenberg, 'Towards a newer Laocoon', p. 42.

27. Barnett Newman, 'Sublime is now', *Tiger's Eye*, Vol. 1, December 1948. Reprinted in Barbara Rose, *Readings in American Art:1900–1975*, New York: Praeger, 1975, p. 135.

28. Clement Greenberg, 'Kafka's Jewishness', in *Art and Culture*, pp. 266–74.

29. Greenberg, *Collected Essays*, Vol. 3, pp. 202–9.

30. *Ibid.*, pp. 209–11.

31. *Ibid.*, p. 211.

32. *Ibid.*, pp. 212–13.

33. *Ibid.*, p. 210.

34. Greenberg, 'Kafka's Jewishness', in *Art and Culture*, p. 266.

35. *Ibid.*, p. 266.

36. *Ibid.*, p. 271.

37. *Ibid.*, p. 272.

38. Chantal Mouffe, 'Pluralism and modern democracy: around Carl Schmitt', *New Formations*, no. 14, Summer 1991, pp. 1–17.

39. *Ibid.*, p. 5.

40. *Ibid.*, p. 11.

41. *Ibid.*, p. 9.

42. Ernesto Laclau, 'Universalism, particularism and the question of identity', *October*, no. 61, Summer 1992, p. 90.

43. Greenberg, 'Kafka's Jewishness', in *Art and Culture*, p. 272.

44. Andrew Brighton, 'Clement Greenberg, Andrew Wyeth and serious art', in *Views from Abroad: American Realities*, New York: Whitney Museum of American Art, 1997, p. 99.

9

The defiant Other: accusation and justification in the work of R. B. Kitaj

I have long since resolved to be a Jew . . . I regard that as more important than my art.

R. B. Kitaj[1]

In 1985 R. B. Kitaj, quoting from Arnold Schoenberg, dramatically announced his stance. His affirmation of Jewish identity was to provoke hostile responses from critics. In *Art Monthly*, Peter Fuller argued, 'on looking at these pictures, Gentiles are likely to feel a sense of exclusion, from the expression of emotion with which they can sympathise but with which they can hardly enter.'[2] In the *Guardian*, Waldemar Janusczak exclaimed coyly,

> There are few subjects in art which I, as a gentile and a coward, feel less qualified to comment upon than the subject of another man's Jewishness. But that is exactly what the new Ron Kitaj exhibition fiercely demands of the spectator.[3]

This much is true: Kitaj's insistence on Jewish identity again puts into crisis an ethic based on universal judgements in art, and yet again tests the limits of liberal democracy and the assimilationist dreams.

Of the 75 works on display at the Marlborough Gallery in London, only 15 arguably dealt with Jewish themes. So it would seem that critics picked up on his words as much as his images, on his intentions as much as the effects of his work. As we have seen already in the discussion of Mark Gertler, *Jew* was inscribed before the painting. The art was then read through that discourse. Likewise with Kitaj, *Jew* became the sign through which the images were explained. This chapter discusses the limits, the traps and the assumptions of identity politics as they emerge through a consideration of Kitaj's problematic project.

Kitaj's art demands attention – to the problems of picture-making and to making meanings. His work is complex and difficult. We cannot look at any one of his works and say with any certainty 'I know what that means'. Yet the temptation is there. He increasingly writes copiously about his art, notably in the *First Diasporist Manifesto*[4] and in the 'Prefaces' to Marco Livingstone's book.[5] As Kitaj himself has said, 'You can't make a canvas that's not redolent of something outside of the picture.'[6] The narratives within Kitaj's paintings refuse to be fixed, to be settled, to be stable. To cite Kitaj again,

> The fact you can get lost in a picture seems very life-like because we all get very lost in our emotional worldly lives. We lose our way in cities, we get lost in books, lost in thought. We are always looking for meaning in our lives, as if we would know what to do with it once we found it.[7]

Kitaj provokes, teases even. Often his writings 'leave out' as much as they 'put in', a necessary condition of the text of otherness, of text as *otherness*. He generally produces carefully edited texts, which suggest colour and frame but never entirely explain the images, except, that is, in the case of his accounts of Jewish art about which he lectured in Oxford in 1983.[8] The text was later published in the *Jewish Chronicle Colour Supplement*:

> Of all the events leading to the Holocaust, the assimilationist tendency in so many of those poor doomed souls took hold of my imagination, at least as much as, and in tandem with anti-semitism itself. It just did not matter if you were a religious Jew or not, or if you thought you were any kind of Jew or thought you were not, or willed yourself not to be. They'd kill you anyway. And they *still* might. A tremendous lesson began to form itself for my art: if it was Jewishness which condemned one and not the Jewish religion, then Jewishness may be a complex of qualities, a force of some kind; and might be a presence in art as in life. Can it be a force one *declares* in one's art? Could it not be a force one *intends* for one's art? Would it be a force *others* attribute for better or worse?[9]

Here Kitaj questions the identity of Jewish art by posing a series of questions which revolve around the notions of authorship and intentionality, reception and interpretation. These themes, of course, are not exclusive to Kitaj's project, but what is specific about them is his fetishizing gaze regarding the Jew, Jewish art and/or artists, which in itself entails questioning Kitaj's representation of Jewish history and identity and negotiating judgements about the nature of his project.

Jewish identity has, for Kitaj, an *a priori* existence which is held within a web of reciprocal relationships. Jewish identity – its definition and self-definition – is indelibly shaped and marked by anti-semitism. Whenever Kitaj writes *Jew*, he seems to mean 'victim': someone trapped, someone imprisoned in and by an identity. His work invites and provokes an interpretation of Jewish experience in the Diaspora in terms which are close to Sartre's no-history thesis, that the Jews are only Jews because of anti-semitism. Kitaj himself has written:

> The subject which interests me most of the time now is vast, and it is as small as I am. I think I can call it Jews in trouble, or Jews in danger. The trouble with Jews is that we are an engendered nation, almost always. Also the hotly debated question – What is a Jew? – has never been resolved except by murderers.[10]

In *Germania (The Tunnel)* (1985) (see Figure 1 on page 10), the ageing, myopic artist is supported by a stick carried in an eloquently gesturing hand. He is watching a child walking on a ledge carrying a book. Kitaj typifies the *Jews* as the people of the book. In the background is an arcade-like tunnel, which is lit at the end. To the right, but cut off from the main incident, is another picture, in which the open, brightly coloured brushwork has been replaced by the closed, deliberate and flat application of dark paint. Leading back, as if on a conveyor belt in a crematorium, lies an outstretched figure, face down, her long dark hair perfectly arranged as if in death. Kitaj represents an infirm man, a woman and a child – the three categories of people who were most likely to have been sent immediately to the gas chambers of the Shoah.

The arcade or tunnel motif combines two identifiable sources, the interrogation centre in Warsaw which Kitaj visited and the hospital in St Remy where Van Gogh had been a patient. Perhaps the tunnel also refers to that one in Treblinka, the tunnel through which the victims of Nazi genocide were savagely ushered to their deaths. The modern Jew of the painting, represented as the artist himself, is haunted perpetually by the memory of that history. The child's presence marks a recognition of the future which is also engraved in the knowledge of past exterminations.

Kitaj's thinking is haunted by the Holocaust and the very real fear that the Jews will yet be annihilated. Moreover, Kitaj has argued:

> I'm not a scholar, though I have been what used to be called an 'amateur' of recent history – right up to yesterday's news, for instance, of a certain gent lecturing thousands of cheering people in Madison Square Garden and warning the Jews yet again of the day 'when God puts you in the oven' (ovation, delight). For some of us you see, that may be just a greater threat than the nuclear one, believe it or not.[11]

The 'gent' to whom Kitaj refers is the American Muslim fundamentalist Louis Farrakhan. The Jewish question is not, alas, merely a problem of history. It continues to be posed. Its Middle Eastern dimension maintains and complicates it. The coming together of these factors and forces have given to Kitaj's project its *raison d'être*, its particular urgency and meanings. And for Kitaj Jewish identity has to be made and made again in and through a history which takes account of these dynamics.

Questions are posed about the nature of the relationship between Jewish identity and the history of anti-semitism in Kitaj's work by Andrew Benjamin in 'Kitaj and the question of Jewish identity', a chapter in his book *Art, Mimesis and the Avant-Garde*. But he also asks the question, 'Is there an affirmative conception that seeks to overcome the continual historical enactment of anti-semitism?'[12] For Benjamin, Kitaj's work becomes the site of the realization of such a possibility.

I continue here by taking up Benjamin's view of Kitaj's project to examine the reliability of the claims he makes for it. Benjamin situates Kitaj's art 'within the space of the heterological',[13] that is to say, Benjamin installs it as the site of a possible philosophical counter-tradition. He concludes his chapter with the claim:

> In the case of Jewish identity, when it is a question posed beyond the logic of the synagogue, and hence beyond the identity given to the Jew, what emerges as central is the space of paradox – space that contains the past but which moves towards the future; the space of process rather than stasis. Thinking this space is the concern of philosophy in the wake of the Enlightenment.[14]

Thus Benjamin insists upon affirmative Jewish identity as something yet to be accomplished. Accordingly it must resist the 'logic of the synagogue' and thereby place itself, be placed, outside or beyond Christendom, in a space which promises a counter-identity: one which articulates the fragmentation between the 'subject' and the 'world', between 'thought' and 'being'. This place is where the 'certainties' and 'truths' represented by the Enlightenment discourses of universalism and reason can be challenged. An 'affirmative Jewish identity' is to be created in the space which lies beyond the dominant tradition of (Western) knowledge which has been founded upon such certitude. For Benjamin the possibility (in the future) of an 'affirmative Jewish identity' resides in its capacity to present a counter to what he perceives as the dominant present configurations of knowledge. He writes:

> Escaping this reductive and self-enclosed conception of Jewish identity necessitates detailing the space where the mirror image of the Jew as transgressor – namely the Jew as transgressed against – is mediated by

the affirmative conception of identity. Even if the latter is the continually always as-yet-to-be-determined conception of the Jew.[15]

This prophetic method is itself a mark of the anxiety which is inscribed in the modern. It is indeed certain that the future will re-read the marks of Jewish identity, but the question remains, in what terms? Historical meanings are determined later, through their inscription in symbolic configurations. So although I share a concern with the issues explored in Benjamin's project, that is to say, the implications of rethinking 'identity' as a question for ontology, I am also concerned that it should be constituted in such a way that it marks a limit to the notion of 'identity' (Jewish and/or other). However, I am not yet convinced that Kitaj's art (including the commentaries) merits the claims that Benjamin makes for it.

Now a further question remains. If indeed Kitaj offers 'affirmation', what is being affirmed, and what is being negated? What is it against? What might be the implications of his insistence upon Jewish identity – which I think are markedly different from those arising out of Benjamin's project. There are other, though related, questions to be asked: What is assigned to that identity? How is that identity accomplished? I shall proceed by discussing *The Jew etc.*, a picture which dates from 1976 (Figure 20). It is here that I shall set out the grounds for my disagreement with Benjamin's interpretation of Kitaj's work in general and of this image in particular.

The narcissistic possibilities of identification inherent in the cultural project of portraiture are the hinges of my argument about Kitaj's refusal of the specific portrait of the Jew. The picture offers an invitation for it to be seen as a portrait. The precise details (marked or unremarked) registered (by absence or by presence) in the way of drawing – the homburg hat, the lowered eye, the straight nose, the slightly flared nostril, the opened mouth caressed by the delicately portrayed hand, the hearing-aid, the ear, the worn laced boots, the crumpled dark suit, the deliberate pose of the man (leaning forward) – these all evoke the sense of a particular man. They promise, or at least give to the image the conviction that this individual (who?) was there (where?) on that day (when?). Yet for all those details we cannot identify that person. The picture denies the means (the attributes given in conventional portraiture) which might place this man, signify him or make of him a referent, make him certain. We are, however, given a title, *The Jew etc.*, about which Kitaj has written, 'I've seen people wince at this title; sophisticated art people, who think it's better not to use the word Jew.'[16]

In Kitaj's portrait the man is drawn in profile. We can see him but he can never face us. If, as Emanuel Levinas has suggested, 'Face and

Figure 20. R. B. Kitaj, *The Jew etc.*, 1976, oil and charcoal on canvas, 152.4 × 121.9 cm, collection of the artist. With kind permission of the artist.

discourse are tied. The face speaks. It speaks, it is in this that it renders possible and begins all discourse', and again, according to Levinas, 'the first word of the face is "Thou shalt not kill"',[17] then this is a man who cannot respond to that fundamental commandment. For Levinas the 'originary' encounter is the discovery of the responsibility for the existence of the Other. 'The self, faced with the Other, is liberated from the self, is awakened from dogmatic slumber.'[18] The face is experienced as a manifestation of divinity – it is also a mark of the possibility of language. The Other is not to be perceived as a threat but constitutes the subject as an ethical being, instituted in dialogue. In this discourse, ethics means 'an anarchical assignation of the particular subject to morality'.[19] Ethical obligation arises not from logic and universal reason but from the uniqueness of the moral situation itself. Ethical individualism is always in tension with universalism, which is itself pre-supposed by ethics. Levinas's work allows new understandings of subjectivity. It begins to chart a path from individuation to universality, a passage from individual responsibility to justice. There can be no overarching concept of justice. It can only be judged in the fullness of each and every moment. The Jew, in the picture, is locked in – in on himself – in a railway carriage, where there is nothing to see or be seen through the window, and yet where he is forever observed.

His existence is announced, proclaimed, by touch – the touch of his own hand upon his face. If this is a mark of self-sufficiency or independence it is dependent upon the same, enclosed within himself, desiring to be just himself alone. There is no Other. This lack of the Other corresponds with 'primary narcissism' which – according to Freud – refers to the moment when a child takes its self-image as its love object before identifying and choosing external objects. This state-of-being corresponds to the subject's belief in the omnipotence of his own thoughts. *The Jew etc.* is self-absorbed and does not identify or face another, and is not offered for mirroring identification. Mikkel Borch-Jacobsen, in 'The Freudian subject', describes the desire of the subject as one of desiring identity and representation. He provides us with a description of the look of envy: 'If I *desire* to be (an) I, if I *desire* myself it must, following elementary logic be because I am not it.'[20] The desire of *The Jew etc.* is marked in and through the gesture of the hand which touches himself as if touching the Other: he is the other of the same.

As Borch-Jacobsen goes on to explain, the ultimate implication of the entire discourse of narcissism is primary identification and incorporation:

> If I am the other, then I *no longer represent him to myself*. . . And at the same time, I have become unable to represent *me*, to present myself to myself in my presence: this other that I am no longer is and never was *before* me, because I have straightaway identified myself with him, because I have from the outset assimilated him, eaten him, incorporated him.[21]

Hence the ethical is rendered impossible; the Other is incorporated and appropriated. He is 'eaten' and becomes the victim of the same. Now Benjamin does not have anything to say about that hand. For him the drama and the potential significance of the image is to be found in the hearing-aid. The ear itself is rendered remarkable by being unmarked, its delineation is scant, sparse, spare. By contrast, the hearing-aid is strongly designated and particularized.

The eye of the viewer, according to Benjamin, is drawn to the hearing-aid, where 'the eye confronts listening'. Benjamin is drawing on Lyotard's writings, where the significance of the distinction made between hearing and seeing is extrapolated and where it is argued 'the readable is not given to the eye but to the ear'.[22] Lyotard continues, 'in Judaism, hearing is dominant. And hearing relates to metaphysics, at least so long as one presumes that Someone has spoken.'[23] Benjamin, taking up this argument, suggests,

> The eye fixes. The ear is always open. It is always already open. Resolving the problem of developing an affirmative conception of Jewish identity must involve a dialectical interplay between the eye and the ear.[24]

Here Benjamin is setting out his claim for the heterological. Hearing is open to endless possibilities of change. What is heard is not what is expected. What emerges does not resemble anything. The eye fixes; sight is static and is dogmatic. The coming back of hearing restores an ethic.

For Benjamin, it is the hearing-aid in *The Jew etc.* which takes the figure beyond 'any status reducible to that of victim. He is more than merely transgressed against.'[25] It is the presence of the hearing-aid which renders the figure both vulnerable but able to overcome the 'weakened ear'. Hence, the hearing-aid becomes, according to Benjamin, a site for the possibility of 'an interpretative differential plurality'.[26] Yet within the terms set by Lyotard, 'the eyes must be closed if the word is to be heard'.[27] In *The Jew etc.* the eye of the Jew is open. He looks and – if the logic of Lyotard's argument is pursued – he cannot hear.

The *Jew* in Kitaj's image is being seen without seeing who sees him; he touches. Touch is the privileged sense/site which, in this image, supersedes either seeing or hearing. This is a constraining touch which locks the figure in and upon himself. He is subject to himself alone. If indeed this image can be understood as an image connoting narcissism, then it could be argued that the Jew's assertion of this self-love is in itself an act of affirmation. This celebration also carries within it the danger of refusal to tolerate the Other and with it the desire to eat, to negate and to obliterate. Hence the denial of the ethical and of the possibilities of change. The *Jew* in the picture becomes, accordingly, the ever-enduring victim and aggressor.

The identity of the name *The Jew etc.* pre-figures and identifies displacement. In the image, as I have already remarked, this man is on a train. By convention, then, the train carries with it a double connotation: the idea of the *Jew* as wanderer, and/or that of the *Jew* as victim being transported to the camps. Neither one of these interpretations can be collapsed into or onto the other. The importance of the choice of this site for Benjamin is precisely because it offers the possibility of a plurality of meanings which disallows a simple, hasty or reductive reading of Jew as victim.

The theme of wandering has also been taken up by Lyotard and used to distinguish further between the 'readable and the visible'. For him:

The wanderings of the Jew express the transcendence of the readable over the visible: 'From that time on, the Holy Writ and intellectual concern with it were what held the scattered people together'.[28]

What makes a Jew a *Jew* is the specific form of intellection prescribed by the Book. The Jew in the Diaspora is saved from total disintegration by the Book. He reintegrates and is integrated by and through the Word. Benjamin also designates *Jew* or *Jewish* identity by drawing on the theme of wandering:

Wandering defers the answer. The Jew remains within the open question. Even the Holocaust cannot close the question of Jewish identity. It is precisely in relation to this that the distinction between contemplation and thought needs to be situated.[29]

Yet it is through this image of wanderer, or wandering, that Benjamin attempts to wrestle the *Jew* away from – in order to surpass – the negative self-image produced by anti-semitism. Benjamin's thought is locked in a double-bind: the *Jew* of the 'synagogue', the *Jew* created by Christianity, must be transcended by yet another identity, the identification and differentiation of thought itself. The wandering *Jew* in this discourse becomes a sign for self-identity. Yet it is surely this perpetually always-in-transit *Jew* which marks him out in advance as victim or virus?

Another train journey figures in *The Jewish Rider* (1984–5). In this painting a man is absorbed in reading a book. It is known to be a portrait of the art historian Michael Podro. Indeed, Kitaj uses the traditional pictorial convention of the book to denote an intellectual. There is a second book perilously balanced on a ledge by the carriage window.

Unlike in the other picture, this window has a clearly delineated view – a second reality; a sepia-coloured landscape, blighted ravines – deep blacks against soft translucent brown. A chimney burns – an evocation of the spectre of the camps, perhaps? The smoke is drawn as if by a wind towards a cross upon a hillside – another Passion? Kitaj once commented on a

train journey someone took from Budapest to Auschwitz to get a sense of what the doomed could see through the slats of their cattle cars 'beautiful, simply beautiful countryside'. I don't know who said it. Since then I've read that Buchenwald was constructed on the very hill where Goethe often walked with Ekerman.[30]

Inside the carriage primary colours masquerade as bright as Van Gogh's palette. The man appears relaxed, urbane, dressed in a lemon-coloured jersey, red trousers, casual white shoes. Assimilated. Whilst the situation itself – the pose of the man – might be calm and innocuous, the paint, the handling, the colour, are turbulent.

A third reality: a steeply rising corridor, chimney-like, reveals at its end a black uniformed guard who wields a whip and represents perhaps authority himself, diminished yet ever-present. Is the guard to be understood as a sign that the new enemy of the Jews is 'black'? Given Kitaj's fear voiced earlier, more specifically Muslim fundamentalists?

The title *The Jewish Rider* perhaps refers to Rembrandt's *Polish Rider* (a late title given to that picture) and is purely conjectural. In Kitaj's painting the head and tail of a horse also figure. Are these allusions to the Rembrandt painting? Is it a rocking horse which is meant to evoke the movement of the train? Could it be an oblique reference to Gombrich's *Meditations on a Hobby Horse*? Podro was a pupil of Gombrich. The painting initiates a game between signs. It is a site of open readings in which the clues Kitaj offers may be misleading or revealing.

Maybe we are being invited to think of those train journeys which took the Jews from their homes to the death camps. Long after the threat to annihilate all Jews, many would not or could not believe that possibility. They were deceived by promises of resettlement, work camps or special provision. Can the image itself be understood as a deception, one akin to the deception played on the Jews?

The theme of exile, wanderer or refugee re-emerges in a painting entitled *Cecil Court London WC2 (The Refugees)* (1983–4). Cecil Court is a small street which runs between Charing Cross Road and St Martin's Lane, London. It is still full of bookshops, many of them formerly – and a number still – run by refugees. Edward Said, referring to a theme elaborated by George Steiner, argues that a whole genre of twentieth-century literature is 'extraterritorial': a literature by and about exiles which has come to symbolize the age of the refugee. Quoting Steiner, Said suggests,

> It seems quite proper that those who create art in a civilization of quasi-barbarism, which has made so many homeless, should themselves be poets unhoused and wanderers across language. Eccentric, aloof, nostalgic, deliberately untimely . . .[31]

Kitaj shares this view of exile and the exile as Diasporist intellectual. He writes, 'The Diasporist feels uneasy, alert to his new freedom, groundless, even foreign . . . the Diasporist pursues the phantom myth of nervous histories he claims for his own.'[32] But surely, as Bauman suggests, rootlessness has turned into a universal condition and with it all particularity has been effaced, 'though not in the way once seen in the dreams of the rootless'.[33] The idea of the intellectual exile is too easy; it presupposes a choice.

In *Cecil Court* we witness a mixing of worlds – in forms, in shapes, in paint, in colour, in texture. Hard geometry marks out the shopfronts like De Stijl paintings. The uniform, flat, coloured shapes which characterize those pictures are broken by a scumbled surface. As in *The Jewish School [Drawing a Golem]* (1982), the paint is applied thickly, more loaded, more charged physically and more overt in its handling than in earlier paintings by Kitaj. His Jewish themes are creating a response in form.

The discourses which have sought to describe expressionist art in the twentieth century have often associated it with Jewish artists and include Soutine's work as a signifier. Could it be that Kitaj is literally loading his paint with a notional tradition that he (and others) identifies as *Jewish*? The paint itself is beginning to provoke. The brush strokes live independently of their subjects and articulate a fractured, discontinuous surface. The street fans out into an open space filled with incident and with people.

This is another world where the strict architectural order is further disturbed by the people. Kitaj comments on the painting:

> I think I have a lot of experience of refugees from the Germans, and that's how this painting came about. My Dad and Grandma Kitaj and quite a few people dear to me just barely escaped.[34]

A man lies outstretched on a Le Corbusier/Perriand *chaise longue* made out of tubular steel and leather. This has an obvious association with modernist design, as do the shopfronts. Functionalist modernism was characterised by Nazi commentators as Jewish Bolshevik design. Kitaj has himself remarked, 'Modernism is dear to me. Fascism and modernism are enemies.'[35] Was not fascism also modern; was it not one of the possible consequences of the processes of modernization?

The man frowns. Under the back of his chair, on the ground, a book has fallen. One of his feet is booted, the other not. Alongside him, floating or lying (it is not clear), is another man, a figure reminiscent of Chagall's *Poet*. His head is cut by the edge of the canvas. Behind him are two children, a girl and a boy. Further back again there is a bald man carrying flowers, who looks down at the squatting figure of a young man whose hand shields his gaze as he looks beyond us and out of the picture. Next to him but small, out of scale, is a figure doing a handstand. To the right, surveying the scene, is a man, carrying a book gripped firmly under his arm. Through and back to the deepening street is an outstretched woman – her limbs dislocated, her legs akimbo, her belly naked, her thighs uncovered. She resembles a disjointed puppet and is perhaps related to images by Balthus. Behind her a man, intent on his work, cleans the street and just visible in the distance is a woman hailing a taxi. But no one and nothing fits here. Everything and everyone is out of place. Estrangement is ordinary here: if everyone is a stranger, no one is.

Could this image also be understood as a comment upon late modernism, with its concentration upon 'artistic breakthroughs' and the banishment of political/social/economic referents from its discourses, and through this the evacuation of notions of identity? Writing to Andrew Brighton, Kitaj commented,

> For some reason, probably boredom with internationalism and its slogans in art and life, I'm very tempted to look at questions of nationality, peoplehood, identity, roots, milieux certainly . . . questioning things that seem richly veined and attractive, where nationality is not.[36]

These three of Kitaj's paintings provoke us to think about and to discover something about the condition of the Jew this century. He pictures rootless people on trains, without property, without a place. The train journey, although it may convey the double connotation of wanderer or victim, does not offer any escape from a pre-given identity (the former associated with Jewish self-identity, the latter with assimilation). In neither case is a way out of the trap of *identity thinking* offered. Indeed the journey itself may signal 'the dying hatred' that forces the Jew to make endless departures.[37]

The refugees are outside in the street. Nowhere do we see a person settled, or at home. What these people share is a name united by an ensemble of limits and constraints, where violence is always a possibility. In these three images of Kitaj's the *Jew* is presented as sharing only the experience of the hostility of the society which surrounds him. If indeed this interpretation of the images is sustainable and viable, then it brings them close to the notion of Jewish identity as elaborated by Sartre:

> What makes a French person is not that he is born in France, votes, pays taxes. It is above all that he uses, understands and connects with the values of society and participates in their creations . . . A Jew is a person who on principle refuses to accept those values. Without doubt the workers' case is the same. But the situation is different: he is still able to reject the values of bourgeois culture. He has his own. The Jew in principle has the appearance of belonging to a social class (bourgeois, petit-bourgeois, worker). He shares their values, tastes and way of life. He is affected by their values but he does not comprehend them. He

lives with them but they do not admit him. The Jew remains a foreigner defined by his *otherness*.[38]

National unity is understood as offering the illusion of a common name and concealing the divisions between people. The Jew is outside those values which bind a nation together. He is, always and inevitably, alterior to the values of the state. He is the perpetual stranger.

Likewise, Kitaj's paintings suggest that wherever the Jews are, over and beyond the diversity of their concrete situations, they share an unequivocal character, a common and unchanging identity – Outsider. Thus, an apparently assimilated intellectual of the 1980s shares the 'Jewish condition' with refugees. Simultaneously they are defined and define themselves merely as products of the hostile society which surrounds them. Halevi points to this paradox when he writes,

> At the very point when Jewish society was breaking up as an autonomous social system, disintegrating into a host of special social situations, the idea spread among Europeans, as among Jews of Europe, of a single Jewish question: a question which always went back, in the last analysis, to the idea that each had a Judaism in general. The idea: at the beginning of the 19th century as, alas, much later, the 'idea' of the Jew replaced the analysis and perception of concrete situations. It was an idea in which the Christian prism filtered and distorted observation. Emancipation inaugurated the era when the Jew looked at himself in the eye of the Western Christian, and integrated the vision of the other into his own representation of himself.[39]

Kitaj's images accept and reinforce a view of the Jews as victims and suggest, by their refusal to contextualize, an account of Jewish history which paradoxically consecrates *Jewishness* (as) Otherness in history. Hence, contrary to Benjamin's view, I consider that Kitaj's imagery is now implicated in this continuing dramatization. In the three paintings I have considered, accusation and justification win out.

Accusation and justification are figured again in *Self Portrait as a Woman*, a painting which dates from 1984 (Figure 21). Kitaj has suggested, in connection with this image, that he wished to make 'woman' the hero.[40] The theme came from incidents concerning those women in occupied France during the Second World War who, having been convicted (or suspected) of consorting with a Jew, were forced to parade in the streets carrying a placard which announced their 'transgression'. The treatment of the 'woman' in the portrait, the violence of the brush marks, can be read as a violation of autonomy and integrity. The image is an appropriation of, an over-identification with 'woman' – another – whom Kitaj desires and envies. The violent brush marks imprint the traces of the frustration of this impossible

Figure 21.
R. B. Kitaj, *Self Portrait as a Woman*, 1984, oil on canvas, 246.4 × 77.2 cm,
H. R. Astrup, Oslo. With kind permission of the artist.

identification. For he is bound to remain the same. In trying to become the Other, in trying to master the Other, he is alienated and lost, yet again a stranger. The image would seem to sanction the violent obliteration of the Other, now designated as 'woman'. This intense over-identification with 'woman' signifies a mixture of anxiety with ruthlessness: a display of inner and outer violence which neither recognizes the violence which seeks to restore grace nor recognizes itself as the object as well as the subject of destruction.

Accusation, again of women, is the tone of Kitaj's painting *The Rise of Fascism* (1978–80). He has written about this picture,

> I used to mean these bathers to allude to the classic fascist period only, but now I don't. The bather on the left is the beautiful victim, the figure of fascism is in the middle and the seated bather is everyone else. The black cat is bad luck and the bomber coming over the water is hope.[41]

These two works are full of violence towards women. His reasoned justification for using 'woman' to stand for fascism is that the central figure is a typical *hausfrau*, a petite bourgeois, a representative of the class which formed the bedrock for Nazism. Further it can be argued that the black cat, and its association in modernist painting with Manet's *Olympia*, makes a further connection with prostitution. It could thus be that fascist politics are represented in terms of a political economy in which women, like the Jews, are always and yet again victims, who must also bear the blame.

Kitaj has said he would like to rework Cézanne and Degas again after Auschwitz. He has been seeking to create a 'symbol' through which the Jewish experience can be encapsulated. He explains,

> The appearance of the chimney forms of my pictures . . . is my very own primitive attempt at an equivalent symbol, like the cross, both after all having contained the human remains in death.[42]

Kitaj draws upon the possibilities of a 'symbolic consciousness' which could achieve 'universally' understood meaning through recourse to the typical. The chimney is clearly not an arbitrary choice through which to 'typify' Jewish experience. Written within it are chains of possible associations which may lead to de Chirico paintings, to a factory, to a crematorium, to Auschwitz. Each image resonates with memories connected with mystery, pain, fear and death. The symbol evokes a collection of images and ideas and yet it is general and singular. For it to be effective and work to accomplish 'symbolic consciousness', it needs to be repeated.

The chimney as a symbol occurs in Kitaj's pictures in different forms, sometimes overtly as in *The Jewish Rider*, at other times obliquely, evoked by the shape of the canvas as in the *Self Portrait as a Woman* and the right-hand panel of *Germania (The Tunnel)*. The chimney functions as an indictment of Christianity. Hence *Jewish* identity in Kitaj's painting is achieved in opposition to Christianity. Benjamin's claim that Kitaj's art 'is mediated by the possibility of an affirmative conception of identity[, even] if the latter is the continually always as-yet-to-be-determined conception of the Jew'[43] has to be understood as a form of identity which, in Kitaj's work, is only accomplished through reproducing the opposition between the *Jew* and *Christian*. It is an identity predicated upon violent negation.

Innocence and guilt: Jew and Gentile. Such oppositions belie the complicity in tension with any individual or collectivity. The tension between intention and complicity sheds light on the recurring opposition between perpetrator and victim. To rephrase the questions which mark Jewish history and challenge oppositions such as these might inaugurate discussion beyond conscience-stricken guilt and contribute to a change in awareness. It is the relationship between these oppositions which is itself significant: guiltlessness and force; impotence and mastery; boundaries of our self-identity and lack of self-identity which are a consequence of modernity and estranged or declamatory politics. From these questions we might come to recognize that we are both subjects and objects of violence and that good intentions merely engender new pieties while leaving untouched our basic complicities. Kitaj's art, through replicating and reiterating the already determined, over-saturated historical identities, remains an accomplice.

If the Jew, since Emancipation, has been concerned to bring the Torah in line with Western thought, is Benjamin suggesting that the Torah now demands something more? Levinas calls for the rebirth of Jewish culture. Judaism is not for him merely another dimension of thought to be added to Western philosophy but is,

> an excess of responsibility towards humanity whose singularity leads beyond any universal value. A withdrawal into itself on the part of Jewish identity or a Jewish state would therefore be the prelude to the exemplification of a Jewish singularity revealing a moral beyond the universal. As such the State of Israel will mark the end of assimilation by bringing us far beyond the concept in a spiritual, and so in a political sense.[44]

Levinas suggests that the special obligation of the Jewish state is to realize the Other beyond mastery. This is, for him, both a political necessity and an ethical proposition. Liberal human rights have destroyed love of the 'neighbour' and resulted in idolatrous collectives. Justice is to be discovered beyond the proximity assumed by individual rights. The tension between identity and assimilation in a modern state is to be transcended ultimately by the 'original' responsibility for the

Other which is beyond universalism and stands against assimilation through which an ethical politics will emerge. This will mark the end of assimilation, identity and the possibility of totalitarianism which, Levinas argues, they indicate and preserve.

Benjamin fails to remark upon the political, or indeed upon the constitution of the ethical, save in terms of affirmation and with it its corollary – negation. For Benjamin, 'affirmative Jewish identity' occupies a space designated as heterological where it has the task of redeeming Western thought. Affirmative Jewish identity is the desire for the Other, for unequivocal selfhood and even perhaps for 'home'. However, the name itself cannot be represented, it is featureless. It is that very name which distinguishes that man, his Otherness, his Jewishness. More, it may articulate a subject who is not given in a specific place or time; one that is always alien, who is bound to a name but lacks property.

For Benjamin, as we have seen, the 'enemy' is the 'synagogue' Jew, that ubiquitous product of Christian dominion. This *Jew* is, I believe, Kitaj's *Jew*. His art replicates this *Jew* and by so doing reiterates the *non-Jew's* representation of the *Jew* and his post-Enlightenment representation of himself. When Kitaj asserts Jewish identity it is predicated upon accusation and justification. This *Jew* is doomed to remain forever outside. He is the stranger, the wanderer endlessly seeking 'home'. In this context, Benjamin's call for the return of an 'affirmative identity' can be understood as a retreat. To affirm is merely to turn negation upside down and to get stuck in identical repetition. While he does himself distinguish between affirmation and repetition, he ends up repeating the antinomy. Whilst 'Jewish thought' may have been organized differently, this is not to say that Jews are inherently different; or at least, they are not any more different than are the same to their other-selves.

The rhetoric of the 'stranger' emerges out of the gaps, limits and difficulties inscribed within the project of assimilation. Bauman describes the limits of the assimilationist project and points to the stark alternatives implicated in its economy and form when he writes,

> If recourse to racism seems to be the natural way of salvaging the *objective* of assimilation programme in the wake of the bankruptcy of its ostensible *means*, so the retreat into 'strangerhood' as a substitute home of rootedness and confidence seems a natural way of salvaging the purposes of cultural self-adaption once the *vehicle offered by the programme have proved ineffective.*[45] [author's emphasis]

At best this 'home' offers a space where questions can continually be posed. Racism may indeed be a consequence of assimilation, which is different from seeing it as the cause. Kitaj seems to long for unequivocal selfhood and 'home'. But all he is left with is an imagery marked by narcissistic satisfaction that could allow for the luxury of the residue of violence which he cannot own and perforce must disown. His work evinces the idea of the original 'nobility' after the Diaspora but only by reiterating the opposited affirmation and negation, *Christian* and *Jew*. There is no possible evocation. What he is affirming is *over* there. The rest is *here*. Everything has a place after all.

Notes

1. R. B. Kitaj, 'A Passion', London: Marlborough Gallery exhibition catalogue, 1985, p. i.
2. Peter Fuller, 'Kitaj at Christmas', *Art Monthly*, December/January 1985/86, p. 3.
3. Waldemar Janusczak, 'Portrait of the artist as a Jew', *Guardian*, 12 November 1985, p. 32.
4. R. B. Kitaj, *First Diasporist Manifesto*, London: Thames & Hudson, 1989.
5. Marco Livingstone, *R. B. Kitaj*, Oxford: Phaidon Press, 1985.
6. R. B. Kitaj, in *Time*, 19 February 1965, p. 72. Cited by Joe Shannon, 'The allegorists: Kitaj and the viewer', in *R. B. Kitaj*, Washington, DC: Smithsonian Institute, 1985, p. 20.
7. R. B. Kitaj, 'A return to London', *London Magazine*, February 1980, p. 25.
8. This lecture took place at Ruskin College, University of Oxford, 25 November 1983.
9. R. B. Kitaj, 'Jewish art – indictment and defence: a personal testimony by R. B. Kitaj', *Jewish Chronicle Colour Supplement*, 30 November 1984, p. 46.
10. R. B. Kitaj, 'A Passion', p. iii.
11. *Ibid.*
12. Andrew Benjamin, *Art, Mimesis and the Avant-garde: Aspects of a Philosophy of Difference*, London: Routledge, 1991, pp. 88, 85.
13. *Ibid.*, p. 96.
14. *Ibid.*, pp. 88–9.
15. *Ibid.*, p. 89.
16. Kitaj, 'Prefaces', in Livingstone, *op. cit.*, p. 151.
17. Emmanuel Levinas, *Ethics and Infinity: Conversations with Philippe Memo*, Pittsburgh: Duquesne University Press, 1982, pp. 87, 89.
18. Emmanuel Levinas, 'Philosophy and awakening', in Eduardo Cadava, Peter Conner and Jean-Luc Nancy (eds), *Who Comes after the Subject?* London: Routledge, 1991, p. 214.

19. Fabio Ciaramelli, 'Levinas' ethical discourse', in Robert Bernasconi and Simon Critchley (eds), *Rereading Levinas*, London: Athlone Press, 1991, p. 85.
20. Mikkel Borch-Jacobsen, 'The Freudian subject', in *Who Comes after the Subject?* p. 66.
21. *Ibid.*, p. 67.
22. Jean-François Lyotard, after Freud, 'Moses and monotheism', in *Gesammelte Werke*, Frankfurt: Fisher, 1962, p. 223. Cited in 'Figure foreclosed', in Andrew Benjamin (ed.), *The Lyotard Reader*, Oxford: Basil Blackwell, 1989, p. 84.
23. *Ibid.*, p. 83.
24. Benjamin, *Art, Mimesis and the Avant-garde*, p. 88.
25. *Ibid.*, p. 90.
26. *Ibid.*
27. Lyotard, 'Figure foreclosed', p. 82.
28. *Ibid.*, p. 84.
29. Benjamin, *Art, Mimesis and the Avant-garde*, p. 89.
30. Kitaj, 'Prefaces', p. 153.
31. Edward Said, 'Reflections on exile', *Granta*, no. 13, Autumn 1984, p. 159.
32. Kitaj, *First Diasporist Manifesto*, p. 89.
33. Zygmund Bauman, *Modernity and Ambivalence*, Cambridge: Polity Press, 1991, p. 97.
34. Kitaj, 'Prefaces', p. 153.
35. Kitaj, in an unpublished correspondence with Andrew Brighton, kindly loaned to me by Andrew Brighton.
36. Andrew Brighton, 'Conversations with R. B. Kitaj', *Art in America*, June 1986, p. 100.
37. Michel de Certeau, *The Writing of History*, New York: Columbia University Press, 1988, p. 314.
38. Jean-Paul Sartre, *Réflexions sur la question juive* (my translation), pp. 98–9.
39. Ilan Halevi, *A History of the Jews*, London: Zed Books, 1987, pp. 129–30.
40. In discussion with me, London, January 1988.
41. Kitaj, 'Prefaces', p. 152.
42. Kitaj, 'A Passion', p. iii.
43. Benjamin, *Art, Mimesis and the Avant-garde,* p. 89.
44. Emmanuel Levinas, *The Levinas Reader*, ed. Sean Hand, Oxford: Basil Blackwell, 1989, pp. 267–8.
45. Bauman, *op. cit.*, p. 81.

Speak, You Also

Speak, you also,
Speak as the last,
have your say.

Speak –
But keep yes and no unsplit.
And give your say this meaning:
give it the shade.

Give it shade enough,
give it as much
as you know has been dealt out between
midnight and midday and midnight.

Look around:
look how it all leaps alive –
where death is! Alive!
He speaks truly who speaks the shade.

But now shrinks the place where you stand:
Where now, stripped by shade, will you go?
Upward. Grope your way up.
Thinner you grow, less knowable, finer.
Finer: a thread by which
it wants to be lowered, the star:
to float farther down, down below
where it sees itself gleam: in the swell
of wandering words.

Paul Celan, trans. Michael Hamburger

(from *Paul Celan: Selected Poems*, Harmondsworth:
Penguin, 1990, p. 99; reproduced by kind permission
of Anvil Press Poetry Ltd, UK, and Persea Books Inc.,
USA)

10

Remembering and forgetting: the sublime Jew and other modern myths

Speak, you also,
speak as the last,
have your say.

Paul Celan

In his essay 'Reflections on forgetting', Yerushalmi, citing Friedrich Nietzsche, observed, 'We must know the right time to forget as well as the right time to remember.'[1] I imagine that most people would assent to this assertion because the point is essentially banal. But, more important, it raises the question – given the need both to remember and to forget, where are the lines to be drawn? So Yerushalmi goes on to ask: how much history and what kind of history? What should we remember? What can we afford to forget? Although, as he reminds us, these questions are unresolvable, they are urgent, and always, in the course of things, apparently resolved. Today, a little more than a half-century since the liberation of the Nazi death camps these questions continue to be crucial. This final chapter draws out and reiterates some of the problems which have already been encountered, through pointing to different tropes and discourses.

A recurring question posed by the Jew in the Modern is how to memorialize and represent the Shoah. During the last few years there has been an explosion of Holocaust memorials: museums such as those in Washington, DC, and Los Angeles; films, such as *Schindler's List* and *Sophie's Choice*; graphic novels, like *Maus* and *Holocaust for Beginners*. Each in its different way tries to expose the events and educate us, by providing explanations for this human-inflicted horror. Each of these representations provokes us to question the ways in which the Shoah is mediated and circulated in the institutions, discourses and the memory of contemporary culture. Yet it is not possible and probably not even desirable to agree upon criteria that can judge the legitimacy of these different endeavours. Rather we might see each as a preferred but temporary solution, and as such open to doubt and critical reasoning. Representation works as an inconstant, changeable and ambivalent sign whose signifiers, like shifting sands, are subject to endless equivocation.

To turn again to Yerushalmi:

> Today, Jewry lives a bifurcated life. As a result of emancipation in the diaspora and national sovereignty in Israel, Jews have re-entered the mainstream of history and yet their perception of how they got there and where they are is often more mythical than real.[2]

People are formed individually and collectively. Myth in this context can be understood as the form of power that comes from bringing together and mobilizing the fundamental forces and beliefs of a people.[3] Myth is the articulation of a deep, concrete and embodied identity. History is one of our myths. It brings together what can be thought and its origin. It combines them in ways that give us insight into a culture's understanding of its own workings. It is a great mistake to think that history is solely about the past.

Jewish identity – and I loosely borrow the following formulations from Gillian Rose in her book, *Judaism and Modernity* – has recently been postulated variously as the 'sublime other' of Modernity, as something waiting at the 'end of philosophy', as the 'terrible essence' of Modernity.[4] The past is brought into the present: past and present intertwine and get caught up with the aesthetic question of representation. As we have seen throughout this book, visual art and its exhibition play a telling role in the processes of narrating the past and mobilizing identity. Kampf's exhibitions demonstrated an exclusive preoccupation with Jewish identity as a return to history. Perhaps Andrew Benjamin's use of Jewish thought as a way out of the impasse of Enlightenment philosophy may be seen as akin to Kampf's venture within art history.

These tendencies seem to be shared by a number of post-modern thinkers, for example, Elizabeth Grosz, who argues that the work of Jabès, Derrida and Levinas collectively functions as a counter-tradition through and in which Jewish identity can be assumed and Western thought redeemed. Whilst it can easily be seen that these writers offer radical critiques and 'deconstructions' of Western metaphysics, is it truly the case that they do so from an entirely *Jewish* perspective, as Grosz would seem to claim?

Grosz herself opposes homogeneity, which is, as she says, symptomatic of assimilation and creates instead a notional 'positive' history for the Jews which figures as self-representation. She argues that the Jew, as an exile,

> automatically has access to (at least) two different kinds of discourse and history, one defined by exclusion from a social mainstream; and one provided autonomously from its own history and self-chosen representations. This is a position uniquely privileged in terms of social transgression and renewal.[5]

She reiterates the Jew as already possessing an identity which itself will precipitate social change and by implication lead to the amelioration of society. Levinas points to the paradox when he writes that the fact of questioning Jewish identity means it is already lost. Moreover, to seek out the 'identity' of Jewish thought is also to assume a 'pure' identity. Hence Grosz posits an incontestable and immutable meaning for Jew.

Against this thinking Gillian Rose describes *Jewish* philosophy in modernity as occupying the same point as Enlightenment Philosophy – both having emerged at the same moment of crisis. She proposes instead

> that the relationship between philosophy and Judaism be explored neither in terms which presuppose self-identity nor in terms of mutual opposition but in terms of their evident loss of self-identity – when they are cast into crisis, chronic and acute; when they are exposed at their deepest difficulty.[6]

Rose is not describing an 'either/or' situation. Nor does she conceive of *Jewish* thought as a component to be added to Enlightenment philosophy but sees it as integral to it and *vice versa*, describing the inextricable indebtedness of each to the other. Hence we can begin to understand that 'loss' of identity can turn into other identities which entail transformation. She goes on to explain that modern philosophy is paradoxically at its most uncertain where it is comprehended as being most certain about its premises, 'finitude, secularity, man'. For at its core lies evasion and ambivalence about each of these meanings. Rose's work offers a radical approach to demystify the *Jew* in the modern and in its effects cautions us against re-inventing and shoring up the Jew in an identity.

The sublime, as we have seen, has re-emerged as a category in art criticism as a way of describing the 'presentation of the unpresentable', as perhaps a way of coping with or displacing the enervation produced by the plethora of images in the 'society of the spectacle'. The rhetoric of the sublime effectively conceals its own contradictions. The emotion it arouses is connected with disordered, appalling, boundless phenomena. Zizek observes that the sublime is 'where the aesthetic imagination is strained to its utmost, where all finite determinations dissolve themselves, the failure appears at its purest'.[7] The sublime then is paradoxical and provides a view, in a negative way, of what is unrepresentable. Is it a coincidence that the sublime, as a notion, has as well percolated through to the representations of the *Jew*? And that these various appeals to the sublime themselves represent not just an avoidance, or discretion, or again not just the limits of rational thought, but also some sort of an emerging consensus about 'how', as well as 'what' it is 'possible' to represent and not?

Correspondingly, does this mean that, after all, there is already in place an idea of what constitutes an appropriate or indeed inappropriate language for the language of memorialization? In the rules and terms of reference of the competition for the monument and memorial site to be dedicated to the Jewish victims of the Nazi regime in Austria, 1938–1945, it was stated that it would be unlikely that 'figurative' work would be recommended for the project: 'the City of Vienna have expressed reservations regarding a figurative design. This is, however, the only restriction regarding the artistic means selected.' [8] A taboo such as this placed upon language or 'means' poses complex questions as to the possible meanings of this foreclosure. It seems to repeat the misguided opposition in modernist aesthetics between 'abstraction' and 'figuration'. However, a regulative and programmatic aim can never regulate itself, and disjunctures are bound to occur. Moreover, it is the very possibilities inherent in language, including visual languages, which open signification to something beyond the logic of a framing identity. Meanings are both organized and unstable, hence we are provided with the very possibilities of meaning. Every work of art offers the prospect of many readings, many interpretations, and in the historical context of both its making and its reception some readings may be preferred over others – preferred by the artist, by the spectator and by the critic. These 'preferences' occur in specific contexts and provide a frame for meanings which do not necessarily define them, restrict them or fix them forever in an identity.

Adorno's declaration that 'to write lyric poetry after Auschwitz is barbaric' is also, of course, an interdiction.[9] But the stricture that he imposed alludes to the danger of sentimentalizing Auschwitz, not to a prohibition on the writing of poetry: 'It is now virtually in art alone that suffering can still find its own voice, consolation, without immediately being betrayed by it.'[10] His thought sets a limit which may be excessive as well as justifiable – insofar as it can be argued that he already anticipated the cultural industry that Auschwitz has now become. His writing contains the demand that serious art should serve the honour of serious thought, which itself deserves serious art. Perhaps, after all, it is only art, for which there can be no recipes in advance, that can disrupt and disturb by analogous possibilities, and can offer meanings that can speak of this still difficult to grasp historical reality – the Shoah. Critical reflections upon these aesthetic questions, which themselves circle and crystallize around the problem of representation and its limits, need to be continually developed and need to embrace the uncertainties posed by critical rationality as well as its antithesis. By taking on these paradoxical risks, our thoughts could then turn to the ways in which signification gets done and meanings are made manifest in specific contexts which can themselves avoid the temptation of giving art a prescriptive identity. Surely one of the important points of art is to undo identity and renounce essences?

In a critical discussion of Kitaj's art in general Michael Podro has suggested,

> Painting is unlike literature because language can be part of political action and at the same time it is saturated with complicated meaning. And the poet or historian can retrace the action through the language. But painting and the historical facts never engage each other so easily.[11]

While his general points are true, they can be understood as a testimony to the difficulties of painting, the problematics and possibilities of visual representation. Up to now I have been critical of Kitaj's project but there are works of his which escape the logic of the contradictions that my text has sought to expose. *If Not, Not* is, I believe, one such work (Figure 22). Indeed at its best an image such as *If Not, Not* tests those limits and can be seen as a 're-affirmation'. It is situated at the intersection of history and narrative. Like a fantasy it tells a story of what has been made in a tradition. It provides a site for a plurality of interpretations. It is an image neither of affirmation nor of negation. It provokes thinking about the Holocaust, yet is not reducible to its narration. The image is a combination of beauty and terror, and the one does not conceal the other. No certainty, not un-certainty is its condition. Abraham is an absence whose presence cannot be presented. The Jew cannot be represented. In the allusive space between presence and absence, the subject is realized. It is not that the work is endlessly open, rather there is an openness *within* the picture. It provokes us to think about certain themes – the Bible, ethics, European history and literature – yet it prompts an awareness of the existence of the blind spot, the 'I don't know' to any one of those possibilities. I think it is a brave painting precisely because it risks identity and fails to secure it.[12] It is bold in another sense as it has emerged at a time when the critical climate, philosophical thinking or more properly speaking, its translation into art criticism has stood against the representational function of art which is not seen as offering a prospect from which critical reflection can emerge. An art such as Kitaj's which seeks to engage so fervently with the grand narratives of modernity is indeed vulnerable and almost bound to receive, in such a context, critical derision.

Figure 22. R. B. Kitaj, *If Not, Not*, 1975–6, oil on canvas, 152.4 ×
152.4 cm, Scottish National Gallery of Modern Art,
Edinburgh. With kind permission of the artist.

Serious philosophical work of the present cannot avoid the demand
that the Shoah continues to make upon thought and the continued
need to contest this very demand. While historical elaboration and
knowledge remain vital, representation and the way it structures
memory and knowledge no longer pertain in an unproblematic sense.
We cannot feign innocence. The Shoah remains as an insult to thinking.
Vigilance is called for, especially in a context which witnesses the
growth of such Holocaust cultural industries as the US Holocaust
Museum in Washington, DC, where the mode of display, the nature of
representation, is a matter for critical scrutiny.

The underlying assumption of the Washington Museum's display is that we relate to history by being implicated in it, by having an 'experience' of it. Accordingly, each visitor receives at random a card with a name, a picture and information about a real victim of the Shoah. As the visitor proceeds through the museum, more information about the assumed person is gathered in an attempt, as Ken Johnson has put it, 'to make you experience the Holocaust from close, personal range, as something that happened to real people in real places'.[13] There is a tragic literalness or perhaps a tragedy invested in the literalness that is being enacted here. The museum experience, akin to that of a theme park, suggests that in order to overcome the loss of memory (history), the loss itself must be actually inscribed. The Shoah is aestheticized by linking it to experience. Jean Baudrillard, commenting upon simulation in general, stages the possibility of a critique of the Museum:

> Thus the prophecy is realised: we live in a world of simulation, in a world where the highest function of the sign is to make reality disappear and at the same time to mask this disappearance. Art does nothing else. The media today do nothing else. That is why art and the media follow the same course, and often become confused with one another.[14]

Simulation is not simply a question of truth or falsity. Signs, Baudrillard argues, now construct the real as simulation. The role of simulation is to camouflage the fact that the 'real' America is already destroyed. Thereby simulation ensures that the reality principle is not threatened. This is an alibi and also a decoy: the lure of projection. The spectator in the Holocaust Museum is a *manoeuvre* of the exhibition. In other words, the notion of disinterested or 'passive' viewing has become, in Baudrillard's diagnosis, suspect in the calculations of some exhibition curators, artists and spectators themselves.[15] And this is because seemingly we are not involved enough. So we are literally projected *into* an exhibition: subjects of it and subject to it. This lack of differentiation between the subject and object forecloses difference. It is the subject's position in relation to the distinctness of the other that is crucial insofar as it provides the axis of the ethical and entails a demand: decision and judgement.

Notions of empathy and identification might on the face of it appear ethically benign. But they can also disguise a tyrannical design. Such 'experience' as we are manoeuvred to have in the Museum assumes that we shall emerge with full comprehension. A well-intentioned aim to give the 'data' of the Holocaust can rebound and produce in its participants a response which produces the reverse of the outcome that the narrative is intended to inspire. In effect, little knowledge of the portentous evil is delivered and the demand of judgement or decision is annulled. Inadvertently perhaps, the Museum display has staged a limit, a limit to identification, by claiming to know and to feel what is in essence unknowable and beyond the reach of common feeling.

In his reflections on mechanical reproduction, Walter Benjamin saw the possibility of the spectator being both more and less critical, more distracted for the sake of criticality.[16] The new technologies, he suggested, shock the viewer into new perceptions. But he insisted on maintaining a space between closeness and distance, for criticality. By 1967, in *The Society of Spectacle*, Guy Debord wrote that spectacle dominates the consumerist West. Then in 1988, a year before the collapse of the Berlin Wall, Debord argued that the spectacle integrated West and East. For him, Benjamin's equivocation had become insupportable: critical distance was doomed. Spectacle had subsumed criticality, which had eliminated distance. Baudrillard asks what is at stake in the hegemonic trend towards virtuality?

> It would seem to be the radical actualization, the unconditional realization, of the world, the transformation of all our acts, of all our historical events, of all material substance and energy into pure information. The ideal would be the resolution of the world by the actualization of all facts and data.[17]

We witness in the Holocaust Museum the 'virtual' and its consequences. Recently, Paul Virilio has argued that Fukayama is right: 'it is the end of history and the start of another history, that of events, of the "live".'[18] If we envisage the annulment of history we are also obliged to take account of the diminution of the field of reflection. One of the traditions of democracy is to have granted reflection as a right. All historians have undertaken painstaking research in books, in chronicles and archives. Contemplative thought takes a long time and understanding and comprehension come slowly: these processes cannot be short-circuited. We must pay attention to the types of history, to the types of engagement and reflection that are brought about. The Holocaust Museum reminds us of the difficulty occasioned by the respectful connecting of memory to history. Moreover, it leaves us with the uncertain task of elaborating a critical recovery in the present of the past which, counter to the Museum's own assumptions, is not assimilable to accessible experience. The importance of remembering is matched by the impossibility of knowing. Never being able to know poses a limit, an experience of a limit – a critical experience of a limit – which the simulated experience fails to know.

Brecht's ideas about theatre, his notions of the 'alienation' technique, provide a powerful antidote to those of the Museum. They were to provide theatre with a method through which the tradition based on empathy could be turned over or displaced. He strove to explode the division between 'emotion' and 'intellect', the very schism that the

Figure 23. Lily Markiewicz, *Places to Remember II*, 1995, photo-sound
installation, Imperial War Museum. Reproduced with kind
permission of the artist.

Holocaust Museum experience would seem to reiterate. The display
uses similar conventions to those of naturalism, and shows real objects,
such as 2000 shoes retrieved from Auschwitz and actual barracks from
Birkenau. 'Realism' did not mean for Brecht representing things as they
are, as in the tradition of naturalism. It means

> discovering the causal complexes of society / unmasking the prevailing
> view of things as the view of those who are in power / writing from
> the standpoint of the class which offers the broadest solutions for the
> pressing difficulties in which human society is caught up / emphasizing
> the element of development / making possible the concrete, and making
> possible abstraction from it.[19]

In other words, as Joan Key explains, it is 'a representation of "what
is real" with the intention of re-ordering our assumptions'. However,
in the rupture between naturalism and realism, as Key goes on to argue,
'between our regular acceptances of appearances and our questioning
of why they may be that way, a testing of reality takes place. This is a
political confrontation.'[20] At this moment of breach, it becomes possible
to ask ourselves why this particular structure of the 'real' is in place
and what are its consequences. So if, as in the case of the Washington
Museum, a narrative is presented in which the inevitability of its own
conclusions are borne out – survival or non-survival; life or death –

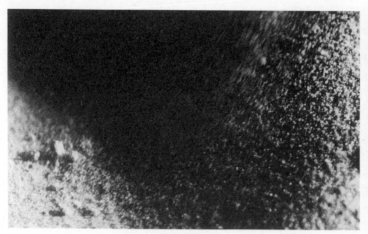

Figure 24. (*above and right*) Lily Markiewicz, *Places to Remember II*, 1995, two black and white photographs on canvas, 1.20 m × 1.92 m each, one colour photograph on canvas, 1.20 m × 82 cm. Reproduced with kind permission of the artist.

assumptions are merely reiterated since the individuals' suffering is not referred back to the operations of power from whence it derived. In a chronological account such as this one, there is always a series of 'befores' and 'afters' which make the outcome appear timely and inevitable. The event just happened. We can leave the Museum secure in our knowledge that after all it did not happen to 'us': unjustly, just to a 'companion', in another time and another place. In the street, as we approach or depart, we can see rubbish bins overflowing with debris – the discarded identity cards – and either way we return home.

Ken Johnson is also concerned about the choice of work by contemporary artists commissioned for the permanent collection of art in the Museum. All but one, Joel Shapiro, shun, as he puts it, 'overtly symbolic' art. Richard Serra, Sol Le Wit and Ellsworth Kelly all make resolutely non-referential works that seem to work in the context of this museum as decoys for endless projection. This poses for him an 'interesting art-critical question'. He wonders why art by, for example, Christian Boltanski, Anselm Keiffer and others such as Jenny Holzer, George Segal and Hans Haacke, who he claims 'have combined interest in issues of politics and morality with innovative ideas about the politics of art', were not chosen.[21] My question is somewhat different: Why include art at all in a museum such as this one? In a double turn, history is again aestheticized and art politicized.

We should take heed of Walter Benjamin's remark to the effect that fascism aestheticizes politics and communism politicizes art.[22]

Young, on the basis of President Carter's speech at the first Days of Remembrance, in 1979, explains the official American justification for a national memorial to the Shoah, in the nation's capital:

> [to] reinforce America's self-idealization as haven for the world's oppressed. It would serve as a universal warning against the bigotry and anti-democratic forces underpinning such a catastrophe and call attention to the potential in all other totalitarian systems for such slaughter.[23]

This was the beginning of what has become, in the words of the Museum's project director, Michael Berenbaum, the 'Americanization of the Holocaust'. The Museum narrative optimistically ends with the 'return to life' theme. America is the standard through which democracy is to be measured. The successful assimilation of Jews is the self-assuming *leitmotif* of American identity.

It is hardly surprising that the Museum has produced diverse responses, and to quote Young again, it has created a competition between the 'various cults of victimization'.[24] Hence, yet again, unable to resist the trap of identity politics, constricted versions of identity emerge to compete over the hegemony's right to memorialize often pitiable pasts. Aggressive counter-attack is affirmed. However, as we have noted, we all belong to many communities and one cannot act as a radical democratic citizen solely on the basis of any one identity. Contained within this logic are always essentialist strands which inhibit rational thought and impede change.

By way of contrast, *After Auschwitz* was a small, carefully crafted exhibition held in the Imperial War Museum, London.[25] The gallery was divided into discrete spaces for each display. Well-orchestrated, the works quietly resounded. Each artist created a work which addressed the Shoah and its aftermath. Jean-Sylvain Bieth's *Phoenix* is a subtle comment on the resistance to management structures and systems that engineered the Shoah. The banality of Melissa Gould's way of drawing *Schadenfreude: The Delight Experienced in Someone Else's Misfortune* denotes what it masks in its horrifying connotations. Pam Skelton in *Dangerous Places: Ponar* tells the story of one survivor. Without beginning or end, endlessly repeated on seven videos in different temporal sequences, the work creates a sense of enervation which is inescapable. *Places to Remember*, a series of photographs by Lily Markiewicz, refuse identification and mark a distancing from one potential meaning at the expense of others (Figures 23 and 24). The exhibition as a whole suggested remembrance of the Holocaust which, in its modesty, avoided glamorizing it. It did not rely upon a 'simulation' of the event. It did, however, provoke. Everything shown was ordinary but precisely extraordinary, as it subverted familiar views of the Shoah. With precision and economy, *After Auschwitz* took us to the boundary of a lingering horror which was, after all, in the details of its operations, prosaic and orderly.

Bauman argues that the Shoah was not 'private property'. It is not simply a '*Jewish problem* and not an event in Jewish *history alone*' [author's emphases].[26] It is rooted in the mainstream of modernity, in the so-called civilizing process. Once Hitler had decided to make all of Europe *Judenrein*, it only remained for the technical specialists to calculate the most effective methods for otherwise mundane organizations to carry out their assigned tasks smoothly. Nazi propaganda deployed modern metaphors from gardening and medicine in its plan to eliminate 'social weeds' and 'diseased parts'. Thus it was that the numerous low-level perpetrators could believe that they were implementing a scientific project of social sanitation. The Holocaust could only happen so long as people accepted and conspired with its own logic and failed to act or exercise moral choice. The world Bauman is describing is one where obedience obeys its own logic and rationality is obedience. This is a closed world, governed by its own laws and rules which may themselves be illogical and irrational or pseudo-rational. Rationality, which is inherent in modern bureaucracy, can easily become askew.

The Holocaust was only thinkable within a modern institutionalized world. Its exceptional character lay in dehumanizing the objects of the bureaucratic exercise so that ordinary diligent workers would regard their victims with moral indifference. Bauman is describing a world in which institutions and discourses have shattered any connections that might have been said to exist between ethics and reason, necessity and freedom, and law.

The Polish historian Franciszek Piper, who has gone to work at the Auschwitz–Birkenau Museum and Archive every day for the past thirty years, cautions:

> Auschwitz can be repeated, not as a camp with barbed wire, gas chambers and crematoria, but as mass murder. Auschwitz happened not because of thousands of men in SS and other uniforms, but because millions were indifferent. Neither the victims nor the perpetrators came out of this with any advantage. Auschwitz is a tragedy. But it is also a great human absurdity.[27]

Perhaps this can only lead us to an unanswerable question: can we really accept that the Holocaust was in its essence 'absurd', or in Hannah Arendt's phrase represented 'the banality of evil'? Or is this not rather our human perception of the appearance of the organizers and perpetrators of the Holocaust, in short, our fellow humans? Or can we suggest that in this there is room for retrospection? We were there without having experienced it, hence, paradoxically, our amnesia. We are implicated as individual agents capable of yielding and assenting to the thrill and pleasures of overcoming but also of opposing and taking on the dilemmas of living politically. As Bauman puts it:

> putting self-preservation above moral duty is in no way pre-determined, inevitable and inescapable . . . The testimony of the few who did resist shatters the authority of the logic of self-preservation. It shows it for what it is in the end – a choice.[28]

In its sobriety, the exhibition *After Auschwitz* said that in the face of the Shoah we should remain silent but cannot.

> Speak –
> But keep yes and no unsplit,
> And give your say this meaning:
> give it the shade.

The voice of Celan returns from the disaster to remind us of what is still critical. He could be telling us to bring things together in the half-light that is the 'shade'. But breaching the abyss between 'yes', affirmation, and 'no', negation, is not to offer us an image of either unity or certainty. For the shade is also the underworld and what might be promised is already belied. The poem offers no consolation, simply the recognition that there are some things which have yet to be said. Celan's poems in general subvert any attempt to crystallize difference into identity and evade decoded understandings. They display the consideration of ethical problems in the more general questions of identity and interpretation. His works acknowledge the injustice and justice of life and death, yet resist judgement in any simple sense. They engage with the difficulties of modernity without trying to avoid them. Celan's work has been described by Philippe Lacoue-Labarthe as immortalizing 'silence'. Perhaps it does memorialize the yet-to-be-named, the unnameable or unspeakable and is poised at the threshold of naming. This is not silence but its intermittence. I am reminded here of Lacan's view of 'intermittences' mentioned earlier, and their effects on man's desire:

> What he desires presents itself to him as what he does not want . . . he transfers the permanence of his desire to an ego that is nevertheless intermittent, and inversely protects himself from his desire by attributing to it these very intermittences.[29]

Lyotard interprets Auschwitz as a 'sign' which imposes silence:

> Myth is not speculatively soluble. It must be (non-speculatively) exterminated and so it has been. But the destruction of Nazism also leaves a silence after it: one does not dare to think out Nazism because it has been beaten down like a mad dog, by police action, and not in conformity with the rules accepted by its adversaries' genres of discourse (argumentation for liberalism, contradiction for Marxism). It has not been refuted.[30]

Auschwitz is silenced because it has been murdered, not refuted. Lyotard presents the proper name, Auschwitz, as an abyss where the genre of dialectic thought is repudiated: 'We wanted the progress of the mind, we got its shit.'[31] The crime signalled by the name is real. It marks the limits of historical knowledge and understanding. In that chasm all narratives fail. Lyotard argues that between the SS and the Jew there is no dispute (*differend*) because there is no common or shared idiom. The inability of dialectics to conceptualize Auschwitz raises the fundamental question about the limits of knowledge. Baudrillard says that Auschwitz is the primal scene of modern society, that it is the murder of the neighbour that cannot be confronted.[32]

Nevertheless we should be cautious, for there is a danger that these kinds of philosophical reflections elevate or denigrate and make it impossible to distinguish, as Rose warns, the 'emblematic objects beyond even mythic meaning'.[33] Thus the Shoah can be represented as displaying all the qualities of myth, that it is unknowable, blurred and vague, and as such it can also be used as a refusal to 'know'. Auschwitz is not just a metaphor, the pre-eminent sign of horror. Auschwitz is not just about refutation or evasion. Claude Lanzmann's film, *Shoah*, makes this plain.[34] This film is, I think, one of the most substantial memorials to the history of the Holocaust. Confounding expectations, Lanzmann uses and subverts the language of 'documentary realism' to create images of extraordinarily powerful poetic resonance. Lanzmann charges his witnesses, both survivors and perpetrators, to answer unbearable questions, for which every reply is inadequate and is at the same time too much. He has written,

> Legends are never laid to rest by pitching them against memory. They must, if possible, be confronted in their inconceivable presents from which they draw their being. The only way to achieve this is precisely by resuscitating the past and making it present, by resuscitating it in a timeless present.[35]

The film mingles past with present in a series of extraordinary interviews and pictures from Auschwitz, Sobibor and Treblinka today. The film defies and shatters chronology. If there is unity in the film it is only figured in the unceasing sound, the rhythm of trains and the voices which refer to them. Unlike sight, sound cannot be fixed. The voices speak of arrivals, of wagons being opened and of bodies falling out, of thirst, of fear of not knowing, of the procedures of 'disinfection', of the gas chambers being opened. Endless repetition but never repetitive. The film has been likened by Simone de Beauvoir to a musical composition in which musical phrases recur and are repeated again and again. But, as she also suggests, this is not a question of aestheticism: rather, in *Shoah* beauty and dread are combined with inventiveness and austerity.[36] Here no traces are obliterated.

There are the voices which tell us with clarity and exactness about the extermination. There is the train-driver who was plied with vodka by the Germans because he could not bear the sound of the thirsty children he was transporting. The Polish peasants who even now are indifferent to what happened on the neighbouring land, and in some cases to their neighbours, whose very homes some of them live in today. There was the state employee who described the holiday or group excursion tickets purchased by the Gestapo out of the Jews' confiscated possessions. The historian Raul Hilberg tells us that the Jews who were 'transferred' were regarded as holiday-makers by the travel agency that arranged the transport. There were the rare voices of survivors, some of whom can hardly speak. The whole work is punctuated by the racket of the trains rushing inexorably to their destinations. For Lanzmann, the Final Solution is not the outcome of an account. It is the account of a point of departure. Through the workings of the film, and in our responses to it, we face the potential of our own complicity in such a disastrous turn in historical events. Lanzmann's painstaking, almost surgical, examination of the Shoah allows us to bear witness and to testify to the undeniable pervasiveness of evil.

Auschwitz was a Nazi concentration camp which functioned as a death camp in Poland in the 1940s. It was and is a reality which it is necessary to remember not only for the victims, the survivors, the perpetrators and our own sakes, but also for revisionists such as David Irving and Jean-Marie Le Pen. Attacks on Jews continue. The sculptural installation by the artist Daniel Buren, commissioned for a site in the courtyard of the Palais Royale, Paris, unleashed virulent opposition which was reported in *Le Monde*: 'It can be nothing other than the work of a Jew, not surprisingly with this Jewish Minister and this government of Jews.' More: 'Jack Lang, dirty Jew, give us back your cash. No one but a Jew or a nigger can understand this aberration.'[37] The last decade has also witnessed the desecration of Jewish cemeteries, for example, in Edmonton, England, and in Carpentras, France. The age-old anxieties, as Adorno and Horkheimer remind us, inexorably return: 'Even the last resting place is emptied of peace. The destruction of cemeteries is not a mere excess of anti-semitism – it is anti-semitism in essence.'[38]

We have been witnessing the processes of forming national identities and the inevitable exclusions these have occasioned. The representation of the Other is itself a political presentation and sets up the drive for a liberating politics which can be figured as a politics of overcoming. The politics of overcoming through the drama of collective identification produces a solution, mastery and suppression. Violent overcoming, in the name of the Master, has been the means of countering the modern anxiety of identity and non-identity. In this discourse, the *Jew* is the hidden Master who is bent on destabilizing the fabric of society. He is the 'terrible essence' of Modernity. Lacoue-Labarthe maintains that fascism mobilized the identificatory emotion of the masses and made itself subject in terms which were absolute. It politicized desire and fear, negated them and obliterated others in a radical synthesis. He interprets the aestheticization of politics as the essence of National Socialism. Quoting Goebbels on this theme, he argues that the work of art does not merely provide the truth of the state but the political is 'instituted and constituted in and as a work of art'. Goebbels declared in a letter to Wilhelm Furtwängler, dated 11 April 1933:

> Politics, too, is perhaps an art, if not the highest and most all-embracing art there is. Art and artists are not only there to unite; their far more important task is to create a form, to expel the ill trends and make room for the healthy to develop.[39]

The identification of the work of art with politics was the most effective way of a nation finding its identity. It assumed that there exists a fixed, unified culture claiming superiority for its own in relation to others. Through the travesty of pseudo-rationalism, racist ideology was further perverted into the actualities of extermination more recently described as ethnic cleansing. *Jew* was the embodiment of ugliness from which the nation must be purged and cleansed. He lies outside of civilization and was the antithesis of European aesthetic values. Racism assumes purity. This is why, as Lacoue-Labarthe argues, racism

> goes hand in hand, no less fundamentally, with a massive unleashing of *techne*, which is in fact its radical transmutation into *excrescence*, which proceeds increasingly to conceal *physis*, whose limits it oversteps, having lost sight of or 'forgotten' them. There is a kind of 'lethal' essence of technology, which means that its 'everything is possible' does in fact end up introducing, that is to say *being about*, if not the impossible, then the unthinkable. Extermination or genetic manipulation – and the latter is still on the agenda today.[40]

The technological features of modern society harnessed to notions of progress and the work ethic provided the constellation of forces for overthrow and destruction. Purification was the means by which fascism strove to mould its subjects. The desire to abolish discord and conflict is precisely the origin of totalitarian seduction: how many murderous acts have been committed in the name of harmony, of *being* without hostility and strain? Fascism made 'false projection' political. It demonstrates the violence of politics when aestheticized, and displays the conceptual beauty of the unified and the universal.

In the realm of politics today, the idea of the universal is increasingly represented as an old-fashioned totalitarian dream. However, politics cannot be adequately represented as a choice between the universal and the particular, or between identity and difference. The ethics of universalism should not be abandoned in their entirety. After all, the universal is only the proliferation of the particular. Ernesto Laclau points out that the 1990s teem with the demands of particular groups which present unique problems and may display their own deficiencies:

> The assertion of pure particularism, independent of any content and of any appeal to a universality, is a self-defeating enterprise. For if it is the only accepted normative principle, it confronts us with an unresolvable paradox. I can defend the rights of sexual, racial, and national minorities in the name of particularism, but only if particularism is the only valid principle, I have to accept the rights to self-determination of all kinds of reactionary groups involved in anti-social practices.[41]

It follows, then, that not all differences can be sanctioned and safeguarded, especially in circumstances where they emerge as forms of domination or subordination of self or others. The terrain occupied by subjects will never be unified and harmonious. Society is founded upon antagonism, which itself provides the shield that prevents democracy from sliding into totalitarianism. Every solution is provisional and temporary, a deferral of a fundamentally unrealizable project that is democracy. By facing the reality of this predicament we might be able to avoid the seemingly inexorable and inextricable cycle of guilt and accusation, attack and counter-attack.

It is important now to consider redefinitions of the horizons of the universal and by so doing begin to sever the assumed or 'natural' connection between the universal and the nation. The work of Levinas may offer a way of breaching the abyss between the universal and the singular, between ethics and individual responsibility. His paradigm of the 'originary' encounter is the discovery of the responsibility for the existence of the Other:

> The explication of the meaning that a self other than myself has *for me* – for my primordial self – describes the way in which the Other tears me from my hypostasy, from the *here*, at the heart of being or at the centre of the world, where privileged and in this sense primordial, I posit myself. But in this tearing, the ultimate 'me-ness' is revealed.[42]

Levinas is describing an event predicated upon violence. This dramatic wrenching gives birth to subjectivity and consciousness. It is this that makes me what I am not: outside of me and different from me. The subject is not the sovereign master of that event. This ordeal is itself the basis of moral consciousness, of the possibility of making promises and of future action.

Hence Levinas proposes the Other as outside the sphere of mastery, neither as in relation to the self nor as a reduplication of the self. He offers a way of thinking the Other as 'responsibility for the other, being-for-the-other'. His thinking presents a challenge to identity thinking which is, he argues, just

> a reconciliation of contradictions: from the identical and the non-identical, identity! It is still the philosophy of the intelligibility of the Same, beyond the tension of the Same and the Other.[43]

Levinas, in Lyotard's words, attempts to 'break this reversible totality and to discombobulate speculative dialectics by reinforcing the dissymmetry of the ethical instances'.[44] Indeed, Levinas himself argues that the idea of the Other as an enemy of the same is an abuse of the notion. He proposes that we should go beyond understanding which is 'equal' (the same) and which seeks to assimilate the other and instead think about the same as 'drowsy in identity' and needing to be woken by the Other. Sheer alterity is presented by him as 'other than being', and is always in excess of itself. It is infinite: 'The absolutely other, is not the other of the same, its other is the heart of that supreme sameness that is being.' The Other is not negotiable, but it is that which constitutes the subject as an ethical being. Levinas's work proposes a reorientation of 'exteriority', which, he argues, is a property of space. He attempts to keep separate and distinct the 'exteriority' of the Other – that which amazes us and is a source of wonderment – and the 'interiority' of self. Between the 'I' and the 'You' lies mystery: 'The other as other is not here an object that becomes ours or becomes us; to the contrary, it withdraws into mystery.' Mystery is not for Levinas either mystification or romance. It is the unbridgeable gulf between the self and the other, demanding not 'clarity' but greater 'intensity'. It is akin to revelation: an awakening.

This form of awakening is obedience. Obedience is irreducible: it derives from love of the Other. I am linked to others by the responsibility that I have towards them. Revelation and awakening and disruption of the same can never be absorbed by the other. Radical responsibility for the other is mine even before my freedom. Ethical obligation arises immediately from the uniqueness of the moral situation itself. It is binding.

The problem here is that such a radical substitution for the other that Levinas calls for is also the command to sacrifice oneself which can lead, as we have noted, to fundamentalist responses. Such denial produces ambiguous come-backs. Indeed as Rose maintains, it is a misunderstanding of the Other insofar as the Other is also distraught and searching for its own forms of ethical life: 'the Other is bounded and vulnerable; enraged and invested; isolated and interrelated.'[45] Misery and intolerance, as well as joyfulness and tolerance, are equally likely answers to the other's call.

Problems are stacking up and are accumulating around the configurations of the Jew as the 'terrible essence' and the 'sublime' Other of Modernity. The 'terrible' or 'sublime' Other cannot be brought into reason, into daily life, into the ordinary, into the commonplace. As I have been arguing throughout this book, *Jew* is constituted in discourse and mediated through institutions. However, I am not presenting an argument against reason, but want to stress that it is the workings of *specific* discourses and institutions which may constrain reason and which can render it antithetical, narrow and closed. The difficulty of reason, as Rose explains, is not with universality, but whether the 'initial abstract universal (the meaning or idea) *comes to learn*'; whether – as Rose goes on to say – '*something can happen to it*'; whether one abstractly universal individual enters into substantial interaction with another abstractly universal individual' (emphasis added).[46] For in so doing each one of us comes up against our own potential violence and fury. This discovery, without glossing it over, gives us the enriched possibilities of working out our relationship with others – not in terms of the impossible demand of the Other but in recognition of the other as flexible and real, as the cause of both distress and delight. Only through exposing misunder-standings or misrecognition can we yield to the true nature of the other and simultaneously subdue our feelings of envy and our sense of dis-appointment and failure.

The choice for Jews, as for non-Jews, concerns what kind of past can be had. My project has not denied Jewish 'singularity' as I have come to understand it, in the sense of identity, repetition and transformation. But more, I would like it to be understood as a refusal to homogenize or reduce it in any way. Or again perhaps I would like Jewish identity to be read so as to stage the possibility of 're-affirming' difference as Jacques Derrida has suggested, but now with respect for others, without giving way to aggression.[47] Yet it is still important to note Edward Said's caution:

> Exiles feel, [therefore], an urgent need to reconstitute their broken lives usually by choosing to see themselves as part of a triumphant ideology or a restored people. The crucial thing is that a state of exile free from this triumphant ideology – designed to re-assemble into a new whole – is virtually impossible in today's world. Look at the fate of the Jews, the Palestinians, and the Armenians.[48]

The idea of a reconstituted people offers the chance to become something else 'for the time being', or the chance to become what they once were. Or even, and most often, to become what they never were.

The desire for cultural identity may be commendable, compassionate or antagonistic – or indeed all three. It may entail real learning about the past and perhaps even self-transformation, but more often than not it plunges into slogans. Edward Said, lamenting the Gulf War, writes:

> My impression is that to be Syrian, Iraqi, Egyptian, Saudi and so on, is a quite sufficiently important end, rather than thinking critically, perhaps even audaciously about the national programme itself. Identity, always identity, over and above knowing and thinking about others.[49]

Identity politics tap into emotional dimensions of 'self' and 'community' which are today as fragile as the rain forests. Precisely because identity is weak, affirmation becomes most desperate. The 'self', as David Reason puts it, is 'the dark twin' of identity.[50] In its name, a potency and intelligibility is conferred upon discussion and action in such a way as to pre-empt rational engagement and moral debate. Since it is true that the cost and the losses precipitated by assimilation may give rise to feelings of regret, pain and anger, it is as necessary as it has ever been to resist the entrapments and seductions of identity politics. While not all groups are necessarily or essentially totalitarian, nonetheless we should proceed with the recognition that totalitarianism may be a consequence, though not the inevitable outcome, of democracy. The

kind of 'loss' which we have seen exemplified in Kitaj's *Jew* as a failure
of narcissism is bound by its own logic to supply the deficit with
exaggerated affirmation. The result of such an idealist formulation is
reductionist and determinist. Kristeva warns:

> Fundamentalists are more fundamental when they have lost all material
> ties, inventing themselves as a 'we' that is purely symbolic; lacking a
> soil it becomes rooted until it reaches its essence, which is sacrifice.[51]

Such sacrificial wounds make their appearance as the almost certain
consequence of modern life and bear witness to the broken promises of
liberal democracies. The development of the modern state has led to
the breakdown of ethics and law generally and the separation between
civil society and the state and evaded the issues of liberty and equality.

Throughout this work I have been reaching limits. At each critical
turn, the Janus-faced trap of representation has been staged. I have
described modes of representation arising from social dynamics, the
structures of Modernity and the relationship of these to political as
well as aesthetic representations. Not to have named would, as I earlier
cautioned, meant not to have written. But I have tried in my naming
to remark upon *Jewish* identity as a process of becoming and dis-
appearance. The Jew has been shown to have been made and undone.
His role has been traced in diverse places as variously a racial, cultural,
social and political category. Yet, as the processes of 'alienization' show,
he is not simply 'outside' but may be outside and inside simultaneously,
and included and excluded, and in turn may include and exclude others.
And again, he may maintain and indeed desire such an ambivalent
relationship to power. There will always be categories of Otherness
related to and recognizable as a specific category. This is unavoidable.
Kristeva reminds us:

> In the fascinating rejection that the foreigner arouses in us, there is a
> share of uncanny strangeness in the sense of the depersonalization that
> Freud discovers in it, and which takes up again our infantile desires
> and fears of the other – the other of death, the other of woman, the
> fear of the uncontrollable drive. The foreigner is within us.[52]

The foreigner signifies the difficulties of living with the self as well as
with others, as another. History has shown us that society depends on
harmonious relations with neighbours, and that this is the contract
upon which it has been founded. To live with others will only be
possible when we are able to tolerate the otherness which is our own.
The other need not be a threat but can be perceived as a way of
recognizing that which is 'strange' within ourselves. The open questions
now are: Can we reaffirm the Other without giving way to
denunciation? And how can we maintain, at one and the same time,

singularity and a relation with the universal, the self and the other, without giving way to sacrifice or mastery? These are the difficult necessities to be confronted here.

Liberating the banal, in its original sense of basic democratic virtue, has been the *raison d'être* of my project. I hope to have provided an alternative to the account of the *Jew* when he is made the criterion of European history, of truth, of reason, of civilization and of their antitheses, of myth, of ugliness, of lies, of perversity and of barbarism. I argue against this form of idealism in favour of the remembrance of the forgotten *banal*. If the Jew is understood in this way the weight of history begins to be understandable, if not necessarily any more bearable.

The banal then has been understood here as a way of remembering and as a way of standing against that other banal which turns the Shoah into entertainment, of forgetting. The *Jew* is not entertaining. I want to affirm the singularity of the Jews which all of them – and all of us – bring to human thought and relationships as well as to the workings of civilized life through daily actions, some of which are momentous, most of which are less so. In this sense they are banal but inspiring. To have begun to have thought in this way may help us salvage something from this blighted and benighted century in the hope that it will not end with the same contumacy from which, at times, it has also sought courageously to disentangle and disengage itself.

> But now shrinks the place where you stand:
> Where now, stripped by shade, will you go?
> Upward. Grope your way up.
> Thinner you grow, less knowable, finer.

Notes

1. Yosef Hayim Yerushalmi, *Zahor: Jewish History and Jewish Memory*, New York: Schocken Books, 1989, p. 107.
2. *Ibid.*, p. 99.
3. My use of the idea of *myth* here is indebted to Philippe Lacoue-Labarthe, in *Heidegger, Art and Politics,* Oxford: Basil Blackwell,1990.
4. Gillian Rose, *Judaism and Modernity: Philosophical Essays*, Oxford: Basil Blackwell, 1994.
5. Elizabeth Grosz, 'Judaism and exile: the ethics of otherness', *New Formations*, no. 12, Winter 1990, p. 87.
6. Rose, *op. cit.*, p. 18.
7. Slavoj Zizek, *The Sublime Object of Ideology*, London: Verso, 1989, p. 203.

8. *Judenplatz Wien 1996: Competition Monument and Memorial Site Dedicated to the Jewish Victims of the Nazi Regime in Austria 1938–1945,* Stadt Wien Kunsthall, Wein: Folio, 1996, p. 113.
9. Theodor Adorno, 'Commitment', in *Aesthetics and Politics*, London: Verso, 1977, p. 188.
10. *Ibid.*, p. 199.
11. Michael Podro, 'Some notes on Ron Kitaj', *Art International*, March 1979, p. 83.
12. See my discussion of this painting, 'Painting another: other-than-painting', in *Other Than Identity: The Subject of Politics and Art,* Manchester: Manchester University Press, 1977, pp. 211–21.
13. Ken Johnson, 'The art and memory', *Art in America*, November 1993, p. 97.
14. Nicholas Zurbrugg (ed.), *Jean Baudrillard: Art and Artefacts*, London: Sage Publications, 1997, p. 12.
15. *Ibid.*, p. 22.
16. In 'The work of art in the age of mechanical reproduction', in *Illuminations*, London: Fontana, 1973, Walter Benjamin argues that mechanical reproducibility threatens the aura of art, its distinctiveness, authenticity, authority, distance, and this withering frees art from ritual, 'brings things closer' to the masses. For Benjamin this collapse of distance had liberatory potential insofar as it allows culture to be shared more democratically but it also has a dark side as it permits politics to become more spectacular. Fascist or socialist? Benjamin asks, in a dramatic twist which brings his essay to a close.
17. Zurbrugg, *Jean Baudrillard*, p. 23.
18. Paul Virilio, 'Un monde surexposé', in Françoise Docquiert and François Piron (eds), *Image et politique: acts du colloque des recontres,* Arles: Actes Sud/AFAA, 1997, p. 19 (my translation).
19. *Aesthetics and Politics: Debates Between Bloch, Lukacs, Brecht, Benjamin, Adorno,* trans. and ed. Ronald Taylor, London: Verso, 1980, p. 82.
20. Joan Key, 'The human body is present by being absent: Brechtian and minimal theatre in relation to the work of Mona Hartoum and Andrea Fisher, South London Gallery, 1993', unpublished essay, August 1997, kindly loaned to me by the author.
21. Johnson, *op. cit.*, p. 92.
22. Walter Benjamin, *Illuminations*, London: Fontana, 1973, p. 244.
23. James E. Young, 'The U.S. Holocaust Memorial Museum: memory and the politics of identity', in Linda Nochlin and Tamar Garb (eds), *The Jew in the Text*, London: Thames & Hudson, 1995, p. 295.
24. *Ibid.*, p. 304.
25. *After Auschwitz: Installations,* Imperial War Museum, London, 23 February–29 May 1995.
26. Zygmunt Bauman, *Modernity and the Holocaust*, Cambridge: Polity Press, 1989, p. x.

27. Edward Serotta, 'The future of Auschwitz', *Weekend Guardian*, 21 January 1995, p. 21.
28. Bauman, *op. cit.*, p. 207.
29. See Chapter 1, p. 3.
30. Jean-François Lyotard, *The Differend: Phrases in Dispute*, Manchester: Manchester University Press, 1988, p. 106.
31. *Ibid.*, p. 91.
32. Jean Baudrillard, 'Hunting Nazis and leaving reality', *New Statesman*, 19 February 1988, pp. 6–7.
33. Rose, *op. cit.*, p. 242.
34. *Shoah*, producer/director and script, Claude Lanzmann, Les Films Aleph/Historia Films, France, 1974–85.
35. Claude Lanzmann, 'Shoah as counter-myth', trans. Jonathan Davis, *Jewish Quarterly*, Vol. 33, 1986, p. 12.
36. Simone de Beauvoir, 'Shoah', *Guardian*, 12 May 1985, p. 25.
37. Reported by Patrick Jarreau, 'La rumeur du Palais-Royal', *Le Monde*, 14 March 1986.
38. Theodor Adorno and Max Horkheimer, *Dialectic of Enlightenment*, London: Verso, 1989, p. 183.
39. Philippe Lacoue-Labarthe, *Heidegger, Art and Politics*, trans. Chris Turner, Oxford: Basil Blackwell, 1990.
40. *Ibid.*, p. 69.
41. Ernesto Laclau, 'Universalism, particularism and the question of identity', *October*, no. 61, Summer 1992, p. 87.
42. Emmanuel Levinas, 'Philosophy and awakenings', in E. Cadava, P. Connor and J. L. Nancy (eds), *Who Comes after the Subject?*, London: Routledge, 1991, p. 213.
43. *Ibid.*, p. 208.
44. Lyotard, *op. cit.*, p. 113.
45. Rose, *op. cit.*, p. 8.
46. *Ibid.*
47. Jacques Derrida, *Talking Liberties*, produced by Patricia Llewellyn, 'Wall to Wall', edited transcript Derek Jones and Rob Stoneman, Channel 4 TV, 1992, p. 9.
48. Edward Said, 'Reflections on exile', *Granta*, no. 13, Autumn 1984, p. 163.
49. Edward Said, 'Empire of sand', *Weekend Guardian*, 12/13 January 1991, pp. 4–5.
50. David Reason, 'Outside intimacy: two exhibitions of Canadian art at the Barbican Art Gallery, London', *SITE Sound*, September/October 1991, p. 30.
51. Julia Kristeva, *Strangers to Ourselves*, trans. Leon S. Roudiez, New York: Columbia University Press, 1991, p. 24.
52. *Ibid.*, p. 191.

Bibliography

Adorno, Theodor, *Negative Dialectics*, trans. E. B. Ashton, London: Routledge & Kegan Paul, 1973.

Adorno, Theodor, *Minima Moralia*, trans. E. F. N. Jephcott, London: Verso, 1989.

Adorno, Theodor, and Horkheimer, Max, *Dialectic of Enlightenment*, trans. John Cumming, London: Verso, 1989.

Adorno, Theodor, *et al.*, *The Authoritarian Personality*, New York: Norfen, 1950.

Agamben, Giorgio, *Infancy and History: Essays on the Destruction of History*, trans. Liz Heron, London and New York: Verso, 1993.

Althusser, Louis, *For Marx*, trans. B. R. Brewster, Harmondsworth: Penguin, 1969.

Appignanesi, Richard, *Postmodernism for Beginners*, Cambridge: Icon Books, 1995.

Areen, Rasheen, 'The other immigrant: the experiences and achievements of Afro Asian artists in the metropolis', *Third Text*, no.15, Summer 1991: 17–28.

Arendt, Hannah, *The Origins of Totalitarianism*, London: George Allen & Unwin, 1958.

Aronowitz, Stanley, 'Reflections on identity', *October*, Summer 1992: 91–103.

Aulich, Jim, 'The difficulty of living in an age of cultural decline and spiritual corruption, R. B. Kitaj 1965–1970', *Oxford Art Journal*, 10(2), 1987: 43–57.

Baker, Leonard, *Days of Sorrow and Pain*, Oxford: Oxford University Press, 1980.

Banham, Joanna, Macdonald, Sally and Poster, Julia, *Victorian Design*, New York: Crescent Books, 1991.

Bann, Stephen, *The Clothing of Clio: A Study of the Representation of History in 19th-Century Britain and France*, Cambridge: Cambridge University Press, 1986.

Barnett, Henrietta, *Canon Barnett: His Life and Work*, London: Longman, 1918.

Barnett, Henrietta, and Barnett, Samuel, *Practicable Socialism*, London: Longman, 1894.

Barthes, Roland, *Mythologies*, trans. Annette Lavers, London: Paladin, 1973.

Barthes, Roland, *A Lover's Discourse*, trans. Richard Howard, New York: Hill & Wang, 1982.

Barthes, Roland, *Barthes, Selected Writings*, introduced by Susan Sontag, London: Fontana/Collins, 1983.

Barthes, Roland, *Camera Lucida*, trans. Richard Howard, London: Fontana, 1984.

Barthes, Roland, *The Fashion System*, London: Jonathan Cape, 1985.

Baudrillard, Jean, *The Evil Demon of Images*, Sydney: Power Institute Publications, no. 3, 1984.

Baudrillard, Jean, 'Hunting Nazis and leaving reality', trans. Material Word, *New Statesman*, 19 February 1988, pp. 6–7.

Bauman, Zygmunt, 'Exit visas and entry tickets', *Telos*, no. 77, Fall 1988: 45–77.

Bauman, Zygmunt, *Modernity and the Holocaust*, Cambridge: Polity Press, 1989.

Bauman, Zygmunt, *Modernity and Ambivalence*, Cambridge: Polity Press, 1991.

Beaumont, Mary Rose, 'Mark Gertler', *Arts Review*, April 1992: 133.

Beauvoir, Simone de, *Adieux: A Farewell to Sartre*, trans. Patrick O'Brian, London: André Deutsch and Weidenfeld & Nicolson, 1984.

Beauvoir, Simone de, *The Second Sex*, trans. and ed. H. M. Parshley, Harmondsworth: Penguin, 1972.

Beauvoir, Simone de, '"Shoah": Claude Lanzmann', *Guardian*, 12 May 1985.

Benjamin, Andrew, *Art, Mimesis and the Avant-Garde: Aspects of a Philosophy of Difference*, London: Routledge, 1991.

Benjamin, Andrew, 'A place of refuge', *Times Literary Supplement*, 10 October 1997.

Benjamin, Andrew, and Osbourne, Peter, *Thinking Art: Beyond Traditional Aesthetics*, London: Routledge, 1991.

Benjamin, Walter, *Illuminations*, trans. Harry Zohn, London: Fontana, 1973.

Benjamin, Walter, *One Way Street and Other Writings*, trans. Edmund Jephcott and Kingsley Shorter, London: Verso, 1992.

Benjamin, Walter, *Selected Writings, Volume 1 1913–1926*, ed. Marcus Bullock and Michael W. Jennings, London: The Belknap Press of Harvard University Press, 1996.

Ben Uri Gallery, anon., *Mark Gertler*, London, 1944.

Berger, John, 'Jewish and other painting', *New Statesman and Nation*, 12 December 1953, p. 53.

Berger, John, and Mohr, Jean, *Another Way of Telling*, London: Writers and Readers, 1982.

Berger, Peter L., and Luckman, Thomas, *The Social Construction of Reality: A Treatise in the Sociology of Knowledge*, Harmondsworth: Penguin, 1971.

Berghahn, Marion, *Continental Briton: German-Jewish Refugees from Nazi Germany*, New York: Berg, 1988.

Berman, Marshall, *All That Is Solid Melts into Air: The Experience of Modernity*, London: Verso, 1983.

Bernasconi, Robert, and Critchley, Simon, *Re-Reading Levinas*, London: Athlone Press, 1991.

Bettelheim, Bruno, *Recollections and Reflections*, London: Thames & Hudson, 1990.

Bhabha, Homi K., *Nation and Narration*, London: Routledge, 1990.

Bhabha, Homi K., 'Freedom's basis in the indeterminate', *October*, no. 61, Summer 1992: 46–57.

Bhabha, Homi K., *Location of Culture*, London: Routledge, 1994.

Black, Eugene C., *The Social Politics of Anglo-Jewry 1880–1920*, Oxford: Basil Blackwell, 1988.

Blackburn, Robin (ed.), *Ideology in Social Science*, London: Fontana, 1972.

Bohm-Duchen, Monica, 'The stranger within the gates', *Third Text*, no. 15, Summer 1991: 11–15.

Booth, Charles, *Life and Labour of the People of London*, 17 vols, London: Macmillan, 1902.

Borzello, Frances, *Civilizing Caliban: The Misuse of Art 1875–1980*, London: Routledge, 1987.

Bourne, Jenny, 'Homelands of the mind: Jewish feminism and identity politics', *Race and Class*, Vol. 29, no.1, Summer 1987: 1–24.

Braudel, Fernard, *Civilization and Capitalism: 15th–18th Century*, London: Collins, 1981.

Briggs, Asa, *Victorian Cities*, Harmondsworth: Pelican, 1973.

Brighton, Andrew, 'Conversations with R.B. Kitaj', *Art in America*, June 1986: 99–104.

Brighton, Andrew, 'Clement Greenberg, Andrew Wyeth and serious art', in *Views from Abroad: American Realities*, New York: Whitney Museum of American Art, 1997, pp. 99–105.

Brody, Baruch A., *Identity and Essence*, Princeton: Princeton University Press, 1980.

Bryson, Norman, *Calligram: Essays in New Art History from France*, Cambridge: Cambridge University Press, 1989.

Bryson, Norman, *Looking at the Overlooked: Four Essays on Still-Life Painting*, London: Reaktion Books, 1990.

Bryson, Norman, *Vision and Painting: The Logic of the Gaze*, London: Macmillan, 1991.

Burgin, Victor, *Thinking Photography*, London: Macmillan, 1982.

Butler, David, and Butler, Gareth, *British Political Facts 1900–1985*, London: Macmillan, 1986.

Cadava, Eduardo, Connor, Peter and Nancy, Jean-Luc (eds), *Who Comes after the Subject?* London: Routledge, 1991.

Celan, Paul, *Selected Poems*, trans. Michael Hamburger, Harmondsworth: Penguin, 1990.

Certeau, Michel de, *Heterologies: Discourse on the Other*, trans. Brian Massumi, Minneapolis: University of Minnesota Press, 1986.

Certeau, Michel de, *The Writing of History*, trans. Tom Conley, New York: Columbia University Press, 1988.

Cesarini, David (ed.), *The Making of Modern Anglo-Jewry*, Oxford: Basil Blackwell, 1990.

Chagall, Bella, and Chagall, Marc, *Burning Lights*, trans. Norbert Guterman, New York: Schocken Books, 1974.

Chagall, Marc, *My Life*, London: Peter Owen, 1965.

Chagall, Marc, Unpublished letters to L. Koenig 1920–55, trans. C. Abramsky, London, Koenig Archive, with kind permission of the late G. Koenig.

Colls, Robert, and Dodd, Philip, *Englishness, Politics and Culture: 1880–1920*, London: Croom Helm, 1987.

Compton, Susan, *Chagall*, London: Royal Academy of Arts/Weidenfeld and Nicolson, 1985.

Compton, Susan (ed.), *British Art in the Twentieth Century*, London: Royal Academy of Arts, 1986.

Corbin, Alain, *The Foul and the Fragrant*, New York: Berg, 1986.

Cork, Richard, *Vorticism and Abstract Art in the First Machine Age*, London: Gordon Fraser, 1976.

Cork, Richard, *Jewish Artists of the East End*, video, London: Whitechapel Art Gallery, 1985.

Cork, Richard, *Bomberg*, London: Thames & Hudson, 1987.

Couzens Hoy, David (ed.), *Foucault: A Critical Reader*, Oxford: Basil Blackwell, 1986.

Dews, Peter, *Logics of Disintegration*, London: Verso, 1988.

Dickens, Charles, *Oliver Twist*, London: Chapman & Hall, n.d. [1842?].

Douglas, Mary, *Purity and Danger: An Analysis of the Concepts of Pollution and Taboo*, London: Ark Paperbacks, 1989.

Duveen, Joseph, *Thirty Years of British Art*, London: Studio, 1920.

Elias, Norbert, *The Civilizing Process: The History of Manners*, New York: Urizen Books, 1978.

Eliot, George, *Daniel Deronda*, London: Panther, 1970.

Endelman, Todd M., *Radical Assimilation in English Jewish History 1656–1945*, Bloomington: Indiana University Press, 1990.

Epstein, Isidore, *Judaism*, Harmondsworth: Pelican, 1973.

Epstein, Jacob, *Let There Be Sculpture*, London: Michael Joseph, 1942.

Feaver, William, 'Art war and roses', *Vogue*, January 1992.

Feldman, David, and Stedman Jones, Gareth (eds), *Metropolis London*, London and New York: Routledge, 1989.

Fishman, William J., *East End Jewish Radicals 1875–1914*, London: Duckworth, 1975.

Fishman, William J., *East End 1888*, London: Duckworth, 1988.

Fontaine, Jean La, 'Countering racial prejudice: a better starting point', *Anthropology Today*, 2(6), December 1986: 1–2.

Forster, Hal (ed.), *Postmodern Culture*, London: Pluto, 1985.

Foucault, Michel, *The Order of Things*, London: Tavistock, 1970.

Foucault, Michel, *The Archaeology of Knowledge*, London: Tavistock, 1972.

Foucault, Michel, *Discipline and Punish: The Birth of the Prison*, trans. Alan Sheridan, Harmondsworth: Penguin, 1977.

Foucault, Michel, *The History of Sexuality*, Vol. 1, *An Introduction*, trans. Robert Hurley, London: Allen Lane, 1978.

Foucault, Michel, *Power/Knowledge*, ed. Colin Gordon, New York: Pantheon Books, 1980.

Foucault, Michel, *The Foucault Reader*, ed. Paul Rabinow, Harmondsworth: Penguin, 1984.

Foucault, Michel, *The History of Sexuality*, Vol. 3, *The Care of the Self*, trans. Robert Hurley, Harmondsworth: Penguin, 1986.

Frascina, Francis, and Harrison, Charles, *Modern Art and Modernism: A Critical Anthology*, London: Harper & Row, 1983.

Frascina, Francis, and Harrison, Charles, *Pollock and After: A Critical Debate*, London: Harper & Row, 1985.

Freud, Sigmund, *Two Short Accounts of Psycho-Analysis*, trans. and ed. James Strachey, Harmondsworth: Penguin, 1962.

Freud, Sigmund, *The Interpretation of Dreams*, trans. James Strachey, ed. Angela Richards and Albert Dickson, Harmondsworth: Penguin, 1976.

Freud, Sigmund, *Civilization, Society and Religion: Group Psychology, Civilization and Its Discontents and Other Works*, trans. James Strachey, ed. Albert Dickson, Harmondsworth: Penguin, 1987.

Freud, Sigmund, *Totem and Taboo*, trans. James Strachey, London: Ark Paperbacks, 1991.

Frosh, Stephen, *Identity Crisis: Modernity, Psychoanalysis and the Self*, London: Macmillan, 1991.

Fry, Tony, 'Old worlds/new visions', *Transvisual Studies*, Sydney: Hale & Iremonger, 1989, pp. 93–106.

Fuller, Peter, 'Kitaj at Christmas', *Art Monthly*, Dec/Jan 1985–6: 11–14.

Garrard, John A., *The English and Immigration 1880–1910*, Oxford: Oxford University Press, 1971.

Gartner, L., *The Jewish Immigrant in England 1870–1910*, London: Allen & Unwin, 1960.

Gay, Peter, *Freud, Jews and Other Germans*, Oxford: Oxford University Press, 1978.

Gay, Peter, *A Godless Jew: Freud, Atheism, and the Making of Psychoanalysis*, New Haven: Yale University Press, 1987.

Gertler, Mark, *Gertler: Selected Letters*, ed. Noel Carrington, London: Rupert Hart-Davis, 1965.

Gertler, Mark, *Paintings and Drawings*, London: Camden Arts Centre, 1992.

Giddens, A., *Sociology: A Brief But Critical Introduction*, London: Macmillan, 1986.

Gilman, Sander L., *Difference and Pathology: Stereotypes of Sexuality, Race and Madness*, Ithaca, NY: University of Cornell Press, 1985.

Gilman, Sander L., *Disease and Representation of Illness: From Madness to Aids*, Ithaca, NY: University Press of Cornell, 1988.

Gilman, Sander L., *Jewish Self-Hatred: Anti-Semitism and the Hidden Language of the Jews*, Baltimore: Johns Hopkins University Press, 1990.

Gilman, Sander L., *The Jew's Body*, London: Routledge, 1991.

Gorelick, Sherry, 'Jewish success and the great American celebration: the Cold War vs. the World War in social science', *Contemporary Jewry*, 5(1), 1980.

Gramsci, Antonio, *Selections from the Prison Notebooks*, trans. and ed. Quintin Hoare and Geoffrey Nowell-Smith, London: Lawrence & Wishart, 1971.

Greenberg, Clement, 'Self-hatred and Jewish chauvinism: some reflections on positive Jewishness', *Commentary*, November 1950.

Greenberg, Clement, *Art and Culture*, Boston: Beacon Press, 1967.

Greenberg, Clement, *The Collected Essays and Criticism*, ed. John O'Brian, Vol. 1: *Perceptions and Judgements, 1939–1944*; Vol. 2: *Arrogant Purpose, 1945–1949*; Vol. 3: *Affirmations and Refusals, 1950–1956*, Chicago: University of Chicago Press, 1986, 1986, 1995.

Grosz, Elizabeth, 'Judaism and exile: the ethics of otherness', *New Formations*, no. 12, Winter 1990: 77–88.

Guilbaut, Serge, *How New York Stole the Idea of Modern Art: Abstract Expressionism, Freedom and the Cold War*, trans. Arthur Goldhammer, Chicago: University of Chicago Press, 1983.

Halevi, Ilan, *A History of the Jews*, trans. A. M. Barrett, London: Zed Books, 1987.

Halevi, Ilan, 'Jewish identity through the ages', *Return*, March 1989: 9–11.

Harrison, Charles, *English Art and Modernism 1900–1939*, London: Allen Lane, 1981.

Hayek, F. A., *The Road to Serfdom*, London: Routledge, 1944.

Held, David, *Introduction to Critical Theory: Horkheimer to Habemas*, London: Hutchinson, 1980.

Hess, Thomas B., *Barnett Newman*, London: Tate Gallery, 1972.

Hilton, Timothy, 'A brush with Bloomsbury', *Guardian*, 19 January 1992.

Hinshelwood, R. D., *Clinical Klein: From Theory to Practice*, London: Basic Books, 1994.

Hinshelwood, R. D., and Robinson, S. with Zarate, O., *Klein for Beginners*, Cambridge: Icon Books, 1997.

Hollington, Michael, 'Dickens and Cruikshank as physiognomers in Oliver Twist', *Dickens Quarterly*, Vol. 7 (2), 1990: 243–54.

Hopkins, Eric, *A Social History of the English Working Class 1815–1945*, London: Hodder & Stoughton, 1979.

Hutchinson, Linda, 'The Whitechapel Art Gallery 1901–1983', unpublished MA thesis, City University, London, 1983.

Hyatt, John, *Art Wars*, Rochdale: Rochdale Art Gallery, 1984.

Ishiguro, Kazuo, *The Remains of the Day*, London: Faber and Faber, 1989.

Jacobs, Louis, *Hasidic Prayer*, London: Routledge & Kegan Paul, 1972.

Januszczak, Waldemar, 'Portrait of the artist as a Jew', *Guardian*, 12 November 1985.

Johnson, Edgar, *Charles Dickens: His Tragedy and Triumph*, Vol. 1, Toronto: Little, Brown, 1952.

Johnson, Ken, 'Art and memory', *Art in America*, November 1993: 90–118

Johnston, Boris, 'Europe struggles to stem the tide', *Sunday Telegraph*, 3 June 1990.

Juten, Frederic, 'Neither fool, nor naive, nor poseur saint: fragments on R.B. Kitaj', *Art Forum*, January 1982: 61–9.

Kampf, Avram, *Jewish Experience in the Art of the Twentieth Century*, New York: Jewish Museum, 1975.

Kampf, Avram, *Chagall to Kitaj: Jewish Experience in 20th Century Art*, London: Lund Humphries in association with Barbican Art Gallery, 1990.

Katz, Jacob, *Out of the Ghetto*, New York: Schocken Books, 1978.

Key, Joan, 'The human body is present by being absent', unpublished essay, London, 1997.

Kierkegaard, Søren, *Repetition: An Essay in Experimental Psychology*, trans. Walter Lowrie, New York: Harper & Row, 1964.

Kitaj, R. B., 'Jewish art, indictment and defence: a personal testimony', *Jewish Chronicle Colour Magazine*, 30 November 1984, pp. 42–6.

Kitaj, R. B., 'A passion', Marlborough Fine Art, London, 1985.

Kitaj, R. B., Unpublished correspondence with Andrew Brighton, 1985.

Kitaj, R. B., Unpublished interview with Juliet Steyn, London, January 1988.

Kitaj, R. B., *First Diasporist Manifesto*, London: Thames & Hudson, 1989.

Kitaj, R. B., and Hyman, T., 'Return to London', *R.B. Kitaj*, Washington, DC: Smithsonian Institution Press, 1981.

Klein, M., *The Selected Melanie Klein*, ed. Juliet Mitchell, Harmondsworth: Penguin, 1991.

Koch, Gertrud, 'Notes on Claude Lanzmann's Shoah', *October*, no. 48, 1988: 15–24.

Kozloff, Max, 'Jewish art and the modernist jeopardy', *Art Forum*, April 1976: 43–7.

Kristeva, Julia, *Powers of Horror: An Essay on Abjection*, New York: Columbia University Press, 1982.

Kristeva, Julia, *Tales of Love*, trans. Leon. S. Roudiez, New York: Columbia University Press, 1987.

Kristeva, Julia, *The Kristeva Reader*, ed. Toril Moi, Oxford: Basil Blackwell, 1989.

Kristeva, Julia, *Strangers to Ourselves*, trans. Leon S. Roudiez, New York: Columbia University Press, 1991.

Lacan, Jacques, *Ecrits: A Selection*, trans. Alan Sheridan, London: Tavistock Publications, 1977.

Laclau, Ernesto, 'Universalism, particularism, and the question of identity', *October*, no. 61, Summer 1992: 83–90.

Laclau, Ernesto, and Mouffe, Chantal, *Hegemony and Socialist Strategy*, London: Verso, 1985.

Lanzmann, Claude, *Shoah*, Les Films Aleph/Historia Films, France, 1974–1985.

Lanzmann, Claude, 'Shoah as counter-myth', *Jewish Quarterly*, Vol. 33, 1986: 11–12.

Lacoue-Labarthe, Philippe, *Heidegger, Art and Politics*, trans. Chris Turner, Oxford: Basil Blackwell, 1990.

LaPlanche, J. and Pontalis, J. B., *The Language of Psychoanalysis*, trans. Donald Nicholson-Smith, London: Institute of Psychoanalysis and Karnac Books, 1988.

Lévi-Strauss, Claude, *The Scope of Anthropology*, trans. Sherry Orton Paul and Robert A. Paul, London: Jonathan Cape, 1971.

Levinas, Emmanuel, *Time and the Other*, trans. Richard A. Cohen, Pittsburgh: Duquesne University Press, 1987.

Levinas, Emmanuel, *Ethics and Infinity: Conversations with Philippe Nemo*, trans. Richard A. Cohen, Pittsburgh: Duquesne University Press, 1982.

Levinas, Emmanuel, *The Levinas Reader*, ed. Sean Hand, Oxford: Basil Blackwell, 1989.

Livingstone, Marco, 'Iconology as theme in the early work of R.B. Kitaj', *Burlington Magazine*, July 1980: 488–96.

Livingstone, Marco, *R.B. Kitaj*, Oxford: Phaidon, 1985.

London, Jack, *The People of the Abyss* (1903), London: Journeyman, 1977.

Lowenthal, Marvin, *The Diaries of Theodor Herzl*, New York: Dial Press, 1956.

Lynd, Sylvia, *Mark Gertler*, London: Leicester Galleries, 1941.

Lyotard, Jean-François, *The Differend: Phrases in Dispute*, trans. Georges van Den Abbeele, Manchester: Manchester University Press, 1988.

Lyotard, Jean-François, *The Lyotard Reader*, ed. Andrew Benjamin, Oxford: Basil Blackwell, 1989.

Lyotard, Jean-François, *Heidegger and 'the Jews'*, trans. Andreas Michel and Mark Roberts, Minneapolis: University of Minnesota Press, 1990.

Lyotard, Jean-François, *The Post Modern Condition: A Report on Knowledge*, trans. Geoff Bennington and Brian Massumi, Manchester: Manchester University Press, 1991.

Macdonell, Diane, *Theories of Discourse*, Oxford: Basil Blackwell, 1987.

Maharaj, Sarat, 'Identity', unpublished paper delivered in London, Camden Arts Centre, March 1992.

Marx, Karl, *Early Texts*, trans. and ed. David McLellan, Oxford: Basil Blackwell, 1972.

Mayhew, Henry, *Mayhew's London Underworld*, ed. Peter Quennell, London: Century, 1989.

McCarthy, Mary, 'Hannah Arendt and politics', *50th Anniversary Partisan Review*, 1984: 729–38.

McEwen, John, 'The outsider', *Independent Magazine*, 18 January 1992, pp. 32–4.

McEwen, John, 'Outcast brought in from the cold', *Sunday Telegraph*, 2 February 1992.

Mendus, Susan, and Rendell, Jane (eds), *Sexuality and Subordination*, London: Routledge, 1989.

Meyer, Franz, *Mark Chagall*, New York: Abrams, 1973.

Momigliano, Arnaldo, *On Pagans, Jews, and Christians*, Connecticut: Wesleyan University Press, 1989.

Mort, Frank, *Dangerous Sexualities*, London and New York: Routledge & Kegan Paul, 1987.

Mouffe, Chantal, 'Pluralism and modern democracy: around Carl Schmitt', *New Formations*, no. 14, Summer 1991: 1–15.

Mouffe, Chantal, 'Citizenship and political identity', *October*, no. 61, Summer 1992: 28–32.

Nochlin, L. and Garb, T. (eds), *The Jew in the Text: Modernity and the Construction of Identity*, London: Thames & Hudson, 1995.

Nunn, Joan, *Fashion in Costume*, London: Herbert Press, 1984.

Orton, Fred, and Pollock, Griselda, 'Avant-garde and Partisan Review', *Art History*, Vol. 4, no. 3, September 1981: 305–27.

Packer, William, 'Gertler: a story of doubt', *Financial Times*, 4 February 1992.

Paine, Robert, 'Israel: Jewish identity and competition of tradition', in Elizabeth Tonkin, Maryon McDonald and Malcolm Chapman (eds), *History and Ethnicity*, London: Routledge, 1989, pp. 121–36.

Parkes, James, *A History of the Jewish People*, Harmondsworth: Penguin, 1964.

Pearman, Hugh, *Excellent Accommodation*, London: Industrial Dwelling Society, 1985.

Pemble, John, *The Mediterranean Passion*, Oxford: Oxford University Press, 1988.

Perkin, Harold, *The Rise of Professional Society: England Since 1880*, London: Routledge, 1989.

Pettrson, Torsen, 'Enough to have bodies? Two incongruities in Oliver Twist', *Orbis Litterarum*, no. 5, 1990: 341–50.

Podro, Michael, 'Some notes on Ron Kitaj', *Art International*, March 1979: 18–26.

Poliakov, Leon, *The History of Anti-Semitism*, Vol. 3, trans. Miriam Kochan, London: Routledge & Kegan Paul, 1975.

Potok, Chaim, *My Name Is Asher Lev*, Harmondsworth: Penguin, 1977.

Rancière, Jacques, 'Politics, identification, and subjectivization', *October*, no. 61, Summer 1992: 58–64.

Readings, Bill, *Introducing Lyotard: Art and Politics*, London: Routledge, 1991.

Reason, David, 'Outside intimacy: two exhibitions of Canadian art at the Barbican Art Gallery, London', *SITE Sound*, September/October 1991: 30–2.

Rose, Barbara (ed.), *Readings in American Art 1900–1975*, New York: Praeger, 1975.

Rose, Evelyn, *International Jewish Cook Book*, New York: Robson Books, 1980.

Rose, Gillian, *Judaism and Modernity: Philosophical Essays*, Oxford: Basil Blackwell, 1994.

Rosenau, Helen, *A Short History of Jewish Art*, London: James Clarke, 1948.

Rosenberg, Harold, 'Herd of independent minds', *Commentary*, September 1948: 244–52.

Rosenberg, Harold, 'Does the Jew exist?', *Commentary*, January 1949: 8–18.

Rosenberg, Harold, 'Jewish identity in a free society', *Commentary*, June 1950: 508–14.

Rosenberg, Harold, *The Tradition of the New*, London: Paladin 1970.

Roth, Cecil (ed.), *Anglo-Jewish Letters*, London: Soncino Press, 1938.

Roth, Ribin, 'The Whitechapel Art Gallery: Arts and Crafts or Art Nouveau? Charles Harrison Townsend (1851–1928)', unpublished Open University Project, 1986.

Royal Commission on Alien Immigration, Vol. i: *Report*, cd. 1742 (1903); Vol. ii: *Minutes of Evidence*, cd. 1742 (1903); Vol. iii: *Appendix*, cd. 141 (1903); Vol. iv: *Index and Analysis to Minutes of Evidence*, cd. 1743 (1904).

Rutherford, Jonathan, *Identity, Community, Culture, Difference*, London: Lawrence and Wishart, 1990.

Said, Edward W., *Orientalism*, Harmondsworth: Penguin, 1984.

Said, Edward W., 'Reflections on exile', *Granta*, no. 13, Autumn 1984, pp. 157–72.

Said, Edward W., 'Empire of sand', *Weekend Guardian*, 12/13 January 1991, pp. 4–5.

Sandler, I., *Triumph of Abstract Expressionism*, New York: Pall Mall, 1970.

Sartre, Jean-Paul, *Réflexions sur la question juive*, Paris: Gallimard, 1946.

Sartre, Jean-Paul, *Essays in Aesthetics*, trans. Wade Baskin, New York: Washington Square Press, 1966.

Sartre, Jean-Paul, *Search for a Method*, trans. Hazel E. Barnes, New York: Vintage Books, 1968.

Sartre, Jean-Paul, *Sartre by Himself*, trans. Richard Seaver, New York: Urizen Books, 1978.

Scholem, Gershom, *On Jews and Judaism in Crisis*, New York: Schocken Books, 1976.

Sennett, Richard, *The Fall of Public Man*, Cambridge: Cambridge University Press, 1977.

Serotta, Edward, 'The future of Auschwitz', *Weekend Guardian*, 21 January 1995, pp. 13–21.

Shane, A. L., 'The Dreyfus Affair: could it have happened in England?', *Jewish Historical Studies*, Vol. 30, 1987–8: 135–48.

Sheridan, Alan, *Michel Foucault: The Will to Truth*, London: Tavistock, 1986.

Shmueli, Efraim, *Seven Jewish Cultures*, trans. Gila Shmueli, Cambridge: Cambridge University Press, 1990.

Sims, George, *Living in London*, 2 vols, London, 1902–3.

Sinclair, Iain, *White Chappel: Scarlet Tracings,* Rutland: Goldmark, 1987.

Solomon, Robert C., *Continental Philosophy since 1750*, Oxford: Oxford University Press, 1990.

Sontag, Susan, *On Photography*, London: Allen Lane, 1978.

Sontag, Susan, *Illness as Metaphor: Aids and Its Metaphors*, Harmondsworth: Penguin, 1991.

Sorkin, David, 'What was the Emancipation?', unpublished lecture, Spiro Institute, London, 13 August 1992.

Spiegelman, Art, *Maus*, Harmondsworth: Penguin, 1987.

Stallybrass, Peter, and White, Allon, *The Politics and Poetics of Transgression*, London: Methuen, 1986.

Stedman Jones, Gareth, *Outcast London: A Study in the Relationship between Classes in Victorian Society*, Harmondsworth: Penguin, 1984.

Steyn, Juliet (ed.), *Other Than Identity: The Subject Politics and Art,* Manchester: Manchester University Press, 1997

Tagg, John, *The Burden of Representation*, London: Macmillan, 1988.

Talbot, Linda, 'Mark Gertler', *Ham & High*, 24 January 1992.

Vergo, Peter (ed.), *The New Museology*, London: Reaktion, 1989.

Wesker, Arnold, *The Birth of Shylock and the Death of Zero Mostel*, London: Quartet Books, 1997.

White, Jerry, *Rothschild Buildings: Life in an East End Tenement Block 1887–1920*, London: Routledge & Kegan Paul, 1980.

Williams, Raymond, *Marxism and Literature*, Oxford: Oxford University Press, 1977.

Williams, Raymond, *Culture and Society 1780–1950*, Harmondsworth: Penguin, 1983.

Williams, Raymond, *Keywords*, London: Fontana, 1983.

Wolff, Janet, *The Social Production of Art*, London: Macmillan 1981.

Wolff, Janet, *Aesthetics and the Sociology of Art*, London: George Allen & Unwin, 1983.

Wolff, Janet, 'The failure of a hard sponge: class, ethnicity, and the art of Mark Gertler', *New Formations*, no. 28, Spring 1996.

Woodeson, John, *Mark Gertler*, Colchester: The Minories, 1971.

Woodeson, John, *Mark Gertler*, London: Sidgwick & Jackson, 1972.

Yerushalmi, Yosef Hayim, *From Spanish Court to Italian Ghetto: Isaac Cardoso, a Study in Seventeenth Century Marranos and Jewish Apologetics*, New York: Columbia University Press, 1971.

Yerushalmi, Yosef Hayim, *Zakhor: Jewish History and Jewish Memory*, New York: Schocken Books, 1989.

Young, Robert, *White Mythologies: Writing History and the West*, London: Routledge, 1990.

Zangwill, Israel, *Children of the Ghetto*, London, 1892.

Zizek, Slavoj, *The Sublime Object of Ideology*, London: Verso, 1989.

Zizek, Slavoj, 'Eastern Europe's Republics of Gilead', *New Left Review*, no. 183, September/October 1990: 50–62.

Index

Numbers in italics refer to figures.